Software Quality Management

BCS Practitioner Series

Series editor: Ray Welland

BELINA ET AL SDL with applications from protocol specification
BURNETT Project management methodology
FOLKES Accelerated systems development
GIBSON Managing computer projects
HIPPERSON Practical systems analysis
THE RAISE LANGUAGE GROUP The RAISE specification language
VERYARD Information modelling
WELLMAN Software costing

Software Quality Management

A pro-active approach

John W.O. Brinkworth

Prentice Hall
New York London Toronto Sydney Tokyo Singapore

First published 1992 by
Prentice Hall International (UK) Ltd
Campus 400, Maylands Avenue
Hemel Hempstead
Hertfordshire, HP2 7EZ
A division of
Simon & Schuster International Group

Typeset in 10/12 pt Times
by MHL Typesetting Ltd, Coventry

Printed and bound in Great Britain by
Dotesios Ltd, Trowbridge, Wiltshire.

Library of Congress Cataloging-in-Publication Data

Brinkworth, John W.O.
Software quality management : a pro-active approach / John W.O. Brinkworth.
p. cm. — (BCS practitioner series)
Includes bibliographical references and index.
ISBN 0-13-818444-5 (pbk)
1. Computer software—Quality control. I. Title. II. Series.
QA76.76.Q35B75 1992
005.1'068'5—dc20 92-13320
CIP

British Library Cataloguing in Publication Data

A catalogue record for this book is available from the British Library

ISBN 0-13-818444-5 (pbk)

1 2 3 4 5 96 95 94 93 92

To my parents

Contents

Editorial preface

The aim of the BCS Practitioner Series is to produce books which are relevant for practising computer professionals across the whole spectrum of Information Technology activities. We want to encourage practitioners to share their practical experience of methods and applications with fellow professionals. We also seek to disseminate information in a form which is suitable for the practitioner who often has only limited time to read widely within a new subject area or to assimilate research findings.

The role of the BCS is to provide advice on the suitability of books for the Series, via the Editorial Panel, and to provide a pool of potential authors upon which we can draw. Our objective is that this Series will reinforce the drive within the BCS to increase professional standards in IT. The other partners in this venture, Prentice Hall, provide the publishing expertise and international marketing capabilities of a leading publisher in the computing field.

The response when we set up the Series was extremely encouraging. However, the success of the Series depends on there being practitioners who want to learn, as well as those who feel they have something to offer! The Series is under continual development and we are always looking for ideas for new topics and feedback on how to further improve the usefulness of the Series. If you are interested in writing for the Series then please contact us.

A lot of interest has been expressed in improving software quality and phrases such as 'software quality assurance' are widely used. What John Brinkworth does in this book is to challenge the reader to think about quality issues and to offer sound practical advice about improving software quality. The book is written in an informal style but the message is clear — quality is important!

Ray Welland
Computing Science Department, University of Glasgow

Preface

This book is aimed at two groups of people. All those involved in developing software-based systems, and also those involved in procuring such systems. The book shows how high-quality information technology systems can be constructed today, in the busy and complex world in which we live. The style is informal and aims to inject some life into what can otherwise be a rather dry subject.

Chapters address each stage of the develop process separately. Chapters can be read on a 'stand-alone' basis, as the aim of the book is to be of immediate use to the reader, whatever point he or she may have reached in a development project. Each chapter ends with checklists of issues that should be addressed if the system is to be a high-quality one.

The book may also be useful to people studying computing, computer science, or business. However, it is not an academic textbook; rather, it is intended to be a useful ready-reference to practising professionals involved in the field of information technology.

About the author

John Brinkworth has been involved in real-world computing since 1982. He holds a degree in Mathematics from the University of York, and has dealt with the application of computing to areas as diverse as maximising oil-well recovery volumes, water installation control, international banking, and high-throughput message switching.

At the time this book was first drafted, he was based at Logica's North American headquarters as a Quality Control Consultant. Upon returning to the United Kingdom he joined a leading City of London Derivatives House where he created and manages a Software Development Quality System based on ISO9001.

His leisure interests are remarkably similar to those of the rest of the human race, but do show a slant towards the communication of ideas, the use of quality to improve people's lives, and going down the pub.

Acknowledgements

This book would not have reached you as a reader without the help and support of the following people.

Viki Williams and Mike Cash, my editors at Prentice Hall—Simon & Schuster. Ray Welland of Glasgow University for having the bravery to sign me up for the Practitioner Series; I hope this book repays the faith he placed in my initial offerings. My anonymous technical reviewers, who made many constructive comments and improvements to the content, form and style of the book. My employers for their support. In addition, my father deserves special commendation for his painstaking work in rectifying my multiple abuses of the English language. All remaining occurrences of odd, incorrect or simply trans-Atlantic English are wholly mine.

John Brinkworth
February 1992

1 Job one

1.1 Putting it on the road

In America companies are allowed to identify their competitors in television commercials. So when Nissan launched the 1990 edition of its Stanza model, it issued the 'Nissan Stanza Challenge'. Quite simply, if a customer took a test drive in a Stanza but shortly afterwards bought a Honda Accord or Toyota Camry, Nissan would give the driver one hundred dollars.

What is significant here is not Nissan's generosity, but rather its choice of competitors. Nissan felt that the American car buying public were not aware of the strengths of Nissan's product and that it had to entice the customer away from the established leaders in the market. Nissan had to consider which firms people thought of as the market leaders. Significantly, Nissan reckoned these were not Ford, not General Motors, who were America's two largest car producers, but Honda and Toyota.

This was symbolic of the onslaught that the American domestic car producers were facing. However, they were fighting back, and they were showing signs of already having learnt a fundamental lesson; one which America had itself taught Japan in the late 1940s. The lesson? The best product was not necessarily the cheapest, but was the one that offered the most features for the money, was well designed and reliable; the best product was the highest-quality one.

And that lesson was now evident in Ford's and GM's own advertising. To promote its corporate image, Ford adopted a philosophy throughout the company that was embodied in one simple phrase:

> 'At Ford Quality Is Job One.'

This approach meant that every aspect of its research, development and production placed quality at the top of its list. General Motors came back into the fray with an equally firm commitment. It had carried out a complete redesign and thorough testing of over seventy new models, and so GM was

> 'Putting Quality on the Road.'

1.2 Mission statement

That is what this book seeks to encourage you to do, to make quality a foremost concern in the development of information technology. But not only that; it is of no benefit to place 'Quality' at the top of the list of priorities if the good intentions are not followed through. This book, then, seeks also to facilitate the adoption of workable techniques that result in high-quality systems — 'to put quality on the road'.

1.3 What is quality?

It is only proper that we should try and define what we mean by quality before detailing how it can best be achieved. But, as with many seemingly straightforward questions, the posing of it is far easier than its resolution.

The question can be tackled at a number of levels. This is not the place for a long theoretical examination of quality in a philosophical sense; however, I would not wish to discourage you from such an exploration. Personally I would recommend a starting point that is rather esoteric, but accessible and, most importantly, intriguing enough to sustain one's interest. The book I am referring to is the classic of its sort, *Zen and the Art of Motorcycle Maintenance* [1]. It interweaves the narrative of a novel with a surprisingly wide-ranging introduction to some of the world's major philosophers and an extended discussion on the meaning of quality.

However, it is by no means a prerequisite for understanding this chapter or using this book. This book belongs to a series by practitioners, for practitioners, so it behoves us to focus our examination upon what is of direct utility to you in your day-to-day life, close to the software workface 'hacking out' code.

How can we perceive quality? When examining a system we can take various quantitative measures of it; more of these in a moment. But are there any non-quantitative (qualitative (*sic*)) signposts that we can look out for? I contend that the first place to look is not at the system but at its creators, the people who produced the specifications, crafted the code, built the edifice, and then tested it to prove that it worked. What attributes are evident in these people if the system they have delivered is of high quality? More likely than not, their attitude of mind has governed the way they approached the development. They will have shown an integrity in the way that they approached and dealt with the aspirations of the users they are creating a system for. They will have enjoyed the opportunity to create a worthwhile working solution, enjoyed tackling the challenge they were given; and they will take pride in the deliverables they present.

One aspect of the approach of 'pride in good quality work', that I have just described, is embodied in a rather frequent mis-definition of a term with many definitions. 'Quality Assurance' is a title bestowed by some software-producing organisations to a department that tests the software before it is delivered to the user. There is nothing wrong with the remit of such a department; indeed, there is a considerable advantage to having a pseudo-user, completely separate from the original development team, and thus in a position to subject the software to some naïve tests. However, to title that group as the Quality Assurance Department is to close the stable door just as the horse's tail slides out. The horse hasn't yet bolted, but the effort needed to stop it from escaping is considerable. By this stage in the cycle the cost of correcting an error is far higher than if it was caught earlier. The mistake in giving the title of Quality Assurance to this department is that it assumes, and more importantly implies, that quality can only be checked for at the end of the development process. This is wholly incorrect; the essence of delivering a system that a development group can be proud of is to ensure that quality has been taken into consideration at every stage — from the earliest tentative requirements onwards. Quality is not something that can merely be hoped for and confirmed by testing just prior to delivery. Quality is something that is actively and explicitly designed and built into a system.

In seeking to identify what we mean by a high-quality system, there is one area in which one can define a comparatively clear-cut measure of quality. It is an area in which not only is there a moral case for quality, but in fact, a moral imperative. This is the area of safety critical systems. These are moving into our day-to-day lives more and more. There is a scale of criticality on which they can be said to lie. It runs from industrial process-control systems, which are used to run a nuclear power station, up to the fly-by-wire systems that are right at the heart of the new generation of modern aircraft. But whatever their position on that scale, they all share one fundamental property. Our lives depend upon how they function, and thus there is a clear litmus test of whether these are high-quality systems or not.

Another area where quality can be discerned in a system is evidenced by our growing reliance on information technology in all the other aspects of daily life. Central to this is the use that business and government institutions make of computer systems. The software industry is starting to undertake work for major companies, with project titles such as 'Core System Replacement'. These clients have, over the last twenty years or so, slowly developed a variety of systems that initially covered only one aspect of the organisation's functions. As time progressed, these systems were connected to each other and now cover the whole of the operation's activities, but not as effectively as the client would like. Thus, the core system replacement type of project has arrived on the scene. The critical word here is 'core'. The new systems being built are pivotal to the organisation's success; in many ways, the systems are the lifeblood of the organisation. Should they not function correctly or, worse still, 'go down' and not function at all, the impact on the organisation can be catastrophic. Thus, a system is deemed to be of high quality if it supports the organisation that uses it, when compared against a system that hinders an organisation.

1.4 The absence of quality

On occasions, it is easier to distinguish something by its absence. Let us turn the telescope around and attempt to search out poor quality.

'I'm sorry, we can't take your booking today, the computer's down until tomorrow, please call back then.' A more and more common phrase heard down the telephone, as everybody becomes more reliant on software to carry out their work. And, undoubtedly, this gives the easiest way to define poor quality — the system is down. Is this because of poor reliability? Not enough fallback procedures? Or, just a badly thought-out backup schedule? Whichever, we have a poor-quality system.

But even if 'up', the system may still be riddled with poor quality. One of the worst situations is if it is hard to use, has a confusing interface, or does not implement all of the activities that it was meant to automate and support. And so it is junked, left to sit in the corner, ignored, while the frustrated users develop work-arounds to minimise their contact with the system. Lack of use identifies the system as being of poor quality, and probably poorly designed.

The next danger signal is a system that drives its users up the wall. It is well designed but poorly implemented, and thus replete with a 'zoo-full' of obscure and exasperating bugs. It is unlikely that the developers mistook the users for entomologists, but the developers clearly cared more about getting something — anything — out of the door, delivered and installed, within the deadline. They forgot about the users — the sour taste of poor quality lingered long after the sweetness of meeting the schedule had evaporated.

The next problem is the inverse of the previous one. It comes in the form of a system that is approximately 70 percent nitrogen, '20-something' percent oxygen augmented with a few trace gases. In other words — nothing but thin air. The organisation needs it, but the development has overrun, and it has yet to be delivered and installed. Initial estimates were probably rushed and scrappy, and again the users end up paying the price.

The system is up, just, but you would hardly notice it unless you had the patience of a tortoise. It is well designed, well liked, highly used and thus overworked. When a command is issued, the system takes longer to get back to the users than the users' annual tax rebates. So an attempt is made to upgrade and expand the system, and this is where the brick wall is hit. No one ever expected the system to be so successful, so expanding it will be no easy task, in fact the developers suggest scrapping it and building a new one from scratch.

What do all these scenarios have in common? They are costing the organisation bundles of money and stacks of lost time. They convey more effectively than any other arguments one simple message. The initial expense of considering quality, right from the start, is far less than that of discovering down the road that quality was treated as an optional extra. If quality is overlooked, ignored, shelved, then the organisation will find itself mired in a morass of hassle that will cost it a great deal more to clear up.

1.5 A different perspective

It is instructive to look at software quality from another angle, that of manufacturing industry. First, we should clarify our terminology, as the creation of software is placed by some people into the category of a service industry, since it involves highly specialised professionals charging for their work by the hour, whilst others point to the end product and argue that the software industry is as much a member of the manufacturing sector as many other high-technology specialisms. We shall take the approach that the developments in software production, moving it from an art to a science, result in a playing field that is level enough for a fair comparison to be made between more traditional manufacturing industries and software production. This provides a situation in which software producers can learn something from their smokestack counterparts.

My eye was caught by a report in *The Financial Times* [2] which summarised the findings of a study carried out by INSEAD, the leading French business school. The survey covered 244 large manufacturing companies in fourteen European countries, and sought to discover what actions the companies were taking to improve their competitive positions in the light of the increasingly competitive European market in the 1990s. Two strategies came to the fore. Companies embraced continual change by restructuring, rationalising plant and introducing new production processes. But of even more significance here is that they also committed themselves completely to quality. We owe it to ourselves to take on board their definition of quality. This was:

> a set of techniques for determining and communicating customer needs and translating them into product and service design specifications and manufacturing methods.

So, quality to them was defined as a user-driven activity — 'the customer is always right'. Well, in most cases anyway, but the point is that quality there is not defined in terms of achieving zero defects or some such target, but in terms of users' needs and users' values. We are not looking at the technology as the driving force; rather, people come first and foremost.

Having taken this on board, does an approach including quantifiable targets have value? In the manufacturing world (zero defect targets) and even service industries (zero customer defections), measurement does form a part of many people's definition of quality. However, software is a soft (!) entity, almost living. Trying to measure it successfully is akin to trying to buy the right size of hiking boots for a jelly-fish. It can become a rather irrelevant academic investigation into the theoretical benefits of competing measures (metrics) of software quality. Luckily for us, there are some rather surprising recently published results, based on data gathered in industry, not academia; and they are worth examining [3]. But since they are most applicable to internal design and testing, you'll have to be patient. Meantime, back at the jelly-fish ranch, there is one other item of note arising from the INSEAD study.

To achieve the targets they had set themselves in the use of quality, the companies placed a high premium on training. Why? Because two-thirds of the respondents considered that only their top and middle management had an understanding of the strategies, goals and objectives of their company. And this understanding needed to go much deeper into the company. In other words, with quality as a top priority there needed to be a much more thorough grounding in its use for everyone in the company. For all organisations using information technology (IT), this is what this book aims to help them achieve.

1.6 What the doctor ordered

So what can this book offer? What are my aims here? Well, first we have to be realistic. It should be fairly self-evident that there is no one simple easy catch-all that can solve all quality problems in one step. No magic machine, no universal incantation. Why not? Because if there was, everyone would already be using it.

No, we are living in the real world. We have to accept human limits and fallibility. There is one approach that may hold promise. This is the idea of using formal methods to specify systems. Documents would then consist mainly of mathematical statements using set theory, and various orders of logic. This has the benefit that most aspects of a system can be fully described, and logical inconsistencies, bugs in the design, can be discovered when one tries to prove the design to be logically correct and complete. This needs special design languages and techniques such as Z or VDM. The specifications are next fed into automatic code generators. Testing consists of proving mathematically that each level of refinement in the specifications, all the way to the code, is logically correct. This is itself done by formal-specification checking programs. The testing of the code uses automatic test generators and test capture tools. These enable tests to be rerun and all test cases (I exaggerate — see Chapter 5 'Testing') to be run. Although the users will need to learn some mathematics, there may still be some loopholes since the technique doesn't necessarily address all the 'Attributes' I give in Chapter 2 'Initiation and Requirements'.

So what do we notice about this approach? It is very time, tool and labour intensive. In other words, for the next few years at least, it will be far too costly. I eagerly look forward to the day when this will become the standard approach, but I fear that realistically it will take a number of years before organisations start to adopt it for all their systems.

Where does this leave us? Unfortunately — in the dark ages. Software development is still more of a black art than a scientific or engineering discipline. We can see the renaissance mapped out before us, but it awaits the highly powerful hardware to become more affordable, allowing the logic tools to be put to general use.

This book, then, is still really a mediaeval manuscript. It is a candle with the aim of lighting the way for the moment, until electricity arrives, and we can turn the arc lights on and really see what we are doing. To develop the metaphor, this book contains a collection of soothsayings. These represent the accreted wisdom and insights of various professionals currently active in software development.

In some respects, there is not a great deal that is new here. Most items can be found elsewhere. Most items may already be known to you. There is nothing wrong in this. Quality systems are, for the most part, the codifying of common sense. The sensible application of particular techniques, combined with regular reference to checklists of questions (that should be asked at different stages in the development process), characterise most software quality approaches currently in use. A few supplement this with taking some measurements of certain quantifiable aspects of the development, monkeying around with the numbers, and seeing what conclusions can be inferred.

The restatement of these basic techniques and questions is no bad thing. Most learning is founded on repetition; we rarely pick up an idea or concept fully on the first occasion it is presented to us. It helps to firm up the idea if we hear it again, see it explained in a slightly different manner, view it from a different angle. One of the foremost American specialists in personal skill training and motivation, Tony Robbins [22], who has consulted for the US Army and many major US corporations, recites the following statement many times in his material:

> 'Repetition is the mother of skill.'

It's a cliché, but he makes no apology for using it, because as a cliché it sticks more easily in the memory. Practice does make perfect; the more one studies a particular field, the more one excels in it.

Cigna, the world-wide insurance corporation, uses the following repetition-centred exhortation.

> Take fast. And make it faster. Take smart. And make it brilliant. Believe that no matter how well you do something, you can always do it better. And chances are you will.

In doing so, it is encouraging its people continually to reconsider and improve how well they are doing the basics. So do not ignore and discount some of the information given here because you may have heard it before. The fact that you've come across it before should serve to indicate to you that it is of higher utility than you might otherwise have thought.

1.7 Who should be reading this?

You, fairly obviously. Someone intrigued by software, possibly producing it, probably using it. You have picked this book up and got this far, so it must be of some interest to you. And it will probably benefit you, give you an edge, and hone your skills in this area. But it is a good idea if I clarify the scope of this book a little.

I make one major assumption. The producer and user of the software system that you are involved with are not the same person. You could be either the producer or the user; this book should benefit you whichever hat you're wearing. However, I am not aiming it at a person who is developing a system for his or her own sole use. This is not to say that such a person shouldn't read it since, at a later date, other people could start using the solo-system, for whatever reason. Obviously, then, such a sole user/developer may find that only a subset of sections herein are directly applicable.

The assumption I therefore make is that there are two groups involved here. There may be only one person in each group, or they may be large departments.

These two groups could be in the same organisation, or might be in different ones. The point here is that, in the second case, it is highly likely that a formal legal agreement will exist between the developers and users. It will include specifications of functionality, timescale, cost, and it will be written down. There is a good chance that there will be a clear definition of responsibilities and interactions.

The other situation is far murkier. Within a single organisation, if two groups are to deal with each other, the way in which they interact will be determined by that organisation's culture. This can be anywhere on a spectrum from as formal and legal as if they were not in the same organisation, to completely informal, very friendly and restricted to verbal communications. Obviously, there are risks here.

This book seeks to address both scenarios. There is a great degree of commonality between them, and both can usefully lend to and borrow from the other's way of working. So, whether you are a producer or a user, this book is for you.

1.8 Time for a vocabulary test

This book is part of a series for practitioners, busy people who do not have a lot of time. It is not intended to be an exhaustive statement on every aspect of software quality. Indeed, the danger with such weighty academic tomes, valid thought they are, is that they are not put to use because they assume that the reader has a green field to start on, and is convinced that all the book says should be used. Which is rarely the case.

This book does not take that approach. It presumes the practitioner is part-way through some development, under pressure, and probably sceptical about all this hyperbole on the best way to do things. To make this book accessible to such a reader, it is structured so that it provides, in a relatively concise form, a vocabulary of techniques that can be dipped into and used to improve quality.

Some techniques are very simple, no apologies for this. It is quite common for people to get caught up on the more fascinating, difficult, technically challenging aspects of a development. They are then likely to overlook the obvious, simple steps that, if taken at the appropriate moment, can save a lot of grief later.

This book does not offer one prescriptive methodology that must be followed to the letter. Rather, it requires intelligent mindful reading, and the selection and application of whatever the user considers most worthwhile. I use the word 'mindful' to distinguish from the fact that most of us spend most of our lives as passive consumers of the information we are handed; we become mindless — only dealing with problems when they confront us. On occasion, we might do better if we tried to ferret them out and address them before they blew up out of all proportion.

1.9 Questions, questions

Feel free to skim and browse. This book fails if you read it once, put it away and do not subsequently actively use it.

To encourage interactive use, this book is structured to include, at the end of each chapter, a series of questions. They are not academic exercises. They do not come with answers. Rather, they seek to stimulate thought. They are questions that readers should ask about their own system. Users should ask them of a developer. And developers should ask them of their colleagues and boss(!).

The order of the questions is significant. The fact that the practitioner is busy means that there may not be enough time to ask them all. Thus, they are ordered so that the most useful, most important ones come first. Read them, think about them and 'Put Quality on the Road'.

1.10 Questions

1. Why are you reading this book?
2. How important is quality to you?
3. Are you going to read the rest of this book?
4. When considering the IT systems you are involved with, what and who do your actions affect?
5. What would be the consequences for the organisation and yourself of not working to improve the quality of its systems?
6. What reasons for the production of higher-quality systems resonate with you?
7. Why?
8. When will you start to take any actions on the basis of this book?
9. How will you know if they are the correct actions for you?
10. Will you set yourself target dates to complete reading those sections of this book that you consider relevant to your current needs?
11. Will you involve other people in using this book?

2 Initiation and requirements

2.1 Introduction

2.1.1 Stop reading and do something

Okay, so you've arrived here at the start of Chapter 2, probably by way of Chapter 1. Good idea? Well, maybe — but probably not. You are not a theoretical instance of an idealised developer; no, you are a real person living in the real world. Consequence? It is highly unlikely that you have picked up this book and are reading it at the very moment that you are about to start a major development. More likely, you are half-way through.

So all my pious suggestions, here in this chapter, will strike you as great, but too late. You'll resolve to remember them for next time, but right now you are too busy. And I will have failed.

What we are talking about here is linear thinking or, to be frank, linear coasting. As a harried professional you do the natural thing; almost without thinking about it, you pick up this book and start at the beginning and attempt to work your way to the end. Result? You've read it, but you haven't *used* it.

The application of quality techniques to development requires that we do not drift down the same old stream, get caught in the same ruts, unthinkingly repeat the same mistakes. I want to challenge you to think, pro-actively, laterally (to borrow a phrase from Edward de Bono), and to approach things with a fresh eye.

The linear — straight-line — thinker would read this chapter now. I don't want you to do that. Instead, turn back to the Table of Contents, scan it to see which chapter addresses the phase that your development is currently in. Turn to that chapter (which in all but a few cases will not be this one) and look at the questions at the end of that chapter. Ask yourself the first five questions in the list, preferably jot down your answers on paper. If the questions seem dumb or puzzling, read that chapter, then try them again.

Result? You are *using* this book, interacting with it. It is stimulating you into taking some action, which will have a much larger effect on the quality of the system you are currently involved with than had you stayed put in this chapter and continued to read.

Right, so get to it.

And if it should turn out that you are right at the very start of a development, then — lucky you. You have the chance to get things right from day one onwards. In that case, consider yourself entitled to carry on reading the rest of this chapter.

2.1.2 The art of the possible

The classic truism holds that politics is 'the art of the possible'. Well, technology has caught up with it; the amount of computing power and telecommunications bandwidth available to organisations means that whatever their needs (bar the constraint of cost), anything is possible.

This is crucial to appreciating how quality is bound into the development process. The aim of the potential system under development is to meet users' requirements. If it fails to do so, it falls (fatally) at the first quality hurdle. The users have dreams, hopes, expectations and fears. A high-quality system will meet and fulfil the positive concerns and be so designed that it allays the negative ones.

So, the first step in creating a high-quality system is to know what we are building, and why, and for whom. It's no more than a practical instance of the classic:

> 'How do I get to Birmingham?'
> 'Well I wouldn't start from here if I were you.'

Why not? Because travelling from Manchester to Birmingham is a very different proposition when you compare driving down Britain's M6 motorway to trying to navigate from Manchester, New Hampshire to Birmingham, Alabama (States-side).

Although detail is crucial, you have to start with the 'big picture', and ensure that it is big enough to encompass everything. And, furthermore, that everyone is looking at the same 'big picture'.

So let's turn a wide-angled lens on the user community and try and determine who has a stake in the system, and thus who we need to talk to.

2.2 The distillation of the requirements

2.2.1 The players

A poor-quality system can acquire that mantle by failing to meet the requirements of any one of the groups of users that it purports to serve. To avoid this happening, we must enumerate all the groups of people involved in the development and subsequent use of the system. We would expect that their requirements will, on occasions, conflict, but that is what gives the profession of systems development its bite. The challenge of exercising judgement and determining the appropriate approach to best satisfy all the demands.

Time for a list. I will first summarise the different players in the 'Let's Build a System' game, and then go into their roles and concerns in more detail.

- The users, which may themselves split into different groups:
  - the corporate planners,
  - the accounting department,
  - the data processing (DP) department,
  - the 'true' users;
- Third party external consultants;
- Multiple levels of lead and sub-contractors;
- The developers of the system;
- The bosses of the developers of the system.

I doubt this list is comprehensive, but it should get you thinking, panicking, running for the door. Well, chances are you may encounter only a subset of these people, but time devoted up front, to considering each of their perspectives, will be paid back handsomely later, in the form of fewer crises and reduced grief. Time for the telephoto lens — let's carefully weigh the species up for consideration.

• *The users*. They do indeed divide (often combatively) into different camps. If your system is being developed in-house then the other players in the list won't apply but the user subdivisions will.

You can probably place yourself into one of the above groups. Fear not, I will probably characterise you unfairly whichever group you belong to.

o *The corporate planners*. Let's start at the top. These guys sweated blood to earn their MBAs, their corner offices and more frequent flier air-miles than they know what to do with. They see a world populated with challenges, which are addressed with solutions. Notice the word 'problem' is not in their vocabulary. They also have the attention span of an impatient flea. As far as they are concerned, every picture is BIG. What are their concerns and requirements? The overall corporate bottom line (with the trend to privatisation, this applies as much in the government sector as in private industry). Note I said the *overall corporate* bottom line. These guys are actually the techno-freak's friend. Why? Because once convinced that the application of appropriate technology (even if it's very expensive) will give the organisation an overall saving or that 'leading-edge' position in the market place, they will back the idea and stake their not inconsiderable reputations and move and shake the idea into reality. Note, no one below them in the organisation can be convinced by arguments of 'economy of scale'; they all have their own fiefdoms to defend.

These corporate planners will want the problem couched in business language, without spurious technological detail. When presented with a requirements specification, they will read the executive summary only. The good point about this is that they will favour the simple solution. If presented with a complex technically fascinating option or a simple one that hides the complexity at the lowest level possible, they will more than likely go for the simple solution — it will be easier for them to understand and sell upwards to the board of directors. Why is this good? Because the development process is already fraught with complexities and complexity spells risk, confusion and an adverse impact on quality. One of the basic rules of quality — always keep it as simple as possible.

Now, how do these people define success? They want it all, on-time, to-spec, within budget. Where can you compromise with them? Technical detail — they don't get off on nice-to-have 'bells and whistles', so concentrate on the core of the idea, the central function of the application. Sell the fact that networking all the PCs in the office will improve secretarial productivity; do not carp on about the joys of 'e-mail'. The cost–benefit of the development is at the centre of their agenda; they will discover how the corporate culture is transformed once the 'e-mail' system is up and running; it may turn out to be the biggest benefit of all, but that will not be realised until after the event. Focusing on it now will only muddy the waters and may jeopardise the whole development.

- *The accounting department*. These people crunch numbers and paper, slowly. Unless you are developing a payroll system (unlikely in this day and age), in which case this lot will be your 'real users' as well, the accounting department will make itself felt by exercising negative positional power. It will demand paperwork and numbers, send your forms back to you, do bizarre or unspeakable things with your invoices, but still moan if you are ever a day late with anything. Okay, maybe I'm being a trifle uncharitable. My point is that no development occurs without interacting with the accounting department, and its requirements and turn-around time, although not part of the formal requirements of the 'real users', will none the less impose constraints on the development work, and should be factored into estimates right from Day One (Day One is defined as the day that accounts demand you send them a 'Project Set-up' form to register your work on their database!).

- *The DP department*. These days, it now does an awful lot more than just process data, but the name stuck. Note that it is a service department to the enterprise. The career path of its staff does not usually lead into the main corporate hierarchy. This probably suits most of them fine; they prefer technology over people and business, and most everything else. They define success in terms of dealing with an intractable problem, and solving it and learning something new in the process. Some of the people there will love disciplined methodologies; others will hate them. Although they tend to be technically focused, do not fall into the trap of thinking of them as identikit androids. They may well place cost and user requirements near the top of their list of priorities, but these can become sublimated into techno-awe when presented with some entrancing new marvel. The importance that they give to timescales and budgets will depend on the culture of the organisation. They are most likely to define success by meeting, or exceeding, the specification they have been given. A culture of quality can result in a very self-disciplined DP department, but don't bank on this being the norm. (One last point — if it is developing the system, the DP department will probably maintain it as well; however, maintainability can come lamentably low down on a DP department's list of priorities — until it's too late; you've been warned.)

- *The true users*. They're at the bottom of my list because this is where they shouldn't be. Sadly, though, this is where they often end up. If the idea for the application is originated by the corporate planners or the DP department, there is a serious risk that the real users will not be involved in formulating the requirements until much too late. They may not be given a loud enough voice. It will be assumed they are more technically literate than they actually are. Their concerns about job security or changes in working practices will be brushed aside. They may even be considered too ill-informed to be able to make a worthwhile contribution to the process of developing a requirements specification. This is a sure-fire recipe for a system that the users will not feel at home with when it finally arrives. It will be treated as an imposition, and will be subject to constant attempts to subvert it. Result? The ultimate poor-quality system — an unloved and unused one. Solution? For goodness sake, involve the real users from the very start, talk to them, trust them, and listen to them.

2.2.2 The process

Now we have identified the principal players in what by now may already be developing into a comi-tragic farce, what happens next? We have to write the requirements specification (RS). Think of it as an agreed statement, approved by all the above groups, couched in business language, of what is to be developed. How do we do this? Simple, call a meeting, lock all the players in a conference room, with plenty of paper, a whiteboard or two and a draft RS. At the end of the day, send in the cleaners to mop up the blood and feathers.

There will be one of three outcomes.

- *Failure*. The proposal is deemed daft; a decision is taken not to proceed any further. Everyone retires to lick their wounds and ponder the idea of refining that bit, tinkering with the other bit, and then trying again on the next full moon.
- *Success*. The proposal is deemed fine; a decision is taken to proceed. Fat chance! Far more likely is that no one has any screaming objections, so the development rolls forward by default. Very dangerous, and all too common. To ensure that this will be a high-quality system the RS must be reviewed thoroughly before the next stage is advanced to; more on this anon.
- *Abdication*. The proposal is deemed good, but everyone is too busy to do it themselves; even so, it is such a good idea that it would be great if it could be up and running by the first quarter of next year. So, the committee checks with the accounting department, and yes, there is some spare money in the coffers. The decision is taken, 'We'll go external'. The work will be contracted out. Result? More players! Details to follow.

And you thought it was complicated enough already? Just to remind you, here's the rest of the list from a page or two back.

- Third party external consultants;
- Multiple levels of lead and subcontractors;
- The developers of the system;
- The bosses of the developers of the system.

So here goes.

- *Third party consultants*. These are hired not to do the development but to manage the development. The user organisation, redefined here-on-in as the 'client', may have had a crisis of management confidence and decided to farm out the management of the development as well as the actual work. Or it may not have the time or staff to write its own RS. Or it may prefer to keep itself at arm's length from the developers.

So it hires some (probably expensive) management consultants to write the RS and manage the interface with the development contractors. These consultants, being well skilled in the art of 'business lead' follow-up, proceed to suggest that the client might benefit from a complete impartial study of its technological infrastructure and its positioning in the global market place. 'That'll be 1.8 million, please.' Result? Timescale slippage, the study that leads to the RS will take a while and then, once the RS is complete, the client and consultant will issue the RFI/RFP/ITT (Request for Information/Request for Proposal/Invitation to Tender) and both groups will begin the square dance of proposals, bids and selection of developer.

Does this start to sound like a recipe for confusion? Well, there is a good side to it all. The consultants' RS is likely to be a good document; it is their sole tangible deliverable, their reputation as a consultancy rests upon it. But that doesn't mean that the client is excused the task of reviewing it properly.

- *Multiple levels of lead and subcontractors*. I list this separately because the significant thing here is the levels. If the system is complex, the consultants may decide to spread the load of the work, maybe to meet a schedule deadline. Also, there may be a mix of specialised hardware and software and different vendors might be needed. The trend these days is for the software developers to take the lead; they might even have a choice over which hardware vendor to select. The crucial point is that as the number of organisations increases, so does the scope for misunderstandings, and the amount of paperwork to avoid them.

I am not exaggerating. I once worked on a project where a water utility hired a company of consulting engineers to design and procure a new sewage treatment works. The consulting engineers then selected a specialised building contractor to do the majority of the construction work. The water utility then instructed the building contractor to hire the company I worked for to do the 'process control', i.e. program the computer that controlled the Works. With the number of different interfaces between the different organisations, preventing the proverbial from hitting the rotating air-conditioning device was quite a challenge.

- *The developers*. Even though there may be many levels, there is usually one company charged with most of the programming work. It defines success in much the same way as the corporate planners back at the top. That is, it wants to deliver the system to specification, on time and within budget. Especially if the contract is 'fixed price' rather than 'time and materials'. The actual development team, however, may be more like the DP department, and its project manager or team leader will be charged with the responsibility of ensuring that it sticks to the letter of the contract. The project manager will be motivated to make a profit on the project, so I will highlight one other part of the developer's organisation.

• *The bosses of the developers*. Within the developer's organisation, the project manager will report to a manager concerned not only that the project makes a profit, but also that the project delivers a system that is of high enough quality that the client will call upon the developer on subsequent occasions to do more work. So the developer's boss has a slightly different definition of success from the project manager.

2.2.3 Putting it all together

Okay, so that's everyone, right? Well, nearly. I thought I would save a little surprise till the end. Now remember that we have lots of different organisations involved here, and in the real world no one trusts word of mouth anymore. So all of these organisations interact by means of signing contracts. And contracts mean lawyers! Lots of them, but don't panic, the rule is the same as per the accounting department. Factor in some extra time to allow for negotiations and assume that the development project will be doing system testing before the main contract is actually agreed and signed.

2.3 The driver behind the requirements

2.3.1 The missing user

It's about time we looked at something more concrete and saw how, out of all the groups listed above, the *true user* remains the most important.

I once saw a programme on American Public Television where a reporter travelled the world and rode on her top ten favourite urban mass transit systems. Well, each to their own(!). I suspect my total stands at about half a dozen or so, but even this size of sample points to how designers can forget the central purpose of what they are building — meeting the user's requirements.

London Underground Ltd (LUL) comes in for more than its fair share of criticism; tough. On this occasion I am going to add to it. My gripe is about the new automatic ticketing system installed during 1989. It is, in actuality, a very sensible use of information technology; it integrates London's overground and underground systems into one. A ticket dispensed by a British Rail machine can also be used as a valid London Underground ticket. Good idea, saves commuters having to carry two tickets, and allows the same fare-zones to apply to both BR and LUL. If you have ever seen the multi-coloured spaghetti maps put out by both organisations, you will appreciate the benefits of this simplification.

But, and it is a big but, the hardware was not designed for ease of use by the passengers. Rather, the main design criteria force the user to compromise, when it should be vice versa. The first problem is that the tickets are made out of flimsy light-weight cardboard, which is easily bent. The magnetic strip on them, which holds the encoded fare information, runs lengthways down the centre of the back of the ticket. Result? For the ticket to be read, it must be physically fed into a ticket-reading machine (linked to a barrier) which swallows it, and returns the ticket to the passenger after checking it.

All very straightforward, so what's the problem? The system appears to have been designed on the assumption that most of the people feeding tickets into it are giving it one-journey tickets. Fine during most of the day, especially since London is perennially full of tourists gadding about, making short one-off journeys. But come 'crush-hour' when the automatic gates need to be working at their maximum throughput, regular commuters shun them and opt for the slower queues through the gates staffed by real live ticket inspectors. Why? Because commuters use season tickets which, if issued by British Rail and lasting a whole year, may cost many hundreds of pounds. Now, take the cover of a favourite paperback of yours (no, not this one!) and push the cover in and out of the gap in your kitchen door frame — 700 times. I said this was an interactive book. You haven't got the time? Haven't got a kitchen door handy? Well, use your imagination if you must. Finished? Good, notice anything? Chances are that the cardboard of the cover got bent, mangled, or generally damaged well before you got to 700 repetitions. Good job actually, as you probably wouldn't have had the patience to do all 700 attempts.

This is exactly what the harassed London commuters fear. So, they don't part with their precious season ticket, not trusting a machine that swallows a token worth thousands and might not return it. Instead, the passengers clog up the station whilst rows of gleaming automatic gates sit relatively unused. So we have a poor-quality system. Its designers appear to have ignored the concerns of its users who, in turn, if given the chance, try and sidestep it.

Could this have been avoided? Yes, come with me to the other side of the 'Pond'; to the home of the American revolution, the Red Sox and more universities per square foot than pretty much anywhere else on the planet. Boston, USA. This fair city also has an underground railway system, called the 'T' by those who love it.

This system, not unnaturally, faces the same information-processing challenges that exist in London. However, when the authorities introduced automatic ticket readers, they obviously spent more effort on trying to decide how people would use the system. The result? Their season tickets are made out of plastic, and are credit card size and shape. The magnetic strip does not run down the centre, but rather is much closer to the edge. To see what I mean, get out some of your own plastic money and examine it carefully; I think you'll find the magnetic strip is in a similar position.

This sounds too trivial for words. Quite right, but although minor, it has great significance. The ticket, being plastic, is much more difficult to damage through ordinary 'wear-and-tear' and the strip, being positioned where it is, allows the card to be 'swiped' through the card reader. Slid along a groove without the owner ever letting go of it. Result? People happily use the automatic gates and Boston has far fewer ticket inspectors.

Okay, maybe I am over-egging the cake. The example is not exactly earth-shaking (although Boston is in an earthquake zone!). But the point is crucial. In writing an RS, it is all too easy to get caught up in the exciting technology, to concentrate on the meaty bits. Developers tend to prefer technology, finding it the most interesting part of the design. Not at all unreasonable; that's why they went into software development, rather than politics or journalism or the police. No, let them concentrate on the technology, it's what motivates them; but, in the rush to model the system, do not neglect to model the user. Better still, drag a few in off the street, sit them down and ask them some hypothetical questions. Would they prefer 'interface A' or 'front-end B'? Do they like the idea of the system? Would they encourage their friends to use it? Fly a few kites, ask some dumb questions, and pay attention to the responses. And remember, the earlier you do this in the development, the less likely you are to find that you have barked yourself to a great height and are staring down from the wrong tree.

2.4 Consider failure from the outset

2.4.1 Whilst I'm on the subject of users

This focus group of bewildered users, I trust you gave them a cup of tea (or some such ...) and they are now looking less shell-shocked after being herded into your conference room. If they just came down from the fourth floor, they're probably looking quite happy as you've taken them away from the drudgery of their jobs. Once you have explained the system to them, take a closer look; do any of them appear to be wearing particularly supercilious grins on their faces? If so, you're in luck. You have discovered an instance of that much feared irritant to designers — the malicious user.

To continue our travels around the world's subway systems, let us head south 400 miles from Boston, preferably via AmTrak, as I'm told the landing at Washington National airport can be a trifle unsettling, since the plane cannot overfly the city and so is required to follow the course of the River Potomac; thus, it turns and banks repeatedly before you are finally down on the ground in the capital of America.

The Washington DC Metro is a fine system, apart from the colour scheme inside the carriages — far too 'seventies' for my taste. On one particular visit, whilst I was staying in the city, my host told me this hard-to-believe tale, but I repeat it here in good faith.

The DC Metro ticketing system, as with London and Boston, has a magnetic strip on the back of the tickets. Encoded on it is the station where it was purchased, the amount of money paid and when the ticket was purchased. The system was designed to be flexible, admirably so. If, whilst travelling, you decide you wish to continue further than you had originally intended, this is no problem. When you eventually arrive at your destination and feed the ticket into the exit machine, you are not allowed to exit. Don't panic, you merely go to a 'top-up' ticket machine, insert the ticket and add enough extra money so that you have paid the total fare. The strip now indicates that there is enough money 'on' the ticket for you to have travelled from your start point to your revised destination, and the exit machine will let you out.

Now, even more considerate of the system, say you buy a ticket, go through the barrier, down to the platform and then remember you forgot to put the micro-cassette into the heel of your boots (this is Washington DC remember). No problem, you can head back to your office and get it. But there's the exit machine to contend with. Don't worry, it notes you bought your ticket in the station you're still in, so figures you haven't gone anywhere and it lets you out, and gives you back your ticket to use later. You dash to your office, get the micro-cassette and head off to the Senate Hearing, safe in the knowledge all's right with the world.

Not quite so, or at least not in the initial week or two when the Metro first opened. Washington is full of people far too bright and devious for their own good, and some of the lateral-thinking commuters in the population soon found a loophole in the system that saved them lots of money. All they had to do was buy two tickets, one from their local station and one from the station in the centre of town. This took a bit of planning — that's why the designers missed the loophole. There was thus a 'home station' ticket and a 'work station' one. The commuter's regular journey was then as follows. Leave home, arrive at 'home station', enter using 'home station' ticket, ride train, exit in town not using the 'home station' ticket but using the 'work station' ticket, which the system took to represent a null-journey and so was returned to the passenger. Spend day in office, making sure everyone in Appalachia is eating their oat bran. Leave office. Go to 'work station' and gain entry using 'work station' ticket, travel home, exit 'home station' using 'home station' ticket (again returned to the passenger — this is the inverse of the morning journey). Go home, repeat the next day using the SAME tickets!

So, almost all of DC ended up riding to and from work for next to nothing, never needing to buy fresh tickets. News of this spread fast and the Metro authorities found out, made some changes to the software, and stamped out the dodge. What they did? My host wasn't able to tell me, maybe the transit authority kept it a secret to avoid people looking for other loopholes. I'm still not sure if I believe the story, it sounds too outlandish; after all, it amounts to a system failing to fulfil its primary function — charge people money to ride the trains. So unlikely that it just might be true.

Well, true or otherwise, that's the sort of havoc that a malicious user can wreak. So let's sum up and remind you what you should do to avoid this serious a failure in quality.

Regular users are fine, the malicious ones are more unnerving. Their regular counterparts will meekly follow the instructions given on how to use the system and not try anything that isn't documented in the *User Guide*. Malicious users derive very little satisfaction from following orders, they are only in their element if they are actively trying to subvert your system. Preventing them from doing so is a design consideration that you should address in the RS, not later, but now.

2.4.2 Contemplating failure

What I am encouraging you to do is to devote as much effort to considering what might go wrong with your system as you no doubt will to defining its positive functions. There is a psychological aspect to this, not dissimilar to the issue of having a developer test his or her own code. When effort is devoted to creating something, it is not a pleasant prospect to focus on how it can be broken. People are naturally reluctant to contemplate the failure of something they do not want to fail. Given the chance, there is a strong likelihood that this part of the design process will be skipped over, brushed under the carpet and not given the weight it deserves.

The best way to address this is to involve outsiders. Two varieties can be useful.

The first comes from the group of bewildered potential users you lassoed earlier. They are best at naïve damage — the unintentional sort done by someone who doesn't know any better. You wouldn't do it because you do know better; hence, you might not remember to build suitable resilience into the system to withstand that sort of treatment. It wouldn't occur to you to treat the system that way.

The other variety will come from somewhere in your development organisation, but will not have been involved in the gestation of your system to date. In other words, this person (or persons, preferably) is acting as a consultant to your development work — knowledgeable about techniques, technical niceties and how to do really nasty things to software, but not familiar with the particular problem you are trying to solve. Now (once you have a draft RS) is the time to bring them into the review cycle. Not necessarily the same review group as the participants outlined above. Better, give them a copy of the RS, let them read it over, then (and this is where having more than one person of this variety pays off) put them in a room with some alcohol (pubs are good!) and let them brainstorm, fantasise, ramble. The more outlandish their suggestions the better. Having a group will allow them to spark off each other; you don't want dry careful analysis here but, rather, insightful inspiration.

Let's tie this failure thing down a bit more. Can we get a handle on what exactly we are looking for? There is a book [4] that I am particularly fond of, entitled *Understanding Systems Failures*. It compares various systems, where 'system' is defined in its softest sense. This includes hospital administration and the collapse of companies, as well as the more classic systems like the Three Mile Island nuclear plant in Pennsylvania, USA, and an oil rig accommodation platform that capsized in the North Sea.

The authors begin by defining what they mean by a system. The definition comes in four parts.

> A system is an assembly of components, connected together in an organised way.
> The components are affected by being in the system and the behaviour of the system is changed if they leave it.
> This organised assembly of components does something.
> This assembly has been identified as of particular interest.

So how do we use this definition? The last part is redundant from our point of view; if the assembly wasn't of interest, you wouldn't be working on it — in fact, you'd probably be redundant! Going back to the first point, the crucial word is 'components'. To discover all the various ways your system might fail (as preparation for combating such situations), you need to ensure you have all the components you need. What marks the boundary of your system? The computer room door? What happens if there's a power failure? Is the standby generator in the computer room or elsewhere? The operators' terminal lies on the boundary, but does the system reside on a mainframe computer used for many other applications, some of which own dial-in lines which an enterprising hacker could use to gain access to your system?

Get out a pencil and a big sheet of paper, or a computer-based graphical drawing package and draw a schematic representation of the system. Poke and prod at the boundaries, and keep nudging it until it ceases to say 'Ouch!'. To be a bit more technical, the second part of the definition helps us to clarify the boundary. For each 'suspect' component near the edge, which you think may be part of the system, assume it is, model the system that way, then take the component away. Is the component affected by its removal? And does the system's behaviour change with that removal? If so, then the component should be in the system. Keep going until you've got all the components. Even if it gets absurd, keep going; you can rationalise things later, if you really must, but only by doing this can you be sure that you've considered all possible contributors to a system's failure.

The only part I haven't mentioned, the third, defines what must happen to avoid a fundamental failure. The system must do something. This condition, from your point of view, is necessary but not sufficient. Not only must it do something, it must do the right thing.

This should be enough to identify your system, but I thought I would drop in a few points on failure. Again taken from the book, the idea here is to stimulate your thinking about your system and all the different ways it can fail.

> A failure can be said to occur when disappointment arises as a result of an assessment of an outcome from an activity.
>
> Failure can be a shortfall of performance below a standard, the generation of undesirable side effects or the neglect of an opportunity.
>
> The assessment of an outcome as failure is dependent upon the values held by the person making the judgement. These values affect how much of the performance of an activity is included for the assessment, what quantities or qualities are regarded as significant, and what standards are adopted. The values are liable to vary from individual to individual, and group to group. They are liable to change with time and the occasion of the judgement, and the viewpoint taken.
>
> Failure can occur in a variety of forms, namely: catastrophic or minor, overwhelming or only partial, sudden or slow.
>
> Failure can arise in the past, present or future.
>
> Failure will be found to be multicausal, and to have multiple effects.

2.5 Finding out what the users want

2.5.1 A taxonomy of users

It's time to return our attention to the system's *raison d'être* — the users. Note, the title of this section does not mean that should they annoy you, you can tell them to 'go visit a taxidermist'. No, quite the contrary, you should develop a degree of empathy for them. They can be placed on a particularly significant sliding scale, and their precise location is important. This is the scale of experience. Have they ever used a computer system before? If so, what did it do for them? And crucially — what are their expectations of what your solution can do for them now, and how much work do they think it will take you to achieve it all?

If they have never been actively involved in the design of a computer system, users can have some pretty peculiar notions. Specifically, if they have engineering backgrounds they can assume that you (the developer) can adapt to changes in the details of the specifications as quickly as they can adjust the resistance of the widget–grommet interlinkage assembly by adding a drop of oil. This may well be the case if you are working with an amenable programming language and have correctly softcoded everything you could think of. But you might have hardware or language constraints that make changing things, after the design is supposedly finalised, very costly — in both time and money. Beware, this misconception can be painful; so sit your users down and have a nice friendly chat and ascertain where they are coming from and, if necessary, explain the constraints you are operating under. This could save you from a lot of grief later.

2.5.2 Pass the lightning bolt

So far I've talked about brainstorming to try and make sure that all potential problems are factored into the design. Well, brainstorming is fun — so it would be a pity to use it only for discovering potential problems. It might get a bad name for itself. There is another area where it is important. The positive side of your system. We have yet to address the issue of determining what your system should actually jolly well spend its time doing. So let's get focused.

Remember, the essence of brainstorming is non-linear thinking. It is the flying of kites, together with restraining the urge to shoot them down the moment they are launched. To this end, I cannot give you a detailed prescriptive checklist of what you must do to achieve this. I can only present pointers.

The organisation of these sessions should be informal and relaxed. Unlimited doughnuts, coffee and/or alcohol may well facilitate the thinking process. Everything should be recorded, written down, video-taped if you have the facilities. The participants should be non-judgemental about the ideas that are presented. It may help to have a chairperson who can sit firmly on anyone who starts to evaluate ideas there and then. And try to include people from all the groups that are listed at the start of this chapter. Then subsequently, at least two days later, you can reconvene and assess the validity of the ideas.

You will already have quite a few sources of ideas. What I am going to suggest here are supplemental sources. They should not be read exhaustively; instead, you should dip into them to gain inspiration. They should, with luck, interrupt your present thinking patterns and prompt you to ask fresh questions about what you are trying to achieve.

The first source is a book entitled *Systems, Management and Change* [5]. It is unique in that it is the most graphically orientated business book I have come across. It discusses the context, evolution and design of different systems in a very accessible manner. It can easily be dipped into and almost any page should stimulate some fresh thought.

The other stimulus is a fascinating book called *Age of Unreason* [6] by the renowned specialist in management and organisations, Charles Handy. It covers the changes that are taking place in many disparate aspects of personal life, society and technology, and how these will impact organisations. It should give you some new insights into the world in which your system will operate — as anticipating your system's external context will be as much a determinant of success and quality as addressing the obvious functional requirements that already scream out to be met, as of today. Remember, your system will probably have a ten-to-fifteen-year lifespan.

One other point of note; you need to evaluate the current way the functions of the proposed system are being met. It may be the case that the functions are brand new and not currently implemented in any way, shape, or form; if so, then skip this paragraph. Otherwise, one of two cases will apply. Either the system is already computerised and the aim of the new system is to upgrade it in some way. Maybe speed it up, integrate disparate functions, give it a new user-friendly front-end. Whatever, do make a point of studying the existing system carefully and discerning both what people like about it, and what people dislike; what it does well, where it falls down. The other case is that there is currently not a screen, keyboard or CPU in sight. In this situation, you are automating from scratch, and face a big risk. The danger is that you will automatically model the paper-based system, then replicate it down to the last counter-signature, on the computer. If you do this, you've missed the greatest opportunity that IT presents you with — the chance to enhance people's working lives, to remove drudgery and inject challenge. In this situation, you must ask 'How can we do this better?'. Think laterally. The aim is to take advantage of the opportunity that installing a system presents to review the way the work is currently done, to automate and hide the boring bits, and to enhance the quality of the users' working lives as a result.

2.6 Project planning issues raise their heads

2.6.1 Development approaches

One crucial question that must be answered during the brainstorming sessions is 'What is our development approach?' Although this is more project planning than requirements capture, the two areas do interact since different development approaches will result in different information gathering strategies. There are a number of different tacks that can be taken, each with pros and cons. I will enumerate them.

- *Specification and installation*. This is the classic mode. It is very much a straight-line approach. You write the specifications and, once each level (Requirements, Functions, Internals) is complete it is immediately encased in ice. Frozen for all time and never subsequently changed. Beware, this is often the aim that people set out with, but countervailing pressures push them off this path and an unholy mess can result, especially if they fail to acknowledge that this has happened. If you are going to take this route, ensure that everyone knows, and appreciates, the implications. In addition, get down to the 'personality gym' and do some 'psychological weight training' as you will need a will of iron to succeed.

- *Phased delivery*. Central to this approach is the fact that there is a lot of functionality in the system to be delivered, but also the system is needed very urgently. There won't be enough time to provide all the functionality by the date when the system is due to go live. The solution is to prioritise the functionality; each discrete component is assigned a level of importance. The ones crucial to the system's successful operation are placed on the 'Phase 1' list. The other functions, which will improve the way the system runs, but can be lived without, at least in the short-term, are placed on the 'Phase 2' list. The main consequences of this approach are that certain tasks, such as the later stages of testing, will have to be done twice; more effort than usual will also need to be expended on configuration management (more on this later in the book — much more!).

- *Dummy user interfaces*. This approach can also be entitled 'slanted phased delivery'. Figure 2.1 shows a tree-like structure, inverted naturally, since all computer people fantasise about a world in which gravity doesn't exist and time

Figure 2.1
Slanted phased delivery

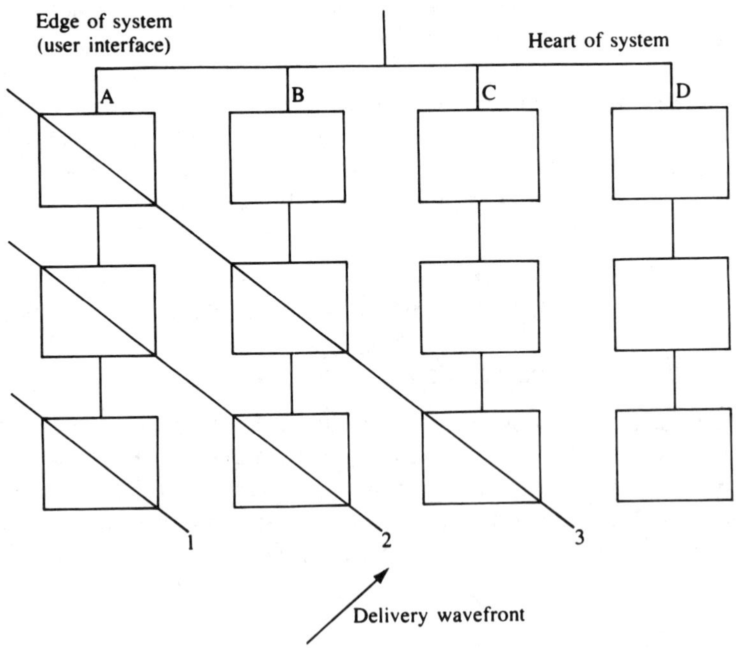

runs backwards. The branches of the tree represent the different subsystems. They are ordered such that subsystem A represents the user interface, subsystem B serves the user interface, and so on, as you work to the right, with the right-most subsystem (D in this example) being at the heart of the system. The diagonal numbered lines represent the 'wave-front' of delivery. The boxes that line 1 intersects with give the 'complete' modules that form part of the first delivery; the other modules are dummy modules. As the numbers increase, so more of the system is 'complete' and less is 'dummy'. In the 'spec and install' approach described above, all four subsystems would arrive at the user at the same time. In this approach, the user interface subsystem is delivered early. It is a dummy user interface, as the other subsystems are not yet complete, so when the user tries out operations on it, it fakes the response. This doesn't matter, as what we are concerned with here is not the core functionality, but giving the users a feel for the interface they are actually going to be dealing with. Because the user interface is delivered first, there is time for the users to give feedback on it; it can be changed and, in the end, will be more to their liking, and hence of higher quality. This approach could be called evolutionary-prototyping, as parts of the system are defined by iteratively building the system. Note, this approach will be time-consuming as it will involve significant reworking of code.

- *Full prototyping*. This approach is the opposite of the 'spec and install' one. Your life will be considerably eased if you have lots of lovely CASE (computer aided software engineering) tools. Preferably, able to generate code directly from specifications; thus, when you amend them the code can be easily and quickly regenerated. You will build a 'rough version' of the whole system, not just the user interface, and let the users play with it. Get their feedback, refine the system, and do it again. The main gating factors on this will be the speed with which a new version of the system can be created, and the amount of time you have to play with before the system must be finally delivered to the users. This approach will involve considerable configuration management, preferably handled by the CASE tools, unless you'd rather live dangerously and junk the previous design each time you produce a refined version. Your choice, have fun.

2.6.2 The dreaded phrase

The what? Yes, it couldn't wait any longer. So here it comes, bounding into the book to take up residency, from here to the appendices.

- *Change control*. Now, the reality of the situation is that requirements change; during the timeframe of the development work, they evolve. The more the system's functions are studied, the greater the understanding that is achieved and the clearer the picture becomes, of what the system must do. This is inevitable, it cannot be avoided. Pretending to be an ostrich, and planting your head firmly in the sand, will only result in your being trampled underfoot by a passing wildebeest, on its way to deliver a change request note to the rest of the project team.

One other point before we get to how to handle change. Distance. The further away a requirement moves from its original formulator, the firmer it will become. That is, the brainstorming session might have resulted in a finely balanced decision, which was taken tentatively and with reservations. Well, by the time the information embodied in this choice has filtered down to the developer, the fragility of the original choice will have been lost. First written on paper, then signed into an agreement, then finally carved in stone. The more layers there are between the user and the developer, the greater the chance of mutual incomprehension when the user changes his or her mind, and the developer retorts that such a change is totally untenable and that to make it will wreck large amounts of work. The sad truth of the matter is that this will happen. The cliché that 'the only constant is change' is one of the defining axioms of the last decade of the twentieth century, let alone the twenty-first.

We can't stop it, but we can attempt to manage it. There is a lot more on this later in the book, so here I will just give the guiding principles. There are three.

- Establish procedures, don't do things on an *ad hoc* basis.
- Write everything down.
- Establish a single authorised individual for each group to act as the point of contact, both for the users and the developers. These two people will be the conduit of communication; they will be aware of all that is happening, and thus stand some chance of keeping control of the forces of change.

2.7 The requirements specification

2.7.1 *'Here we go, here we go, here we go . . .'*

By now, you should be ready to write your Requirements Specification (RS). I've talked at length about how to do it, so it's now time to address what should be in it and what quality hurdles it must jump over before it can be considered complete.

- *Language*. The users' language. No computerese, that can come later (if it must). It will be littered with acronyms, but these will belong to parts of the users' organisation, or represent tasks that the organisation does.

- *Structure*. There should be the following:

  - *Executive summary:* remember the red-braces (suspenders States-side) brigade. Put it at the front, but write it last. Then consider the three elements.
  - *Liveware:* describe the users; who are they, what do they do now, what do they want to do?
  - *Hardware:* what are the essential qualities that it must have? Geography, communication links and other functions are more important than the brand name on the side of the buff-coloured boxes, at this stage.
  - *Software:* remember, the crucial thing at this stage is to state what it does,

but not how it does it. If some functionality could be achieved either in the software or in the hardware, address that alternative.

- *Qualities and issues*. The RS cannot be considered finished until it has been reviewed to confirm that it addresses the following:

- *Complete:* is everything covered? Keep asking this question, as it is very easy to overlook some aspect or other.
- *Verifiable:* can each statement be checked? A vague woolly sentence is not only useless, it is dangerous, as it will breed a feeling of false security. This is essential if you are going to test the finished system successfully.
- *Unambiguous:* is everything stated as simply and as clearly as possible? Could statements be misinterpreted? Are there unwarranted assumptions implicit in the text? Check with a fine toothed comb and, if you are unsure, rewrite.
- *Attributes:* ensure that in discussing the system you address the following.

  - *Expandability:* it's bound to grow with time, don't impose arbitrary constraints, either in hardware or software.
  - *Configurability:* there may well be multiple versions in use, which require different configurations; make changing these easy. Aim to be able to do this on-line.
  - *Capacity:* this is important. Model the system, look for bottlenecks, think 'parallel design'.
  - *Resilience:* walk around it and kick the tyres; does it collapse? If you've looked on the darker side and thought about system failure, this should be a doddle.
  - *Flexibility:* you are bound to want to change the things the system does and how it does them. Keep things soft (as in softcoding) wherever possible. Visit a lawyer and make 'parameterisation' your middle name; it'll sound good at parties, and changes to the system will be far less painful.

2.8 Final thoughts

What's most important from this chapter? Talk to the users, and don't stop. Keep talking to them, involve them, expect them to change things. So plan for change, set up procedures and designate responsible individuals, and maximise flexibility in your designs. And review, review, review.

2.9 Questions

1. When will your RS have to be completed?
2. So when will you schedule the negative, positive and review sessions?
3. How will you rewrite my review checklist, expanding upon it, so you can base your review on something meaningful to you?

4. Who are the 'players' in your development — names and phone numbers are needed — how soon will you schedule lunch with each group?
5. What is going to be your development approach?
6. Who will be your 'information conduits' (see 'The dreaded phrase')?
7. When will you read 'Change Control and Configuration Management', Chapter 9?
8. When will you explain its contents to the rest of your team?
9. Have you ordered the beer for the brainstorming sessions?

3 External functionality

3.1 Introduction

3.1.1 Should I be here?

'As the Knights of the Data Table made their way through the forest of paper that seemed to have grown up around them literally overnight, they stumbled upon a clearing and lo, in the distance, was that not the Castle of MaynFrame, home of the statement of External Functionality?

'They set to their journey with renewed vigour; soon their trusty work-horses had carried them to the entrance to this, the most important staging post yet, on their quest for the ultimate system. There it stood, tall, proud and forbidding, surrounded by a moat infested by nasty looking data-crunchers, with long sharp teeth. How would they get in?

'They worked their way around to the south side, for they had crept up carefully from the north. There they found the main gate, and a guard with a stern look on his face. Seized by a sudden flush of bravery, they boldly marched up to him, declared themselves, and demanded entrance. He looked affronted, but then his rough hewn features turned slightly quizzical. He recognised them as Knights of the Data Table, with their Swords of Analysis and the Shields of Past Experience. A silence fell over the drawbridge, save for the snapping of the data-crunchers below in the murky watery depths.

'He spoke, suddenly, barking out a conundrum, a riddle that took the Knights by surprise. He demanded the key of entry, saying that they were not entitled to seek the Statement of External Functionality unless they first produced for him the Description of User Requirements. Taken aback, the Knights retreated, called a meeting and analysed the situation over a bowl of hot gruel. This was an unforeseen problem, they had hoped to begin their quest with the External Functionality, skipping the easier early stages that were no real challenge to a true Data Warrior. But there was no choice; they had to go forward, but how? At that moment, a thunderbolt ripped the heavens asunder and they were jolted by the realisation of what they must do. Reinvigorated, they settled down for the evening, resolving to return the next day to the castle.

'That morning, with the cool dawn mist swirling around them, they stood again

Executive Summary in the language of the Users, would they be let in? The guard nodded his assent, but he gruffly warned them not to forget the warning at the start of Chapter 2 — upon their return with the said Executive Summary, they were not to bring with them any associates who were already further advanced on the quest. For the quest was an urgent one, and it was not wise to spend time on the early stages if the associates were already further advanced. Lo, the Knights produced the Executive Summary within the hour — for it was a high-level piece of work.

'This presented, the guard granted the Knights access to the castle and they did wander and feast on the delights of the External Functionality.'

Well, all right, I know this metaphor is getting a little 'pythonesque', and just slightly carried away with itself. But you'll have to admit, it's not quite how you expected this chapter to start. A bit unreal, really — but then so is the mammoth effort you're about to undertake. A definition of a system's external functionality needs the dedication of a knight on a crusade if it is to be worth the parchment it's laser-printed on. And you owe it to yourself to know the users' requirements — in writing — before you start.

3.1.2 So what is it anyway?

We are talking black boxes. Not buff boxes, but black. We are not interested in the detail of how this wonderful system will achieve what we ask of it; right now, we are still behaving a little like the users. They know what they want the system to do, but don't care how it achieves the result, as long as it does. The statement of external functionality (SEF from now on) is primarily a work of scholastic translation, giving the developers a techno-speak document upon which the rest of the development will be based. You will take what is written in the requirements specification (RS), in user-speak, and translate it to techno-speak (if you are missing an RS, then grab a user or two and draft up a quick user-speak executive summary (where have I heard that phrase before?) and make that the first section of your SEF).

Given that you now have something in user-speak, note that your translation will be the opposite of TV news translation. On 'the box' English always seems to be more concise than the original language; the overdubbed translation starts later and finishes sooner than the native tongue. For you there's no such luck. A by-product of your translation will be an expansion in the size of the document. Statements that seemed simple and obvious to a user will need careful examination, and will be clarified by the SEF. Note, it will be a clarification only from the point of view of the author of the SEF; the user will find such rewriting either nit-picking, bamboozling or just plain irrelevant. No matter, you need to do it. Not least because, although we are, at this stage, still concerned only with what the system will do (not how it will do it), we must make sure that what we propose is feasible. If we don't check this now, we could find ourselves up to our necks in trouble later down the line. Scrub that, later around the bend; remember — no linear thinking!

Whoops, I've made a big assumption; I really should run it up the flag-pole, just to confirm that you will indeed salute it. I have assumed you've had nothing to do with the system until now. The people who hatched the original idea, hawked it around until it picked up enough support and was allowed to fly, are all total strangers to you. They may be in your organisation, on the seventeenth floor, with their own key to the executive washrooms; or they may be clients (if you in fact work for a firm of software implementors). Result, you are already one, maybe two, steps removed from the real end-users. Their definition of success is probably not yours — be aware of this. If I'm incorrect, as far as you are concerned, and you have been involved in formulating the RS and are now embarking on the SEF, then good, you stand a better chance of delivering a high-quality system.

On the other hand, if you've arrived here via Chapter 2 and were involved in the brainstorming that produced the RS, but have now handed it all over to the developers who work on from the SEF all the way to going live, then don't lose touch. Read this chapter to find out what the developers are up to, and call them up, regularly — keep involved and stay informed.

3.2 Consider this before you write

3.2.1 The dotted line

One other major aspect of the work that you, the developer, are about to undertake is that the document may form the legal basis for the development. If this is taking place all within one organisation, the SEF may supersede the RS as the agreed point of understanding between the users and the DP department as to what is to be delivered. If we are in a situation where the system development work has been contracted out to a different company, then this document will probably give the technical underpinning to the legal contract between client and developer. Even if the work results in other long documents, this one will be deemed (by convention) to take precedence over the other ones, in case there's an inconsistency between the SEF and the RS. When the judge calls the court to order, this document will be the touchstone upon which any dispute between the parties (to the said contract) will be judged. That is to say, what's written here goes.

It becomes obvious that it is crucial for everyone involved to understand what this document is committing them to, and to (hopefully) enter into that agreement happy with their ability to (respectively) develop the system on the basis of the document, and have their needs met by a system that matches the one in the document. A poor-quality system would definitely result from a poor-quality SEF and that would be expensive enough, but a poor-quality SEF could also generate astronomical legal costs — so the motivation to strive for the highest possible quality should be apparent.

3.2.2 *Time to get the pen out?*

Not yet. We must first consider the stages that are involved in producing 'an SEF to be proud of'. First of all, we need to do a little bit of investigation. If we are lucky there will be a well-written RS. Such a document should cover all the areas I outlined at the end of Chapter 2. Check that it does. If so, then it will be a straightforward task to translate it into the language of the developer. Although not a mindless task, it remains very important that every statement in such an RS is questioned, probed and its implications considered. Remember, the developer is in a much better position than the user to spot interactions in requirements which may be of benefit, as they can be implemented more easily than the user imagined; or they may be a potential source of trouble, as there might be latent conflicts that the user wasn't even aware could exist. Do not assume that every statement has been thought through already and is cleared for take-off. Indeed, don't take my words at face value, question me. Why am I asking you to do something? Have I guessed right about the nature of the organisation you are in and what it is demanding of you? How might it be necessary to amend my advice to increase its utility to you?

The other case is where you have a pile of paper which would be more aesthetically pleasing if it were still part of a glorious coniferous expanse sloping down to some peaceful lakeside. But I digress, you are faced with an RS not worth the paper it is written on. What do you do? Cry; then call the user. Why cry? Not from sorrow, but joy! What? Yes, because this means you will have to get the information from the horse's mouth, not rely on what she might have dictated to the stable lad. You will have to interact with the user — this will keep you on your toes. The SEF will be more likely to reflect the actual requirements of the user.

3.2.3 *Buff boxes and what to put in them*

Now is not too soon to start to gather some of the wisdom that defines the true information systems professional. Sink your teeth into a few trade journals, go on a junket around the European trade fairs, and visit a vendor or two. You need to know what technology, both hardware and software, is out there to augment the capabilities of you and your development team. Get visiting.

Discussions with the users and vendors represent the first stage in the production of the SEF — investigation. The central point here is that it is not enough to automatically copy what you find in the RS. Critical thinking must be applied so that areas of concern that are external to the RS are also taken into consideration.

3.2.4 *Production values*

Armed with the RS (or, should it prove to be worthless, the information you've gathered), you should start to consider how you are going to write the document. Building a skeleton document early on — just section headings — is a very good idea. This will mean that your investigation findings won't be floating around the office scribbled on little scraps of paper. The more important they are, the more likely they will be to get lost and prove to be the most difficult to replicate.

This means you need to start thinking about word processing. You may be lucky enough to be in an organisation that is geared up to provide you with an IPSE (integrated project support environment) and that will include decent word processing facilities. If this is not the case, then you have a series of questions to answer.

The first is — how graphic do you want your SEF to be? People reason about information in many different ways — some can handle page after page of text with little trouble (you are probably in that category, otherwise you would have put this down already!), others are much more at home with graphical representations of ideas. There is no right or wrong here. A judgemental attitude on how best to present information, resulting in a decision that one approach is better than the other, is inappropriate. Remember, irrespective of who you expect to read the SEF, people as yet undreamt of will enter into the development project and also need to understand the material presented in the SEF. It behoves you to make the document as accessible as possible to all its potential readers.

The main dividing line is between word processing packages that allow you to include graphics drawn using 'art-tools' and those that restrict you to 'character graphics'. In the first case, we are talking about the classic Apple Macintosh style interface, which originated from Xerox's Palo Alto Research Center (PARC) in Northern California. Characterised by windows, icons, menus and a pointer moved by a 'mouse', the look and feel of this type of interface has been duplicated by various PC-based packages. If you are on a Macintosh, almost all packages allow you to import items from other packages, so your selection of drawing tool need not restrict the choice of word processor. On a PC, interchangeability is less guaranteed and, as usual, since the aim here is to keep things simple, you want to aim for the eventual print-out of the document to be the 'last act'. If you subsequently need to cut and paste, or recollate output from different sources, you are setting up a chore for yourself that you will not enjoy and very soon not do, and your document is at risk of not getting updated properly and getting out of step. So the central point is 'inter-operability', choose tools that can work together on the same platform.

If you intend to use 'character graphics', then I will give you a little demonstration. This is what the word processor I am using to write this book provides me with:

```
 - - - - - - - - - - - - -
|                         |
|   Here's your example   |
|                         |
 - - - - - - - - - - - - -
```

Not nearly as nice as the other graphics, but maybe adequate if all you intend to do is draw boxes and straight lines. However, it does restrict your creativity as diagonal lines look messy and, by that point, you've already reached your limit. With the range of desk top publishing tools available, I have to admit, I think it's a shame if you limit yourself to this. But this is a judgement for you to make — remember, you are the boss, at least as far as this is concerned.

One last group I shouldn't forget, the people condemned to work on the word processing packages set up on their mainframe machines. These probably came with the operating system; some of them look like they came straight out of the Ark. My advice in this situation, try screaming — not at walls — but more carefully targeted screaming, at the person in your organisation with the power to authorise expenditure on better equipment. The one good point on this, however, is that it makes configuration control of your documents easier (see Chapter 9).

Most important is output, the very paper the document appears on; almost all mainframes these days can have laser printers hooked up to them, and the use of laser printers and PCs by secretaries in offices is exceedingly commonplace. So? So there's no excuse for your print-out not to be of laser-printer quality; it looks much more professional, and is easier to read and photocopy (compared to fanfold print-out from listing printers).

3.2.5 Production process

The production of the document will undoubtedly be iterative. You'll find yourself producing a series of drafts, and each one will be reviewed, resulting in corrections and refinements. The reviews should involve representatives from all groups who will interact with the system.

- *The users* are crucial to the whole exercise; however, that doesn't mean that they should be allowed to drive the contents of the document, particularly with reference to the language that is used. They already have their own statement of what they want, the RS. They are entitled to express a preference over the executive summary, but as you go deeper into the SEF, their role becomes one of ensuring that your understanding of their requirements is correct, rather than one of influencing how you choose to express their requirements in your own technical language.

- *The designers* are, I guess, the main target audience for this chapter. To say that they should be present at the review is in some respects almost tautologous; but I do so to point out that sending the document out to people, letting them produce written comments, reading (and possibly ignoring) those comments, then reissuing the SEF does not constitute a review. Instead, that scenario is really a case of non-interactive feedback. Notice that I use a negative phraseology in my definition; I want to emphasise that central to the review process is the interactive discussion of the document. The designers can't hide away, rely on the postal service, send out copies, get back comments and consider the document to be reviewed. The designers must be involved right at the heart of a series of lively, possibly controversial, but certainly interactive meetings. I said involved, I did not say convening; the designers are necessary participants but that does not mean to say that they should co-ordinate and run the review meetings. This is best done by a third party, probably the project manager, who is able to concentrate on the art of facilitating a good review session — not an easy thing to achieve (more on this in Chapter 10) — while the designers concentrate on presenting to the other participants the thinking underlying the design.

• *The implementors* may not be the same set of people as the designers. The worst case scenario would be where the users are in company A, the designers work for consultancy B, and the implementors are part of software house C. It is crucial that they have a say, as they may be the only people aware of some subtle technical constraints that may prevent certain functional objectives from being achieved in the way the designers were envisaging. They may also have input on how easily different design approaches can be implemented within the timescale constraints the development is operating. However, these detailed technical points, although resulting in particular design approaches being adopted over other ones, may not be appropriate for the SEF. They should be noted in the written review record, which provides a log of decisions taken and the reasons underlying those conclusions; but the technical detail of the implementation (the 'how it does it', rather than the 'what it does') should be left for the next level down in the development project's documentation set.

• *The maintainers* should be brought in at this stage as well. In some cases, they will be the same people as the implementors; in other cases, they may come from a separate division within the DP department and rarely have contact with the development division. As a group, the maintainers' views will carry more weight in the reviews of the documents defining the system's internals. But by that point, time will be tight (not to say that it isn't already!) and precedent-setting decisions may already have been taken. These decisions could lock the implementors into an approach that results in code that is very difficult to maintain. The best way to avoid this is to bring the maintainers in at the current stage. One design issue on which they have an entitlement to voice an opinion is the presentation of error messages, not only at a user console, but into an error message log (be it to a terminal, printer or a file). The format and content of these messages will provide one, maybe the only, source of information the maintainers have when trying to troubleshoot and fix a problem with the system after it has gone live. It is crucial that this log presents all the information that it can, in a form that is of maximum utility, and thus that it be given due consideration during the design of the system — not left as an afterthought. It is no good devoting hours of effort to designing and specifying the system's functions if, when it goes wrong (as it will — they all do), there is no effective way to discern why it's gone wrong, what's happened and thus how the situation might be rectified.

• *The operators* are often neglected. This is a shame. It is also a bad idea, as they provide the first-level support to all the live systems that the users' enterprise runs. The operators can facilitate the system's functioning if it presents them with meaningful information ('primary data file 95% full, please load new disk pack'), or they can be left as helpless observers ('system abend — error condition dat008432z'). The psychology of many organisations relegates the operations staff to the bottom of the corporate heap. The only power they are granted is negative positional power — not uncommon for a service function in an enterprise. They are a hygiene factor; their presence is not noticed if everything is functioning fine, but should they fail to do their job, or deprive the users of the system because of an operational problem, then and only then are they noticed, and promptly cursed by all affected. However, they are very valuable; if the new system can be designed to integrate with their current operational working practices, then they can provide an enhanced level of support to the users. Ask them how they currently handle disk crashes, disks getting full of data, processor crashes, power failures, backup cycles. I provide a more detailed discussion of this below, but these examples should serve to underline the nub of my argument — involving the operators at the design stage is crucial to the success of a system.

Okay, so you've reviewed the SEF. What next? You then cycle (no, not on an exercise bike, at least not now, maybe later . . .). I mean that you repeat the writing and reviewing sequence again, and then once more. You have one important criterion to assess this activity against. The point here is, when is the document complete? The answer is not when you reach the 'document complete date' in the project plan. All that means is that you've met the schedule and reviewed the document a bit, but not necessarily enough. The definition of completeness has to be a little more rigorous and demanding. This chapter will provide you with such a definition. A high-quality SEF will cover all the structural elements I list and will address all the issues I enumerate in the rest of this chapter. I will allow you a little leeway; it is not the SEF that must cover everything, it is the review process. Take this book into your reviews and use this chapter as a checklist of items you should check the SEF for. But don't only use this chapter, let my questions start you thinking about issues of unique concern to you and yours — augment my list with an extra one of your own.

3.3 The statement of external functionality

3.3.1 Outlining the structure

So how would you organise what you put into the SEF. Preferably in the same way as the RS was organised. But I am rather presumptuous in assumption here; the last statement applies only if the RS is organised along the lines I adumbrated in Chapter 2. In case it is not, here they are again:

- Executive summary.
- Liveware.

- Hardware.
- Software.
- Development schedule.
- Actual functionality.

- *Executive summary*. This is included for one simple reason; you and everyone else you interact with already have too much to read. Unless you need to get down to the nitty-gritty level of detail, this section should provide you with all the information, in the SEF, that is of relevance to you. Although short in length, there is no reason why diagrams should not be used to show the system's context. Indeed, as these can sometimes be better at transmitting information to the less technically literate members of the SEF's readership, I would positively encourage you to maximise your use of diagrams. In fact, there should be one to summarise each of the sections in the rest of the document.

In the situation where there is no satisfactory RS, the executive summary will serve an additional function. In all cases, it will have two parts; the distinguishing factor is the weight that will be given to each of them. The first part is a summary of the users' requirements of the system, the second is an abstract of the rest of the SEF. The first part will be written before any other bit of the SEF, the second part left until the SEF is complete. If there is a satisfactory RS, the first part need only be short; however, if the RS has gone AWOL, this part will need beefing up.

- *Liveware*. The SEF is, in essence, a model of the system you are going to build. And since the system exists to satisfy the needs of its users — people — they should not only be included in the model, they should be considered before the other components. But what are we aiming for here? We need an abstract summary, in technical language, of the users' interaction with the system. You will need to identify the different groups the users may belong to, and thus the different ways in which they expect to interact with the system.

This is where you should discuss the user interface — in detail, preferably using plenty of diagrams. It is not satisfactory just to assume that the users will use the terminals and keyboards that come with the computer hardware that the system will run on. Not least because your system may have some very specialised function that requires the user to interact with a non-standard piece of hardware. You what? An example — the ticket-barrier machines I mentioned in Chapter 2. Here is not the place to describe the detailed workings of their innards, but it is imperative that you do address the way in which the users will use them. And, in reviewing the SEF, this sort of hardware/user interaction needs to be considered especially carefully — because the uniqueness of the specialised hardware means that the particular series of interactions that the users are being expected to carry out may never before have been tried, and thus proved workable (or not). Remember that the document isn't complete until it has been reviewed by everyone involved and it has jumped the necessary quality hurdles.

The fundamental aim in writing the liveware section of the document is to ensure that the user interface is central to the system, rather than an afterthought. The interface should make the system easy to deal with. It should present users with a consistent approach to the system in terms of aspects such as naming conventions, screen format, presentation of prompts, error messages, use of menus, use of colour. If the system does specialised things, the most appropriate technology should be harnessed to support those functions. The users should not be forced into compromising by having to use inappropriate equipment. I am talking about devices such as touch-sensitive screens, text scanners, light pens (for drawing on screens), drawing/digitising pads, specialised keyboards (colour-coded keys), tracker balls, mice (or mouses — I'm not sure the conventional plural necessarily applies!), colour printers, voice recognition interfaces, cameras (still or video); the list could continue for a while yet, but I think you get my drift.

As far as colour is concerned, I tend to the view that a colour monitor should be used, unless a very good case can be made that colour would be of no benefit whatsoever to a potential user. Whatever the system, consistent and intelligent use of colour can increase the usability of a system, particularly for novice users. A simple example is the presentation of messages on a screen — a monochrome screen can only give text, reverse video or maybe flash the text on and off. Colour, on the other hand, can be used as a background so that purely informational messages could have a green background, warning messages yellow, and error messages red. But do remember that a percentage of the population is colour blind; we tend to forget this fact as it doesn't show, except when they run the occasional red traffic light(!). So, in this example, include a code letter in the message to distinguish the type, say the first letter, 'I' for information, 'W' for warning, and 'E' for error. This does, though, introduce the 'person with two watches problem' — 'the person with one knows what the time is, the person with two is never quite sure', as the two watches will never tell exactly the same time. By being tautologous and presenting the same information twice, we run the risk of a bug (or two) when the information conflicts, e.g. an 'E' for error on a green for information background. Don't worry, it's all right really; this is just another little challenge to keep you on your toes. Solution? Design the system so this possibility can't arise.

A system may have different types of user — administrators, operators, true users (both regular and infrequent). The analysis you've gone through to assess the most appropriate devices and technology for the liveware interface needs to be repeated for each type of user. Their level of sophistication with respect to the system's functions, and their degree of computer literacy, will result in significantly different interfaces being designed; otherwise, each type will not be working to the peak of its ability.

At this point, think also about 80/20 shortcuts. You know the truism — we spend 80 percent of our time on using only 20 percent of a system. When you're designing something like a series of menus that users would follow to navigate their way around the system, make sure that it is enabling not disabling. By this I mean that it has 'back-alleys' and shortcuts that the experienced user can nip down to save time. Think about which are the most trafficked routes the users will take around the system — the ones they will spend 80 percent of their time on. Try and group them logically together. If this can't be done, then ensure that the screens can be hopped between without all the rigmarole of going back to the top of the menu tree.

• *Hardware*. This isn't just the good old buff boxes, or maybe even ergonomically tasteful grey; there's the odd cable or two to be considered as well. One of the most significant facts in the information technology world today is that computer hardware continues to get more powerful and simultaneously becomes cheaper (the price/performance ratio continues to fall). But software development does not follow the same curve. Its development costs remain fairly static — there is no ongoing improvement in programmer productivity.

This has implications on the trade-off you will find yourself having to make when you design the system. One of the basic driving requirements in development is to ensure that the overall costs of a project are kept to a minimum. But there are different configurations of the hardware and software that may cost the same but will impact you quite differently in the long run. When I talk about processing power, I do so in a general sense, covering both disk space, raw MIPS (millions of instructions per second), number of parallel processors, amount of core storage — any and all of these measures of hardware performance.

You need to get a feel for the amount of functionality your system involves. And how many users it will have. The aim here is to do a basic sizing to determine what sort of size of machine will it run on, how fast will it need to run, how many concurrent users will be busy degrading the speed?

You are faced with a trade-off. There is a sliding-scale that you will find yourself on. Each location has pros and cons — there is no one correct location, merely the most appropriate one to meet all your needs. Note that, whatever your location, you will still be spending the same amount of money (all of your budget — and then some!), the only difference is what you spend it on.

One end of the scale can be characterised by a system that uses the cheapest possible hardware, and that minimises the number and size of disk drives it uses. Such a system, to meet its performance requirements, then has to accommodate the restrictions the hardware places on it by being smart. It will need a truck-load of whizz-kids to code it. They will delight in using assembly language (very low level, very complex but very fast) and lots of data compression routines so that as much data as possible can be packed on to the limited number of disk drives. The result of this approach will probably be a system that will be difficult to develop and test, and a nightmare to maintain. It does, however, represent nirvana for certain of the programming and design staff. So beware, they will try and nudge you in that direction.

If the defining characteristic at one end of the scale is that the performance requirements are met through smart code, then the other end of the scale eschews this religiously and goes for as much high-performance hardware as can be afforded. This stuff will run fast, and there will be more disk space than in an Iowa wheat field. Result? The code can afford to be inefficient, not a bad situation, in fact probably good, as the code can be laid out clearly, be easily maintainable, but not intrinsically fast. The hardware will look after that. As you can probably tell, I am biased towards the latter end of the scale. But this is a matter for your judgement.

Next, remember time. Normally you think of it as your enemy, but there is one situation in which it acts as your friend. Indeed, the longer your project the nicer the surprise you might get. But you need to prepare yourself to make the most of it. Japanese consumer products are running rings around those of many other industrial nations because of their length of their product development lifecycles. The Japanese have this down to a blend of art and science, augmented by the 100 metres sprint. What? I mean they are able to come out with a new product in half the time it takes most of their western competitors. Back in the isolated, hermetically sealed hothouse of your development you select your hardware, then labour away through the stages I will elaborate on in subsequent chapters; however, not a million miles away, your hardware vendors will also be sweating this, that and the other to shorten their development lifecycle and produce the successor to the hardware you have selected. It will be physically smaller, but by the wonders of miniaturisation it will have a larger storage capacity, run faster and cost less. Instead of having the ground cut out from under you, you will find that a hill will have been formed where you stand and you will have been lifted into the clouds.

The average project from inception to full-scale live running is spread over at least one if not a number of years. I worked once on a development where we proposed hardware which we knew about under the terms of a non-disclosure agreement, but which in reality had yet to be demonstrated in public. By the time the system came to be installed for the client, two to three years later, the hardware vendor considered what was originally proposed to be obsolete. It had already been superseded by a much more powerful and compatible new model. Lessons? Whilst you are trying to settle on hardware vendors (and from then on in), talk to them on a regular basis to find out what is in their pipeline. Ensure that you don't design your system to rely on obsolescent features, or to function in such a manner that it cannot take advantage of radical improvements in hardware performance. And don't buy the stuff! Lease it, beg it, borrow it, ensure that you can upgrade the buff boxes the moment bigger, better ones come along, and that this does not involve an extortionate cost penalty.

There's more to life than boxes. At this point, you mustn't forget wires as well. More specifically, communication devices. Most new IT applications involve a degree of connection to some telecommunications networks. The system might be geographically distributed, people might dial-in to use it, there could be remote fallback sites if the main one goes down. The hardware section should address communications as thoroughly as it does computing power.

- *Software*. This is the most obvious of the sections. But this section should not be the one that focuses on what the system does, that comes later; there are other concerns that this section should address.

These days, selecting your hardware does not necessarily tie you to a particular operating system. Vendors may have different ones available, for the same machine, to suit different types of application. And almost all vendors have a version of UNIX* that conforms to one of the standards promulgated by the various vendor alliances. So don't stumble into using the one that comes with the box, unless it really is the best one for your needs (or you have no choice due to an unhelpful/self-interested hardware vendor). Best? Ease of use, handling of concurrent processes, fault tolerance, security against hackers, staff experience. These qualities apply as much to operating systems as to other aspects of the development.

There are shelves and shelves and shelves full of existing products. Packages put together by various software houses, the hardware vendors themselves, universities, other computer users marketing their own in-house systems. You might be able to pick one of these up, install it, and run with it straight away. It could meet all of your needs and you'd never have to write a line of code (shame! eh?). If you said 'yes' to my last exclamation, then be very careful in your analysis of these packages. My ever-so-scientific little personality test, back there, may just have labelled you as one-of-those who like to define themselves solely by what they code, rather than what they develop. Be sure to check that someone else hasn't already developed something that meets your needs — it could save you a lot of grief.

The next step down the slippery slope towards doing it all yourself is integration. No-one produces a product that quite meets all your needs, but if you lash package A on to tool B, and bolt-on front-end C, then you might be home and dry. If so, do so. I would encourage you to make use of existing software, wherever possible. If for no other reason, it saves you development time because it's already there and, being out in the market, other people have been testing it and getting the vendor to strip the bugs out of it. Yes, that's the downside, it will have bugs, but then so would your stuff if you attempted to duplicate it with an in-house development, from scratch. The most important aspect of the approach outlined here is to gather as much information as you can on the detailed technical workings of these products; only then can you be confident that you can integrate these disparate items into one system.

Sometimes it helps if these different products all come from the same vendor. They're more likely to work together. Talk to that vendor. Do your ideas of integrating the products conflict with the vendor's medium-term strategies? Where does the vendor want the products to go? Will the next releases still be able to talk to each other? On the flipside of this issue, are you maybe doing the vendor a favour? Integrating these items into a fresh new product — might the vendor give you some financial backing? Technical support? Take over the results of your development and resell it around the world? With the royalties accruing to you of course.

Only now do we arrive at your coding it yourself. Don't start hacking yet. Try

*UNIX is a trade mark of AT&T.

these issues for size. First of all, consider your development platform. Should you be doing the development on the same hardware as the system will eventually run on? There are plenty of cross-compilers on the market these days (and I've run across some pretty angry ones before now). Come on, admit it, the 'techie' in you would love to work on a spanking new high-powered work-station. If not a work-station, what about a plain old PC, acting both as a terminal and, when coupled with file transfer software, capable of acting as an off-line editor that is much faster than on the development machine. Your team would probably produce nicer documentation as well. And you don't have to buy it, there are plenty of PC rental companies.

Mind your language or languages. Do you really want to use COBOL again? Don't stumble blindfold down the same old familiar alley. Is there a new, more appropriate one, Modula-3, C++, a 4GL or whatever? Learning a new language will improve staff morale, reduce attrition and improve maintainability. What was that last claim? Yes, the code will be better because, although comparative ignorance will result in a few howlers of bad coding, the staff won't be familiar enough with it to do lots of smart tricks. You know, the ones that look neat and only disgorge their innards at 4.55 on a Friday afternoon, causing the whole system explicably to hang. As I keep saying, a high-quality system is one that keeps everything as simple as possible.

Note, I said appropriate language, the downside of such a choice is that it may reduce staff inter-project mobility and the scope of code reuse. At this point, you might need to consider current staff skills, whether you want to/need to recruit, and the organisation's attitude to training. Be bold, go on, try something appropriate but new (though don't let your choice be driven by the office 'techno-freak').

- *Development schedule*. It doesn't hurt to summarise this here. I advocate you write a separate project plan, but you can guarantee that most people will put it into their cylindrical one-day filing cabinet (the trash can!). But if they stumble across it in the SEF, they just might look at it. I cover what should go in the plan in Chapter 10. Duplicate or summarise whatever of that you see fit and place it here.

- *Actual functionality*. At last! Yes, and with the other sections to address the other issues, this can be kept blessedly simple. Lots of diagrams, show the context, show the data — model it (try entity relationship diagrams), state what's going in (input), what happens (processing), and what comes out (output). Do this in a hierarchy of layers. I will give a little more detail on this when I discuss methods and methodologies later in this chapter.

3.3.2 *Clarifying the issues*

Okay, we've looked at how the SEF should be put together, and what should be covered in each section. We must not forget, however, that there are a number of issues that spread across the system. These may not be easy to pigeon-hole, which tends to result in their being left out of the SEF; not a good idea. I will enumerate them, stimulate you to think about them a little, and give you pointers to where in the SEF you might want to place them. However, don't take those as instructions carved in stone; if you prefer, it's fine by me if you choose to have an extra section in the document just called 'Issues'. Indeed, such an approach may well encourage you to think of other points, since you now have somewhere to document those concerns. So, let's begin.

- *Legalities*. These may end up in the contract if the project involves more than one company. However, what the SEF should address is not so much the legal responsibilities of the parties (to the contract) to each other during the development, but the necessity of making sure that the system meets the legal requirements where its functioning interacts with the law. What on earth is this author guy on about now? Well, the issues will vary from system to system, but let me present you with a couple of practical examples. Say your system is a real-time process-control installation that controls a water treatment plant; then, remember that the water company has legal obligations upon it with respect to water quality. If it fails to meet these, it might be liable for prosecution, so it is imperative that the system is designed to take this into account. It might be configured so that its safe-states are such that the water quality would not be compromised, irrespective of what happened if the software crashed. In addition, it might monitor the output of the plant and issue warnings (of a unique severity level) should the installation appear to approach the point where it would be stepping over the legal 'line in the sand'.

Let's take another situation, a payments system for a bank. If the system 'goes down' at 3.25 p.m., just before the deadline for payments to be made, and doesn't come back, then the bank will fail to make the payments. The bank will then have broken the contracts it has with its creditors — not a pleasant situation in which to find oneself. So this requirement focuses the design of the system; in effect, the different functional elements become ranked in terms of the priority the users assign to them or, more exactly, the legal consequences for the users should the system fail to fulfil these functions.

Now, if the developers belong to a different company from the users, and if one of the situations I've just described arises, then the developers could find themselves devoting more time than they would care to in preparing a legal defence to some sort of lawsuit. It would be prudent for such developers to review their corporate insurance for such situations, and explicitly specify in the SEF the degree of legal liability their legal counsel considers them to have.

One other legal point. The users might care to stipulate that the developer does not include a time-sensitive code that switches the system off if the user fails to pay the developer for the system. Or, more specifically, since the inclusion of such devices is hard to detect unless they are triggered, that should a device be triggered, it would not damage the system's data files or any other program on the client's hardware; instead, all that would happen would be that a 'graceful shutdown' was executed and the system then remained shut down until the dispute was resolved.

- *Sizing*. It is crucial, if you are to create a high-quality system, that you make sure you build onc that is the right size. You will need to cast your nets far and wide if you are to obtain decent estimates from which to build. Do not just count the number of people in the user departments. Further, don't look at the last five years' worth of changes in staff levels and project those ahead into the future. You need to go and find the corporate planners (remember them from the last chapter?) and determine what their strategic plans are for the enterprise one, two, five, ten, fifteen years hence. Then think about the system, remember you are developing a high-quality system and as such you are not going to be mindlessly replicating people's activities using keyboard and screen.

Your system will alter the way the task is done, the way people work, the amount of information that can be processed. You will need to start not with the number of staff and the planned staff growth (or shrinkage), but instead with the tasks these people will perform once the system is implemented. You will need to use the corporate level strategic plans to assess the likely change in the 'task-load' the enterprise will be faced with. Then you can start your more detailed estimating: how many people, will they be working twenty-four hours a day — via shifts; how will you distribute the processing between mainframes and work-stations; might people be working from home and dialling-in and what capacity of dial-in lines, modems and similar items will that require? Does it make sense to characterise the system's tasks in terms of standard industry-wide 'transactions'? If so, then you can gain help from the manufacturers of the hardware with their own statistics on performance.

Of course, this section wouldn't be complete without a comment about margins of error; time and again, estimates seem to be out by 'orders of magnitude' rather than marginal percentage differences. I would agree that such scenarios tend to be so discouraging that people consider estimating the sizing to be hardly worth the effort, and instead choose to make a few uneducated guesses. The downfall here is that you aren't learning anything. It is better to try and estimate, and afterwards review your degree of success. If things turn out to have been a gross overestimate or underestimate, then determine why (it could be something specific to your organisation) and factor this into the estimating for your next development.

Also, remember there are computer-based tools on the market that you can use to model a system and derive sizing estimates. If you already have a system and you are replacing, upgrading or enhancing it, then you may be able to attach these modelling tools to the system to analyse its current performance, and gather sizing data with which to start the exercise.

- *Expandability*. We've just talked about sizing, and I was emphasising the point that you should not just be sizing your system for today, but for the whole of its projected lifespan. However, your efforts to develop a high-quality system will be thwarted if, having estimated the sizes that the system will need to be, you fail to design it so that it can easily handle changes in its size.

The key here is one word: soft, soft, soft. Now, having said it thrice, let's think about what it means. The technique is softcoding, the use of parameters, the avoidance of writing specific constant values in a program where a variable value would do just as well (and, in fact, a great deal better). But it applies to the design of the external functionality as well, and is underpinned by one central assumption. This is that everything should be alterable. In trying to expand a system at a later date, you may well find yourself having to amend things that you had taken for granted would not change. Disk volume labels, computer node names, date-formats, time-zones in which the system runs; the list could go on. If these aren't softcoded, you could find yourself diving down into the code, with all the risks inherent in changing the code of a system that is in live use (see regression testing later in this book). But if you've got everything softcoded, then all you have to do is alter a few parameters. Now, don't try and second-guess yourself and the future by selecting only some things to softcode; cover yourself and go for everything.

Note I said time-zones, date-format. What was I getting at? Another of the truisms of our age is the continually shrinking world, the internationalisation of all aspects of life. Your organisation may well already have an international dimension or, if reorganised or taken over, may acquire this new outlook. Work on that assumption (and without necessarily developing this aspect now), design in enough flexibility so that the system can operate in other countries, in multiple time-zones, with different date-formats, and different spoken (and written) languages. We need to think about qualitative expansions (changes in the nature of the system) as well as quantitative expansions (changes in the size of the system).

Do not forget parallelism in the design. If the system can handle multiple copies of a process running simultaneously, then all you will have to do is configure a few more copies of the requisite processes. But don't overlook the handling of contention should these copies of the same process need to access the same database. If this sounds more like internals than externals — you're right. I've wandered a little from the path, so the SEF should be addressing this at the level of ensuring that configuring multiple copies of a process is easy to do.

- *Configurability*. This brings us neatly to a closely related issue. You may not want to change the size of a system but you will, on a fairly regular basis, need to change different things to do with how the system is being run: where the data files are located; removing the registration of a user who has left the organisation; the names of the ports into which the terminals (hooked into the mainframe) are connected; the time that the daily backup occurs. A system that is well designed will allow you to achieve this, mainly house-keeping, functionality whilst it is still up and running. Note the fact that most of these tasks are house-keeping-orientated, and as such are likely to be neglected since they do not represent the primary functions of the system. There is a risk that they can be overlooked initially, resulting in your having to completely stop your super-dooper system merely to add a new user.

- *Performance*. Haven't we already talked about that in sizing? Well, yes — but there's more. Specifically, how will you know if your system is performing well? Are too many processes trying to access the same data at the same time, resulting in a bottleneck? If it is running slow, why is it running slow? Are we about to overflow the crucial data table at the system's very heart?

The only way you'll know, and when it's up and running you'll want to know, is if you design in the necessary checks now. Think about how the system is going to run. Where would it be sensible to collect statistics about the system's performance? How would you process them? What could be inferred? How often should such monitoring take place? Should operators be able to request it whenever they feel they need to? How would they do this? How best can the information be presented? Remember, here is a great place for graphics and colour. Lies, damn lies and performance data? It's up to you . . .

- *Reliability*. This is an area where requirements vary a great deal. At one extreme, we have the classic safety-critical systems that must be completely reliable — people's lives depend on them. Then we have systems that are essential to the functioning of a business or organisation. Eventually, we arrive at systems that do not need to work all the time; if they are down for half an hour, it doesn't really matter. Although, to be honest, people's expectations are rising, and fewer and fewer systems now fall into this category.

The basic question to ask yourself is, how long could you be without your system? What would it cost your organisation if it were without the system? Using the answers to those questions, you can then decide if the additional cost of increasing the system's reliability is worthwhile. You should aim to state your reliability requirements in as abstract a way as possible.

To help, I will, however, sketch the different ways a particularly high level of reliability can be achieved. Computer designers address the problem of reliability by the use of redundancy — having more than one component capable of doing the same task. The word 'component' can refer to hardware or software (and different levels of software). Usually, components are duplicated, but there is no reason why there cannot be three, four, or more instances of some components. On occasions, these are developed independently (but to the same RS) to weed out certain types of systematic errors. This is particularly true for in-flight computers used on board aircraft. Up to five may be asked to do the same task; each one goes off and does it, and only if the results of all of them match is the result accepted. Remember, we need to address both hardware and software reliability. We have lots of computers in case one of them 'goes down', but we also need to ensure that they are working correctly even when up, so that is why their 'answers' are cross-checked with each other. Even this does not provide total safety because they all may be subject to an error in the original specification (a systematic error for those who remember school physics).

The simplest form of component redundancy is to have duplicate copies of processes running in the same processor. And to have extra processors available that these processes can be swapped to. The work is only done once, but there is a shadow or standby component available at each stage of the operations. To programmers, this level of duplication is apparent and they have to deal with the consequences of having standby copies of processes. The next level is where all the hardware components are duplicated within the same computer — two processors, two disk drives, etc. These run in parallel, and so the programmer sees only one process. This process checks itself at the hardware level and, if the parallel copies of it have divergent results, the process enters a manageable error state. Finally, complete computers can be paired together, so that the duplication is such that it is all handled in the operating system, and a user can transfer a system developed on a single instance of this type of computer on to one of the fault-tolerant pairs; and the system will continue to run, with next to no changes needed to it, and it will have gained the protection given by the fault-tolerant hardware.

Reliability can be further enhanced by carrying out preventive maintenance on the hardware. Most of the vendors of this fault-tolerant hardware include an option where they can install a link directly to their own service centre, and they will periodically carry out a remote examination of the machine to confirm that all is well. Indeed, if this is not the case, the machines can sometimes diagnose the problems for themselves and 'phone home' to the vendors, informing them of the problem, and the service rep. will arrive without the user needing to be bothered with the hassle of calling directly.

Explore these options and determine if you consider the benefits they offer are something that you need.

One particularly significant aspect of the way the vendors create these reliable hardware systems deserves to be highlighted. This is transaction auditing. A transaction is an update to a file. Auditing it consists of keeping a record of the change that was made to the file and keeping a 'before the change' image of the file. That way, should anything go wrong, the change can be backed-out and the previous version of the file recreated. Also, should a version of the file be completely lost (e.g. the classic nightmare of a disk-head crash), an earlier version of the file can be brought together with the 'audit trail' of the changes and the file can be 'rolled forward' and the latest version recreated. This sort of software can often be purchased to run on regular hardware that isn't fault-tolerant.

In addition, this is quite a good point to place some explicit markers declaring that care will be taken in the development to avoid the classic software nasties: dividing by zero errors, programs that tinker with the operating system, and ones that carelessly generate stack (memory) overflows. Ensuring that these can be recovered from is one of the aspects of the next section.

- *Resilience*. Having just designed in reliability, also make sure you cover resilience when writing the SEF. Reliability is designed to avoid disasters; resilience is the ability to bounce back from them and keep on running. And you should expect that you will experience disasters — most systems do at some point. I will talk about this in more detail when I cover installation in Chapter 6. At this point, we need to ensure that the system has been designed so that it meshes well with the disaster recovery procedures that you will implement as you install the system and go live with it.

So here I will list some of the more important points you should ponder on. Backups are obvious, but what will you back up? Who will do it? How often will they do it? What degree of automation will be involved? How will this mesh with live running and the work schedules of the users? Are there other sites involved? What are the fallback procedures?

Remember to think of unlikely, but really nasty, contingencies — like fires and burst pipes! And remember, you have options for how the live installation is to be run. You might want to involve a facilities-management company — so ensure that you retain enough flexibility in the design in the SEF so that this approach can be adopted.

• *Security*. A survey published in *The Financial Times* [7] at the time I was writing this highlighted that, in the United Kingdom, the attention paid to security issues is at last increasing. In 1986, security features amounted to 5 percent of IT expenditure; by 1991, this had increased to 9 percent. Similarly, in 1986, an amazing 25 percent of companies spent nothing on security; by 1991, this was down to 5 percent. They were beginning to become more aware that passwords alone were not enough.

The problem faced in designing systems so that they do not suffer from breaches of security is twofold. Firstly, the technologies of sabotage and counter-measure play a game of eternal leapfrog. One gets ahead, the other one leaps over it and gains the advantage, the first bites back — and so it continues. Secondly, the more complex you make the security of the system, the more it will irritate the users. It's no good having a database that tells a user his or her password is too obvious, and a more complex one should be entered (that a dial-in hacker with a database of passwords to try wouldn't guess) since the user will probably end up writing the password on a scrap of paper and taping it to the terminal.

Determine the level of security that you need. The hierarchy (that you must now be finding familiar) will probably apply, with safety-critical needing the most, closely followed by systems that handle money, and then ones that companies depend on. If you need a lot of security, get an expert. What I write here will not be detailed enough for you, will be out of date (this area changes very quickly) and will be available for all and sundry to read. You need to keep your security strategy quiet, or it becomes an exercise in futility.

So here is a sampler of what might go wrong, and how you might counter it. Use it to get yourself thinking; after all, if you come up with a unique original idea and keep quiet about it, you've immediately made the saboteur's job an awful lot harder.

Let's assume you do use some sort of password. These are a few 'do's' and 'don'ts' that should stand the test of time. Will you make sure you don't echo it back to the users when they type it in, both when they logon on and when they choose a new one? Will you force them to update it regularly? Will you allow them to reuse a previous one? Will you reject obvious ones when they select a new password? Will you encrypt it when you store it? Will you prevent the storage from being dumpable? If they forget it, can the operators look it up and remind the users, or can the operators only delete the current one and assign the users new ones?

Other issues. Could a rogue operator with super-user access to the whole computer delete your whole system? Might you use keys (you know the small metal things) to lock up rooms and individual terminals? What about smart cards and fancy things like body-part recognition (finger prints, retina images) if that's not too James Bond for you? What about general building security? Access to the site — window cleaners, regular cleaners, security guards, school trips(!). Note how this is straying away from the conventional narrow definition of a system — but if not addressed, the rest of your effort on the SEF could be for naught.

Just to add to your nightmares. Don't forget terrorism and the requirements of state security (if you're in the government sector). The risk of hackers coming in over dial-up lines and modems is now legendary. Fascinating cases of people freeloading across networks around the world have resulted in investigations being undertaken by US Congressional Committees. Oh yes, and don't forget viruses; this is one area of IT that is rapidly acquiring a very bizarre and somewhat tasteless set of bio-medical jargon. And I categorically refuse to indulge it by giving examples here.

- *Have you gone Green yet?* Yes, you mustn't forget the environment. Specifically, computing uses far too much paper; can you minimise your system's appetite? Electrical power likewise. Remember not to forget about the ergonomics of the users' interfaces. Screen glare, keyboard and mouse design, and similar issues, can all impact user productivity.

To broaden the scope of my use of the word 'environment', you need to consider how the system is to be housed. Do you need a bigger computer room? Do you have a computer room? What about power supplies? Think about these at this stage because they will have as long a lead time as the development of the software.

- *Don't forget.* These are a couple of small but significant items that don't really have a home anywhere else. Leap years can throw you. As I understand it, the formula for calculating them is as follows. It is a leap year if divisible by 4, but not if also divisible by 100, except if also divisible by 400. But I might be wrong; the point is, let your system rely on the computer's internal clock and be able to handle months of any reasonable length. Don't depend on February always having twenty-eight days. One other issue, the year 2000. Not really an SEF issue, but that is the best place to state that the system should function just as easily in the twenty-first century as it did in the twentieth. The important point is not to use the last two digits of the year as an index into a table or for any other sort of calculations; use all four digits. I place this here so that the users remember to check the SEF for it when reviewing an SEF produced by developers from other organisations. Forgetting these points could be expensive and embarrassing.

3.3.3 'Parlez-vous Spec-ese?'

You should be quite careful about the way you phrase the sentences in the SEF.

There is a particular reason for this. It is not dissimilar to the list for the RS about clarity and ambiguity, etc. But the SEF, out of all of the documents produced during a development, will act as the basis for the test specifications and scripts. So it is crucial that the statements in the documents be testable. What is a testable statement? Easy, take the sentence and preface it with the words 'Confirm that'. If the new sentence makes sense and provides you with a do-able test, then the original statement was testable or, if you prefer, 'an affirmation of functionality'.

3.3.4 What about methods?

Fair question. Let's start with the less formal. By which I mean things like Yourdon, Jackson Structured Development, Information Engineering, SSADM (Structured System Analysis and Design Methodology), etc. These all tend to consist of a supporting framework upon which is hung a selection of techniques, notations and procedures that define a particular approach to the process of systems development. The procedures outline what has to be done, the techniques cover how the particular methodology achieves those goals, and the notation details how the design can be recorded and transmitted to others. There are plenty of detailed descriptions of them elsewhere; if you need to know more, they will keep you pretty busy. But the essence is this, provided you choose one that matches the nature of the development you're doing (real-time versus data-crunching) and you follow it intelligently, treating it as a means to an end, not an end in itself, then using it is probably a good thing for you. Consequence? Your SEF will be written using its language, diagramming conventions and structure. Just don't be so slavish to the method that you forget to think about some of the more obscure but significant issues I've raised here.

The nice thing about methods is that they often come with automated tools. Goody, goody — these can save you boring work and reduce the likelihood of errors. Grab them with both hands.

Formal methods? Yes please. But bear in mind my warnings in Chapter 1, the introduction. These tend to be expensive to use because they are time-consuming, involve a learning curve of mathematics and logic, and absolutely positively must be used in conjunction with tools. That caveat given, I encourage you to give them a try. Most developers seem to be pleasantly surprised by how useful the approach is once they've got the hang of it.

Whether you choose to be formal, informal or whatever, still think about computer-based tools. CASE (computer aided software engineering) will, amongst other things, help you with your diagrams and might even generate the next level down of your specifications and your code!

3.3.5 Let's get lateral

Methodologies are very good at disciplining you. That's what they are designed to do, to ensure that in the headlong rush of development your enthusiasm doesn't get the better of you. But discipline on its own is not enough. I keep carping on about lateral thinking; I thought it might prove useful if I gave you a more concrete example of what I mean. This actually includes a little bit of speculation on my part because, as usual in the real world, we are working with incomplete information.

There is an organisation in the United Kingdom that is responsible for gathering weekly ratings of TV programme audiences. It's called the BARB, British Audience Research Bureau, and it has recently upgraded the technology it uses to gather the necessary information.

Originally, ratings information was gathered by sending out written questionnaires which a selected group of viewers completed and returned. This is error-prone, slow and subject to cheating — people might be watching programmes they don't want to own up to. So this was in time replaced by a communications link to the various households. A small box on top of the TV set recorded information about which channel was being watched, and that data was transmitted back to the headquarters of the ratings company.

But there was still one loophole. The ratings organisation didn't know if everyone in the family, or merely Spot the dog, was actually seated in front of the television whilst it was on. So they added one extra piece of equipment to the configuration. A small TV camera was placed on top of the TV set, so now it became the family watching the TV and the ratings TV watching the family.

But you can't afford to have someone sitting at a TV monitor in 'Ratings HQ' for each TV family. There are quite a few thousand TV families; that would be a lot of monitor watchers! So the next step was to employ some more technology. This particular technology is still in its infancy, the science of facial recognition by computer. You've seen the science fiction films where the domestic robot opens your front door, looks at you, figures you are the real you, and lets you in. Well, the problem (this is where I am speculating, but it seems like a fairly reasonable series of inferences) was that the technology of facial recognition is not yet very advanced. It was only possible for the system to recognise someone if they were staring directly at the camera; the system needed the data from a full-face to be able to make a reliable determination of who was looking at the camera.

Now, the designers could have considered this to be unsatisfactory, since people don't do that in real life, so they would have to wait until algorithms were developed that would enable people to be recognised with only partial information available. But no, this is not what they did. They realised that the technology was appropriate to those needs if they thought carefully enough about their needs. In actual fact, it was important to tell how much attention the viewing family were paying. If they were reading the paper, canoodling on the sofa, or eating a TV dinner, they wouldn't be paying enough attention to the programme (and the commercials!) for them to warrant classification as 'viewers'. So this is how the system was set up. When a family member stared directly at the TV, the camera recognised them and logged the fact that father was now watching the News. If he picked up the paper, the system could no longer identify him, but could infer who he 'used to be' and would log 'father ceased to pay attention but remained in the room'. If a friend visited, the system would log 'stranger entered room' and if the friend sat down and watched, 'stranger watched "Cheers"' would be recorded.

So, in this example, a limitation in the available technology did not hold a system back. Instead, a lateral approach to defining the requirements of the system enabled an improved system to be implemented.

In writing the SEF, you will be aiming to meet users' requirements. You may consider that you do not have the appropriate technology. Or, you may have a choice of approaches. Try to avoid straight-line reasoning; this tends to result in a lot of sledgehammers being used to crack far too many nuts. Better, think about the requirements, how they can be refined and revised (continuing to be in contact with the users helps a lot here) and try to think laterally. That is, don't automatically throw technology at requirements, it may be possible to amend the requirements.

3.3.6 Don't get cross, get a reference

The most important part of the SEF is actually one of its (no doubt many) appendices. It is a two-way cross-reference of every statement in the RS to every statement in the SEF, and vice versa. Yes, I know it will take an army of labourers a year and a day to construct, but it will be the most useful part of the writing of the SEF; having an SEF-structure that corresponds to the RS may reduce this somewhat. In producing it, you will ensure that you are making provision to implement all the requirements in the RS. Further, you will be controlling the scope of the development work; you will not be starting off down any paths that the user didn't even ask you to walk along. In addition, it will form the foundation for complete traceability within the development, from requirements to (eventually) code.

I know it sounds like a horrendous undertaking, but the payback will be enormous. If you act on only one piece of advice from this chapter, make it this piece of advice. Now, go write your statement of external functionality.

3.4 Questions

1. What's the deadline for the completed SEF?
2. Who's going to write the cross-reference?
3. When will you schedule a review of the SEF, with *everyone* in the same room?
4. Who are your users, designers, implementors, maintainers and operators?
   Again — names and 'phone numbers are needed.
   When will you schedule a trip to the pub with each group?
5. What sort of word processor will you work on?
   What diagramming tools will you use?
6. Have you produced a standard comment form so all non-interactive review comments can be logged and tracked?
7. Do you know your local hardware salespeople?
   Ditto software?
8. Are you going for a method? (If so, now's your last chance; any later will involve a lot of reworking and be too late.)

4 Internals and coding

4.1 Introduction

4.1.1 *Do you have the key?*

If you've looked at some of the other chapters, this first section may start to seem familiar. Good. If you are to get the most from this book, you need to be looking at the chapter that corresponds to the stage that you have reached in your development.

So do you have the key that entitles you to open the door to this chapter? You need to have the externality of the system specified, preferably both in user language (business-speak) and developer language (techno-speak). That is, if your development has paralleled this book, you should have an RS and an SEF.

But, on the other hand, you may have already gone too far down the line for this chapter to be useful. If you're in the thick of testing, then go to the next chapter; but if anyone on the development team still has a few lines of code they haven't yet written, then stay here, read this and ensure that all the people involved with hacking code out of the software workface are familiar with what I present here.

4.1.2 *So who are you anyway?*

This is not quite such a fatuous question as it may appear at first sight. It is important you realise that, in all likelihood, the people who write the documentation covering the detailed technicalities and internals involved in the implementation of a development will have had little, if anything, to do with the higher-level documents. This is a shame. People who are two levels removed from the users' requirements are bound to have less of an emotional involvement in what the system they are designing and coding is actually meant to do. They are more likely to perceive specifications as fixed documents, and to resent having to rework code if changes filter down. There is also a significant risk of serious misunderstandings by the time that everything has been translated from user-speak, through high-level techno-speak, into more detailed techno-speak.

Consequence? You need to ensure that the work done in this phase is carefully controlled. By now, the costs of correcting errors are already getting high. This is the pivotal stage in ensuring that the system you develop is of high quality. Poor detailed design and bad coding will result in over-runs during testing and a never ending stream of bug reports once the system finally goes live. So let's see how we can make sure the internal design and coding results in quality that everyone can be proud of.

4.2 The internals specification

4.2.1 *Not more trees*

So how many more forests is your documentation collection going to consume? There is no hard and fast answer, since it very much depends on the complexity of your system. The issue here is whether you wish to create two levels of internals documentation before starting to code, or whether one will be adequate. Remember, each level you go down within the system, the larger the documentation will be for a particular subsystem, since there are more details to attend to.

The two-level approach would entail a document giving an overview of the internals of a system, describing the overall data, data-flows and processes. This would be supplemented by a set of more detailed individual documents covering each individual process. Such documents can be thought of as instructions to programmers; they could pick up one of these documents and, with only a few references to the higher levels of documentation, would be able to do their coding straight from the individual specifications.

The one-level approach would be best suited to a small system, programmed by only a few people. In this situation, all the information could be lodged in one document which would be a good thing, as the processes might well be less specialised and compartmentalised. This would mean they interacted more with other processes, and so would the staff who coded them; consequently, it would be good for the staff to have a feel for the complete system.

This issue is primarily a matter of judgement on your part. Which approach you choose is not as important as ensuring that whatever is written covers all the areas I will discuss in this chapter.

4.2.2 *'My words mean what I want them to mean'*

So said Humpty Dumpty to Alice in *Through the Looking Glass*. Lewis Carroll was, after all, an Oxford mathematics Don and, in the Victorian age, was working in one of the few fields where new terms could be coined pretty much at will. Nowadays, this is also true in the world of information technology. And I am going to indulge myself by giving you a series of definitions. The words are so common you're almost bound to have come across most of them already. The scope of my definitions is, however, limited; I claim no particular validity for them outside the confines of this book. I make the definitions, not so much to persuade you to adopt them, but to make sure that it is clear what I am talking about in this chapter when I start to get nearer the nitty-gritty workface frequented by the 'real' information technology professional.

- *System*. This is the whole caboodle. Everything involved in the installation. The people, the hardware and the software. You can go back to Chapter 2 for a more detailed discussion on what constitutes a system. The point is that we need a term that is all-encompassing, and 'system' fits the bill nicely.

- *Subsystem*. Here we are talking about a logical grouping of functionally related tasks. The system will be composed of subsystems. I prefer to have this decomposition 'user-driven'. Thus, we would have the 'client database subsystem' and the 'passenger check-in subsystem', rather than the 'transaction record roll-forward subsystem'. A high-quality system would, anyway, have been designed such that it was decomposed in line with user functionality rather than the technicalities used to achieve the functions.

- *Process*. A process is deemed to be what runs on the computer as a self-contained program. Simple systems may have only one process, complex ones may have many in each subsystem. The process is the almost living entity which is the embodiment of a program that is running at a particular instant.

- *Module/unit*. Here we have the basic building block. It is not uncommon for a process to consist of many modules or units bound in together. In this case, we are distinguishing between object code that has been compiled, but cannot run on its own (a module or unit), and a process which consists of a collection of modules which have been bound together (or link-edited) to create the executable process.

- *File*. We shouldn't forget this one. It's the place that the code, data, object, executable or whatever else takes our fancy, is kept in.

- *Procedure/routine*. We're now down to the building blocks of the individual programs within files of code. Most languages allow you to structure these in a hierarchy with a main procedure or routine that calls subprocedures or subroutines.

Okay, that's our vocabulary clarified a little. Now we can proceed to use it in outlining what should go into the various detail-level documents you are about to write.

4.2.3 Write the right stuff

The internals specification should consist of the following:

- Introduction.
- Overview.
- Data descriptions.
- Subsystem descriptions.
- Process descriptions.
- Issues.
- Quality check cross-references.

- *Introduction*. This can be nice and short. The aim is to set the scene for anyone involved in the development who picks up this document without having first seen the RS or SEF.

- *Overview*. Now, more so than in the SEF, diagramming comes to the fore. The overview is the classic place for some good clear artwork that depicts the external interfaces the system has, together with the internal structure of interrelated subsystems.

- *Data description*. This comes next to ensure that we don't put the cart before the horse. I know that the activity of designing systems is iterative, and that you sometimes have to figure out how you are going to process the data before you really know how best to organise the data. That's okay; you will find yourself doing this, because it will be necessary for the internals specification to be subject to quite a few trips around the review, revise, reissue loop. So don't worry — but do start off by trying to detail the data the system is going to manage. Processes only exist because they have data to process and not vice versa. Again, make plenty of use of diagrams to illustrate the way the data is structured. You could try using entity relationship modelling or third normal form analysis — both these techniques are pretty standard and someone in your office ought to have a book about them. Remember, some methodologies encourage you to match the structure of your processes to the structure of your data — so ensure you get the data right.

- *Subsystem description*. This is where the multi-level nature of design comes into play. Call it step-wise refinement, call it structured programming; whatever mantle you choose, note that what you are doing is basically the same type of analysis at repeatedly more detailed levels. Eventually, you'll find you hit code!

In describing the subsystem, first cover the global data that it uses, i.e. data that is also used by other subsystems. Then cover the data local to the subsystem; this will be shared between its constituent processes, but not passed to processes in other subsystems. Clarify where this data will live. Always in files on disk? Sometimes in core memory? If so, make sure you address how the two are kept synchronised.

Next consider the processes in the subsystem. Define any necessary hierarchies, in terms of which processes call which other processes. Start with how the subsystem is kicked off. Having described the data, deal with how it will be used; for each process give all of its inputs, and specify clearly what are valid and invalid inputs. For invalid inputs, explain how the process will respond — make the response as graceful as possible. For all valid inputs, detail how the process will manipulate this data — make the most of any diagramming techniques available to you. Try state machines, decision tables or good old flow charts. If you do use flow charts, try and make them structured, i.e. wherever you find yourself in the chart you should know what has happened to put you there. Charts become dangerous if you can reach a particular point by two different routes, as you may want to do significantly different processing depending on how you arrived at that point, but that cannot necessarily be shown on the chart. In Figure 4.1, I show the components of one diagramming technique that I have found useful.

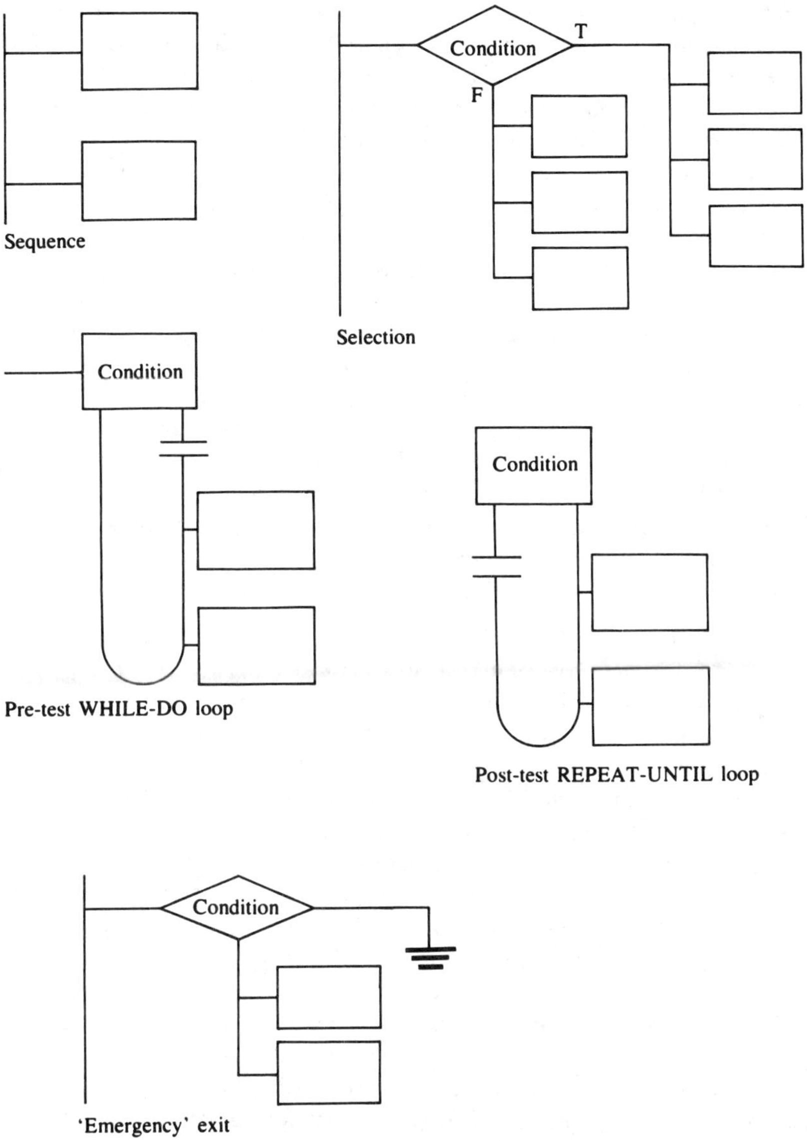

Figure 4.1 Diagramming technique elements

Figure 4.1 possesses standard constructs to represent the main constituents of structured design. Specifically, a direct sequence of operations, a selection between two or more paths of operations, and the repetition of a sequence of operations. The looping construct allows you to show pre-test (WHILE-DO END-DO) loops and post-test (REPEAT-UNTIL) loops. When the end of a sequence of operations is reached, trace the line back to the departure point from the previous sequence of operations. I have only used what I suspect to be a subset of the complete vocabulary of this diagramming language. Exits from procedures under error conditions are sometimes hard to show. I have augmented it by adopting the electricity earth-grounding symbol, indicating that the flow of control reverts to the previous path. Noticc that it is difficult to draw GOTOs with this technique; this is deliberate, so as to encourage structured programming. It is not very good at representing the data being manipulated — but then nothing's perfect!

I make no special claims for this technique other than the fact that it allows you to see where you came from, tends to encourage structured programming, and I have found it useful over a number of years [8]. When you find yourself replicating structures with it, you probably have good candidates for sections of processing that can be broken out as separate, functionally discrete processes or procedures.

Back to the description of the processes in each subsystem. After detailing the processing that they do, you should list all the output produced by each type of processing.

Also, consider the context of the process within the subsystem's flow of control. Specifically, explain how the process is started, under what conditions it continues to run, and how it terminates both normally and in abnormal error conditions. Think of how it will behave in nasty situations. Say an operator mistakenly deletes the executable of the process whilst it is running; what state will the rest of the subsystem be left in? How will it recover and resume normal running?

- *Process descriptions*. The subsystem descriptions covered the internals of the subsystems and the purposes of the processes, but should have treated the processes themselves as comparatively opaque (if not black) boxes. Now, you repeat the analysis and go down a level to examine the processes and the procedures that make them up. Address all the same issues as for the subsystems.

This is the section of the document that you may prefer to break out into a second-level set of process specifications. Now there is an additional function for these documents; they are the instructions to the programmers. Depending on the extent to which they have been involved in the system design up till now, it may (or may not) be appropriate to include a pseudo-code description of the functionality (of the actual files of code) in the process specifications. It could also be the case that the programmers will be handed the internals specification and required to write the process specifications themselves, including pseudo-code, prior to coding. This approach helps to focus the thinking on the logic issues before all the complexities of coding and compilation and syntax start to intrude.

As you can probably guess, I'm not particularly fond of coding. The aim behind this approach is for all the tricky issues to be ironed out in advance; as a result, the code should almost drop out of the process specification with very little effort, and shouldn't need to be changed because of gaps in the logic resulting from a skimped analysis stage. Obviously, if the system development approach is based on prototyping, there will need to be reworking of code, but I am presuming that one of the other approaches has been taken.

- *Issues*. When the SEF was written, a whole series of issues was considered. The internals specification now has to address how the concerns embodied in these issues will be addressed by the implementation. As there is quite a lot of detail on the issues in the preceding chapter, all I will do here is mention them again. The actual implementation of these will be very specific to your installation.

So here's your memory jogger:

- sizing;
- expandability;
- configurability;
- reliability;
- resilience;
- performance;
- security.

Make sure you address all of them.

- *Quality check cross-reference*. As with the SEF and the RS, there should be a two-way cross-reference between statements in the SEF and the detail of their implementation in the IS. If the process specifications are broken out into separate documents, then a cross-reference will be needed between the subsystem sections of the IS and the relevant process specifications. This will pay you back considerably when it comes to testing the system.

4.2.4 *Are we done yet?*

Now, the same applies to the internals specification documents as to the previous documents. They need to be reviewed, critically and constructively. Further, meeting the deadline for producing them does not mean that they are finished. In reviewing them, you should be asking questions about completeness, ambiguity, testability and traceability. If you want to, you can also get 'quantitative' and apply the results of some research into metrics for measuring the quality of detailed software designs. Once you are satisfied with all of these design documents, then and only then can you actually, finally get coding.

4.3 The quality of the design and coding

4.3.1 *Scholarly aside No. 1*

A recently published book [9] has identified a few numbers that it might benefit you to pay attention to. The advice needs to be considered when reviewing internal and process specifications, and before starting coding; so it slots in here very naturally.

The book's author considers data gathered from a number of projects carried out by NASA. These were real projects, resulting in a whole clutch of 'attitude determination systems' for spacecraft in near-Earth orbit. This is solid research data — from which we can draw some startling conclusions.

The author talks about modules (which he calls the smallest independently compilable section of code), for him FORTRAN subroutines. Investigating some common suggestions about 'good' design and coding, he determines the extent to which following them affects the number of errors that result. Let's enumerate the advice and the book's conclusions.

- *Be strong*. Give your module a 'singleness of purpose'. There was a (statistically significant) correlation between taking this advice and the number of errors; specifically, single function modules had fewer errors. So do this, avoid modules that perform two or three unrelated tasks.
- *Limit your span of control*, the number of modules you call. Again, there was a correlation between taking this advice and fewer errors. Again, do this. Initially, the book suggests no more than seven calls, but later analysis, seeking to minimise a metric the author calls 'relative complexity', results in the advice of restricting 'fanout' to none, one or two calls (only!).
- *Minimise coupling*. Instead, pass all data through parameter lists. This yielded no correlation. In other words, following or not following this advice seemed to have no effect on the number of errors. It could be that long argument strings introduce extra errors, balancing up any improvements arising from using shared global storage (which is usually presumed to be more confusing as it is not so clear which processes access which data). Anyway, this one's up to you.
- *Keep modules small*. Shock horror — negative correlation. The statistics showed that large modules had fewer errors. Small ones had lots, or none if they were so small as to be trivial. So the advice here is not to worry about size, don't introduce artificial constraints (e.g. module must not exceed a page). But beware, larger modules may be harder to maintain; so don't get carried away.

This is all solid stuff — based on empirical research. If it whets your appetite, go read the book, it's very compact. You'll even get some graphs you can draw to help you determine how complete your design is.

If you're a little uneasy about following this research data, then hold your horses. In a few pages' time, I'll articulate the more classic orthodoxy and you can choose.

4.3.2 Back to the nitty-gritty

High-quality code can be actually quite dissatisfying. It looks simple and obvious, doesn't take advantage of the smarter aspects of the language being used, and isn't so esoterically constructed that the 'signature' of the coder is instantly apparent. To be frank, good code is bland code. But then code is not a statement of the coder's personality; that's what clothes and hairstyle are for.

Corporate culture has a lot to do with the way a system's code will look. Some organisations impose a strong corporate orthodoxy on their employees from day one. This will result in comparatively uniform code across the programming staff. Others treat their staff as free spirits pioneering their own creative way through the jungle of information technology. Conventional wisdom has it that the latter approach is the more satisfying. I think that's a heap of junk — or at least that's what the organisation risks ending up with. I don't claim that it will; some people will naturally discipline themselves into producing good code. But, left to their own devices, and without explicit guidance on what constitutes good code, there is a strong risk that 'programmers will be programmers will be Italian chefs'. What? Yes — it's spaghetti time!

So what I'm aiming to do in this part of the chapter is restate the obvious. Of course, it's only obvious after it's been read — if raw programmers are left to fathom this out for themselves, the classic colony of an infinite number of monkeys and typewriters stand a fair chance of producing their copy of the complete works of Shakespeare first. Anyway, enough polemic — let's get down to it.

4.3.3 What do we want?

The basic aim is to produce code that is easy to read and understand. Such code will then be easy to test, easy to debug and easy to maintain. The extra time spent thinking about how to keep it clear and simple will be saved many times over when it is subsequently looked at by programmers who had nothing to do with its original creation.

4.3.4 Files

Before we even get into a file, we need to establish sensible naming conventions. Most (but not all) systems allow you a two-part file name. Sometimes there is a restriction on the number of characters, but increasingly this is something very big and silly, like eighty characters. Try and avoid things like:

VERY_BIG_AND_LONG_AND_RAMBLING_NAME.EXTENSION

It only confuses the situation, because it can rarely fit on to one line if it is part of a command or a line of code. The best bet is to decide on a standard separator, since you are often allowed any and all of — and _ and ^ . A three-character extension is usually sufficient, and should be reserved to denote the contents of the file. If this is done, make sure it matches the standard abbreviations for file contents for this particular type of computer; it will help the default compiler to be invoked more easily.

Whether you have a tree-like file directory structure (the way you organise the files on disk) or not, decide on how the files can be named so that name length can be kept to a minimum, whilst still being intelligible. The flipside of this is when there is a ridiculously short limit on file name length; in this situation, make sure that every letter counts. You may think you have spare letters now — don't bet on it. As the system expands, new file types and functions will spring up, and you'll need all the available characters to be able to distinguish between the different varieties you are now bamboozled with. If you need to omit letters, drop vowels, retain consonants. CNSNNTS is far easier to pronounce, remember and understand than OOA!

If you do have a tree-like file directory, consider the location in the tree to be part of the file's name. In other words, it is only obvious what the file does when the directory location of the file and its name are married together. Be consistent in the way you name both the directories and the files. It should be possible to infer a great deal about the system from a well-named set of directories and files.

In doing all this file naming, think also about the development environment. That is, the fact that you may well have more than one version of the system in existence at the same time. How can you distinguish clearly and easily between them if they are running on the same system? Here is a good time also to think about process naming. When processes or tasks are declared on a computer, there is usually a very limited number of characters in the name. When designing your system, don't be tempted to use all the characters right away. If you do, you may find that they will all be necessary for you to achieve a unique name for a process, and thus you will not be able to run more than one copy of that process. In fact, there are two types of multiple copy of a particular process that you should allow for. The first type is within one instance of a system, where you want to expand the capacity of the system, and run two or more copies of a process simultaneously within the same system. Then, at the same time, you might want to have multiple instances of the system (each with multiple copies of that process) running on the same computer. So, at its crudest, if you have *N* characters to play with when concocting process names, only use *N*-2 of them, and save the other two for the multiple copies to come.

If you are going to run multiple versions of a system and you have a tree-like directory structure, make the top of the tree (the logical root directory!) the one that varies in name, or part of its name. Then keep the structure below it standardised and the same.

If you have more than one programmer working on a system (quite likely really!), arrange the configuration of the system such that all programmers use the standard version of the system and such that an individual's code, which is still under test, is not available to anyone else. There are various strategies to achieve this, which I will cover in more detail in Chapter 9, 'Change Control and Configuration Management'. The essence, however, is to make sure that the standard tested version of an executable does not become overwritten by a more recent untested version of that executable. Instead, both versions should exist, and the tester should be configured to use the untested one, and everyone else the tested one.

As you can start to see, parameterisation within configuration files can be of great benefit in this sort of situation.

4.3.5 'You *might say that,* I *couldn't possibly comment*'

The annotating of code with sensible, apposite comments is the very essence of producing a high-quality program. Luckily, there are very few people left in the information technology community who still believe that their programs are perfectly intelligible to everyone else without comments. The problem is that, even so, they reckon that they can understand what they did without needing to place comments and, if they are not expecting anyone else to be looking at their code at a later date, we still end up with very poor code.

The rule of thumb must be that all code should be considered as destined to be maintained by someone else. Only with this approach can we ensure that everything will be commented.

Comments come in many forms. The most basic is the file header, placed in the file before any coding even begins. It should include the following.

- *Name*. Blatantly obvious, but should some malicious so-and-so happen to rename the file, then it could get lost in the system. Not as far-fetched as it may sound. Also, the name of the program or process that this file contributes to may not be the same as the name of the file; if this is the case, then all the appropriate names should be given.
- *Location*. Where in the file directory structure is this file held?
- *Language*. What particular dialect of hieroglyphics are the instructions in this file coded in?
- *Date created*. When did the file first see the light of day? Use a date-format that works internationally, i.e. 10 Apr 94, not 04/10/94.
- *Author*. Who was the person (or persons) who originally coded the file?
- *Configuration management hooks*. Many tools to manage multiple versions of files allows fields to be set up in a file header that are filled in by the tool, when a particular version of that file is retrieved from the tool's library.
- *Function*. What is the file intended to do? But not how it actually does it.
- *Inputs*. What data goes into the file (this may be a data-file or data processed by a program)?
- *Processing*. If this is a program, how does it do what it does?
- *Outputs*. What data comes out of the file?
- *Emergency exits*. How does the file (and process if applicable) behave under abnormal error conditions?
- *Called by*. Which files or programs have access to this file?
- *Calls*. Which files does this one want to get at?
- *Depends upon*. When the system is built, which other files need to be in existence, or built, before this file can become part of an executable process?
- *Copy libraries*. What library files holding common code does this file 'source-in' from?
- *Change history*. A blank one, i.e. a collection of column headings. The existence of this will encourage its use when the file comes to be amended. In fact, you could give it a first entry signifying the file creation. The change history columns should include date, version number (of file), name of coder who changed the file, reason for and nature of change, and relationship between the file's version number and the system's overall version/release number.

4.3.6 Coding guidelines

It is a well-worthwhile exercise for a senior technical member of the development team to produce some coding guidelines *before* anyone starts to do any programming. If more than one language is to be used, the same material will need to be covered for each language, as they all tend to have their idiosyncracies. This means that my comments can only be given at a very general level. One advantage of having guidelines is that they provide a ready checklist that can be used when the code is reviewed. Now, don't tell me you weren't planning to review the code prior to testing it by running it? More on this in Chapter 5 on 'Testing'.

• *Naming conventions*. What? Is this author person repeating himself again? No — previously I was talking about files and file directories. Those are likely to be named by the senior designers; the more junior programming staff will have such entities presented to them on a plate. The area where the programmers will have discretion is in the naming of the local (non-global) data-structures that their programs use, and the names of the procedures (subroutines) that are in their programs. Conventions for these should make use of all the facilities of the language to maximise the intelligibility of the names (make them meaningful), whilst keeping them as short as possible. A policy decision on the use of upper and lower case letters (if the mixing of both is permitted in the language) should be taken at the start. One kind should be used consistently to represent certain types of language elements (such as data-item names or reserved words) and the other kind used for all other types of element. Global data might be in upper case with local data in lower case; just a suggestion. The way certain types of data are named should be considered; a standard first couple of letters for all error message text or all loop-counters would pay dividends. You might have a language that implicitly types particular data-items on the basis of name; don't try to subvert that feature, you'll confuse the maintainers who come later.

• *Errors*. Talking about error messages, it would be a good idea to centralise these in some sort of copy file so that they are 'sourced-in' to all programs that need them, while at the same time they are all available in one handy location. This would prove to be of inestimable benefit to the poor documentation specialists faced with writing the guides to your system (not least ensuring that they've covered all the error messages!).

Placing all the error messages together will also improve the consistency of their presentation to the user. It will be possible to grade them all by one set of severity criteria, and define consistent ways of handling all error messages of the same severity level. The language in them is also more likely to be meaningful, and centralising them can act as a starting point for an on-line help facility that can provide more explanation to the poor bewildered users about the catastrophe that may have just befallen them. Similarly, the basic error handling routines should all be grouped together in a library, since these are modules that could be frequently reused.

• *Comments*. You should also discuss the placing and contents of comments. First, lay it on strong that code will not be deemed complete unless it is properly and completely commented. Define standard places where comments can be given, i.e. the layout of the comments. Only if they consistently occur in the same locations in all files (of the same language) will they be found by the emergency support staff who have ten minutes to fix a bug before the system must be back up to print this month's payroll. Also, clarify the use of upper and lower case letters; I think it can be left as a matter of house-style as to whether complete sentences are required or merely the odd word or two. But whatever the standard of grammar, ensure that the content is appropriate. The basic rule of thumb should be to assume that the person reading the code knows the programming language. After a few minutes of study, the reader will be able to work out what is happening; she or he needs to know why it is happening. A comment like 'START LOOP HERE' is pretty useless. 'CHECK EACH CUSTOMER RECORD FOR SATISFACTORY CREDIT LIMIT' would be much more informative, and is to be preferred.

• *Layout*. As with comments and the intelligent use of upper and lower case letters, a consistent approach to code layout will prove to be very beneficial. Try and develop this house-style so that not only do files written by different programmers have the same look and feel, but the number of programming errors is reduced. How? Develop a layout style that doesn't hide potential sources of error. For example, the use of the = sign varies from language to language. In some, = means assignment, whilst in others, = means comparison and := means assignment. Compare X=X and X = X. If you leave space between the variables in the code, the symbol can be more clearly seen during the code-walkthrough reviews, thus avoiding a nasty debugging mess later on.

And, for goodness sake — INDENT! I still have fond memories of various coders I've met in my travels who loved particular variants of languages that allowed them to stuff seven instructions on to one line. Sure their files were short, their print-outs saved paper, but you had to work for Interpol to be able to tease out the truth of what their programs actually did. Sensibly laid out blocks of code, preceded by an explanatory comment, and all associated with the function in the comment, are a lot less painful. Indent, by a standard number of spaces (set up the same tab definitions on *everybody's* editors), to show whenever the next level of control (loop or 'if statement') has been entered into. Inconsistent indenting is a sure-fire recipe for confusion — beware. You could try using style-checking programs to catch offenders!

• *Parameterisation*. This is the point at which to plug softcoding. With luck, a lot of items will have already been defined as global parameters; in addition to this, encourage all possible numerical constants to be declared as variable parameters at the top of the program as local data. For instance, don't allow a loop to iterate ten times with

```
loop-counter := 1 to 10
```

instead, declare loop-start and loop-end variables; this will make amending the code far easier later. Similarly, declare constant values used in computations at the start of the program, in case the units in which the calculation is carried out change at a later date. For example, the USA still uses the Fahrenheit temperature scale, but may one day switch to Celsius. Defining variables such as 'FREEZING-POINT' and 'BOILING-POINT' builds in a great deal more flexibility than hard coding 32 and 212 all over the system.

• *Structure*. This is where I enumerate the classic heuristics of structuring code. Since you are a mature adult (I presume!), I offer you a choice; you may take this traditional advice, or live a little more dangerously, walk out on a limb, and follow the research advice from a few pages back — although some of it's counter-intuitive, there is a research base to it.

Anyway, my thoughts cover a myriad of sins. The first one, not unreasonably, is close-coupling(!). Sadly, in this context, this is no more than a measure of the extent to which different processes interact with and depend on each other. The less close-coupling the better. Encourage programmers to keep their procedures and subroutines self-contained. There should be a clear calling hierarchy. We do not want code in which two procedures flip-flop around the system calling each other repeatedly until they've dug themselves into a deadly embrace, from which they can be released only by killing the process they are both part of.

Associated with this are the cases of procedures that recursively call themselves. Boundary conditions need to be thought about very carefully here, since these are prime candidates for infinite regressions, which can also be alleviated only by the aforementioned drastic remedy.

One of the skills here is to keep processes compact and self-contained. They shouldn't cover more than a few pages of listing paper. They should not have more than half a dozen (or so) levels of nesting (of loops or 'ifs').

One good approach is to limit how far data roams. If procedure A calls procedure B, and A doesn't need to know about some of what B does, then all the data that B uses for that internal purpose should be declared in B. In other words, declare data at the lowest possible level of procedures. Hand-in-hand with this is an injunction against having low-level procedures monkey about with high-level global data without admitting to this in their parameter lists. Basic rule: if a procedure changes any data that is not local to it (it may not be global — it may be local to the calling procedure one level above), then the data must be declared in the procedures parameter list.

• *Bugs*. If you adhere to good programming guidelines, you can minimise the number of bugs in the system, as well as making it easier to find the ones you will, even with guidelines, still succeed in introducing. Some of these bug-avoidance issues will be very language specific, so think hard and talk to the maintenance staff — they've seen most of them before now. What I can present is more general in nature.

Loops have a natural tendency to run forever. Ensure that the loop counters are of the correct data type. New-fangled languages that allow mixed-mode comparison operations can get you into all sorts of trouble here; rounding errors on a thirty-two digit variable may mean that, although it should be equal to the test value on the last trip around the loop, it may in fact already exceed it and, since you've plumped for a cold stark = sign, you'll miss your exit and loop forever.

Another common failure results from incorrect assumptions about the way the language will evaluate a complex sequence of arithmetic operations. Mathematical order of precedence is the name of the game, and the details, in some suitably cryptic form, can be found somewhere in the manual produced by the vendor on how they've implemented the language. Don't even try — take the easy way out and make sure; whenever there is the slightest room for doubt, use brackets, brackets and more brackets.

Every vendor likes to add a few non-standard extensions to the language. If you use them, you will be guaranteed to need to port (reimplement) the system on another vendor's hardware, and whoops, they don't have the same extensions. So behave yourself and stick to your knitting.

4.4 Final thoughts

4.4.1 An apology?

No way! Those amongst you who love assembly programming and know a stack overflow when you see one will probably be quite horrified by now. Yes, I freely admit, the approach I am advocating will not lead to the most efficient code. No problem, that isn't the aim — what I want is manageable code. If there are performance problems, they can be addressed by taking advantage of the march of progress in the world of hardware and the falling price/performance ratio. Get a bigger buff box!

4.4.2 More opinions

In the reference section, I list some of my favourite programming books. They reflect some of the languages I've worked in. I treated each book as my main reference point for that language when I was immersed in it. I make no outlandish claims for these books; they are good, there are probably other ones as good and maybe better. No matter, the point is these are tried and tested. They give similar advice to mine here, but in relation to the specific language in which they are aiming to teach you to program. They are also not necessarily very recent (they may not even still be in print), but again no matter. Never mind all the great new super-duper languages; most people are still stuck in Cobol, and will remain so. Anyway, if you want to check them out, they cover: VAX Assembler [9], C [10], Cobol [11] and Pascal [12].

4.5 Questions

1. Has anybody started coding yet?
2. Have you stopped them?
3. Have you got someone to write language-specific coding standards?
4. Have you decided whether to adopt programming pairs?
5. If so, have you explained this approach, and the reasoning behind it, to your people?

Now we've stopped things running ahead of themselves, we can return to a semblance of order.

6. Will you split your internals documentation into two levels?
7. When must each level be complete?
8. Who will review them?
9. Where's the checklist?
10. Have you mislaid the standard comment form used on the SEF?
11. Will you use a structured diagramming technique?
12. Do you intend to use pseudo-code?

5 Testing

5.1 Introduction

5.1.1 Read this now

Given that the book has fallen open at this page, I see no reason why you should not start reading. I know that the other chapters are prefaced with little examinations which determine your entitlement to proceed further, but in this case testing is so central that it's never too early to start thinking about it, and for that matter never too late. What?

It's never too late because even if your system is alive and kicking, it is unlikely to be perfectly behaved (the occasional misdirected kick?) . . . yes, bugs! And the consequence is that you'll be devoting effort to fixing these bugs. And having changed the code, how will you know if you've successfully restrained your recalcitrant software, and for that matter, not taught it any other bad habits by mistake (introduced new bugs!)? The only way you'll manage to achieve either is through testing.

Until your system is consigned to the dustbin of computer history you'll find yourself involved in some sort of testing or other. You have no excuse not to read this chapter right now.

5.1.2 'A test by any other name . . .'

Would no doubt smell as sweet. You know what a test looks like. You've run plenty of them in your time, testing systems that run the gamut of application areas from battleships to paperclips. You could run them in your sleep. You've proved that your software does what it should do. You know about testing. So why is this author guy belabouring the point?

If you ever find yourself in southern California, drive north on the San Diego Freeway, and just after you pass Los Angeles airport, turn west on to Interstate 10 — The Christopher Columbus Memorial Highway (it runs east all the way to the Atlantic!). You'll pass through a dark tunnel, and exit blinking at the sun reflected off the ocean as you merge on to the Pacific Coast Highway. Ahead of you will be an arched bridge; the section above the far right (slow) lane has a sign on it stating 'IMPAIRED VERTICAL CLEARANCE'. What? When I saw it I was expecting something more like 'LOW BRIDGE'! But which is better? How can one tell? They are both notices that convey the same information, the same warning; the only way one could tell is by seeing which was more successful. Here defining success is easy. Put each sign up for a few months and the one which results in the fewest large trucks wedged under the bridge is the one that can be deemed a success.

So how about tests. Obvious really, a successful test is one that proves the software does what it's meant to. Yes? Don't you dare not read the rest of this chapter. Wrong, wrong, wrong. Tests are not about proving that a specification has been fulfilled, as I will elucidate in a minute. Tests are about demonstrating where a system departs from its specification. A successful test is one that finds a bug.

Why? Well, if we were to try and prove that your widget classification and distribution system did everthing that its SEF said it should, and nothing that it shouldn't, we'd need to test every single path through the system, with all possible types of valid and invalid data. Sounds like quite a big undertaking. Bigger than you might ever imagine.

5.2 What is testing?

5.2.1 'The' work of reference

Imagine a program that takes three integer values, treats them as lengths of the sides of a triangle, and outputs whether the triangle is scalene, isosceles, or equilateral. How many tests would you have to run to prove that the program worked correctly. Three? Four? There are at least seventeen! And there may be more; these seventeen merely detect errors that have been found in various versions of the program. There may be other possible bugs. I haven't told you what these test cases are. Indeed, this puzzle may look vaguely familiar. It comes from what I consider to be one of the best books on testing that there is.

The book I have in mind acts as the standard work of reference in anything to do with the testing of software systems. I have seen it in use on both sides of the Atlantic. It is *The Art of Software Testing* by Glenford Myers [13]. A fair proportion of the material I cover here is explored by Myers in much greater detail. I've not given you the answer to the puzzle, as I want to irritate you enough for you to go and find a copy of the book and look at it in more detail. If you haven't got the time, get someone else in your team to study it; they'll probably become so enthused that the pay-back will be more than worth the cost of the bus fare to the library.

But I mustn't forget that you're in a hurry, you're a busy practising professional. So this chapter will attempt to cover in a few pages the essence of the message about testing.

Back to the definition of success. If the triangle program needs at least seventeen test cases, how many will be needed to cover every possible way your widget-shuffling system may behave? And how long will this take? If there's a nice sandy beach nearby, with powerful arching waves crashing down on it, then feel free to exclaim that you have from here to eternity.

Since I suspect you'll be out of luck on this score, you have no other option but to consider life's most unforgiving task master — time. You only get today once, and you only have a limited amount of time before your system is to be delivered. You can't run every possible test case. There simply isn't enough time. So every test must count, be worth expending your time on; in other words it must test an important part of the system in such a way that if a bug exists, it is uncovered. That is why we choose to declare a test to be successful if it finds a bug; this test has been a good use of your time. In all of this you have one very useful asset — your intelligence.

5.2.2 *Creative narcolepsy*

Yes, I know you can run tests with your eyes closed, but if you do you will not be making the most of your time. Selectivity is at the heart of the activity. Testing is one of the most challenging, creative, yet emotionally ambiguous parts of the software development process. Challenging because you need to ensure that you have exercised the paths through the heart of your system, creative because you need to fabricate test cases to catch those obscure and infuriating little errors that everyone makes, and — emotionally ambiguous?

This isn't a book on overcoming co-dependent relationships. What has emotional ambiguity got to do with the nice clean hard discipline of building software systems? People! They do the testing. I used the word 'discipline', not the word 'science' because (just in time) I remembered my claims in this book's introduction. Software development is still a black art, only high-power CASE (computer aided software engineering) tools, coupled with formal methods, will entitle us to treat it as a science. Once we have these to hand, we can let the machines get on with testing the systems. Machines are heartless; they don't mind that the definition of a successful test is one that finds a bug. People do mind, particularly the developer of a program.

If you've just spent a number of weeks, maybe months, of hard effort carefully crafting your masterpiece of code, you'll feel pride in it. You have a heart; you've probably developed a soft-spot for all those 0s and 1s carefully arranged at your behest, to carry out your bidding. Almost parental, certainly protective and affectionate, these feelings are perfectly reasonable; they're more commonly characterised as motivation, enthusiasm, and dedication. But they naturally result in a blind-spot (to go with the soft-spot). You are not at all well motivated to start to pick your masterwork to pieces. To kick it, prod it, stretch it, bend it, strain it, overload it, confuse it. There's a part of you in that code and you really cannot be that clinical, detached and downright nasty to something you've created. This is the psychology of testing, quite simply — if you wrote it, then you won't test it properly.

This incidentally is why people tend to conceive of testing as the act of exercising the stated functionality. Your program carries out photo-recognition of the local zoo's elephants and rhinoceroses. So you take it to the zoo, plug in your laptop, put Nelly in front of the camera, and the program promptly declares that it sees Nelly the Elephant. Your creation does what it's been asked to do; there, you've tested it. 'It works!' sounds good and positive, whilst 'It doesn't not work' just doesn't have the same ring to it. You feel you are rewarded by those higher up your corporate tree for getting things right, so you are inclined to concentrate on that aspect of testing.

I've belaboured the point. I hope it sounds plausible. Try and think back to when you last derived real satisfaction and enjoyment writing a whole suite of tests to really kick the hell out of one of your own programs. My guess is that was a while ago, if ever. Where does this leave us? Delegation time! In this case sideways is often best. More on this in Chapter 10 'Management of Development' — but in summary, low-level testing is best done by pairs of programmers who have worked together such that they each write a module specification, then they code each other's modules, and go on to test the modules they originally specified. This provides for a more unbiased approach, without sacrificing too much in terms of unfamiliarity with what is to be tested.

5.3 Teasing testing apart

5.3.1 Levels

I just mentioned low-level testing. What did I mean? This is a good point to give a few more definitions. All sorts of different types of test-names crop up in conversation with professionals, but how best can we tie these different types of test into the rest of the software development process? I will list the main test levels in chronological order of their use in a development.

- *Unit tests*. These are of the very lowest level of the system. They might use test harnesses, i.e. other programs written specifically to mimic the environment in which a particular unit may run. This is often done if the rest of the system is not yet available. However, if the rest of the system is already tested and available, then it is perfectly valid to use the system. The word 'unit' connotes the fact that the item under test is the unit, and it is the item rather than the choice between test harness and system that is essential to the test being a unit test. The defining document against which the unit is tested is the process specification. It is okay to have a unit test, although the terminology I defined in the preceding chapter identified a process as the smallest runnable entity. Unit testing implies that we are testing only certain aspects of a process. If unit testing covers everything it becomes a process test.

- *Integration tests*. These involve testing the way different processes interface to each other. In a single-process system this will be fairly trivial, but in all other situations there is quite a lot to consider here. Again, harnesses are perfectly permissible; they may be able to behave more predictably than a real process,

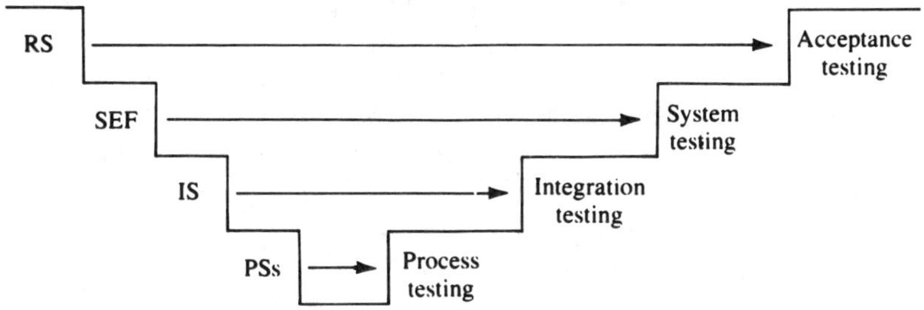

Figure 5.1
The specification and testing valley

particularly where the generation of error and non-standard data is concerned. Here the document against which integration testing is done is the internals specification.

- *System tests*. These tests treat the system as a whole. They are the first to pay less attention to the internals of the system. Because the system is tested as a whole, harnesses can now be used only to mimic entities beyond the boundaries of the system. The defining document here is the statement of external functionality (SEF). Notice this document describes the 'what' of the system without explaining the 'how'; the system tests reflect this. These tests can sometimes be thought of as dry-run acceptance tests.

- *Acceptance tests*. These are not necessarily run by the developers. Here's where the users may make a reappearance. Whoever runs them, the aim is to confirm that the users are happy enough with the system to take delivery (but see the chapter on 'Installation', Chapter 6). They may refer to the requirements specification, or if it has been declared as the 'defining specification' they refer to the SEF. As with the system tests these are high-level tests, but they need not be the same tests as the system tests.

I like to think about these diagrammatically as shown in Figure 5.1. Extending the waterfall model of development, where we have level defined on the vertical axis and time on the horizontal, I think of the process as one of descending down into the valley of detail, then climbing back out again, with ropes strung across at various levels linking the different stages of specification-writing with corresponding stages of testing.

5.3.2 Rope bridges across the valley

On the downward slope we have the design specifications, on the upward slope the testing specifications. How do we straddle the valley and link the two?

This presupposes that you were planning to write down the tests, on paper (no less), before you actually run them. I trust this isn't too radical a proposition. None the less it's worthwhile giving reasons why you should do so.

Firstly, there is the age-old art of keeping records. Write down what you've run, and the outcome; and not only do you have proof that such and such a path through the code was exercised (traceability), but you have also made use of the best weapon to attack complexity. Buzz word and bane of the industry, the management of complexity is an inevitable challenge that you will face because software systems are inherently far too complex for the good of most people's mental health. You only use between 3 and 5 percent of your highly prized grey matter. We are all very poor mental jugglers, unable to keep more than about half a dozen thoughts at the front of our minds simultaneously. With being able to keep so few things actively in mind, you then have to rely on your memory. Who was the second man to walk on the moon? It's in there somewhere, you've heard it many a time in the media; even if you weren't paying direct attention, you did store it. But how long will it take you to recall it? The only safe option is to write down your tests and test results. This is, though, a very negative reason for getting out the quill and parchment. And yes, I know that, in the final analysis, any pop-psychologist worth his or her weight in invoices will tell you that sicks are more effective than carrots; but I would still prefer to enthuse you into this activity with a more positive reason.

So, secondly, there's time. Not much of it left by now; you're well behind in the development schedule and if the delivery date is still to be met the testing must be pared down to the bare essentials. Selectivity now becomes almost god-like in its importance. You must make the most of your time and choose the most effective tests. If you run headlong into the computer room, spin around on the ninety-seven-way adjustable chair and start hammering the keyboard — chances are the tests you select won't be the most effective. Writing requires thinking if it's not going to end up as a mere stream of gibberish. Writing out your test specifications will demand of you that you first think about which tests would be the most appropriate. Which tests will exercise the most critical parts of the system? Probe the hiding holes most beloved by the varieties of familiar silly mistake bugs? Here, as with everywhere else — failing to plan is like planning to fail (although don't forget, right now we do want failure; the successful test is the one that uncovers a bug). But don't try to find bugs by chance; write yourself a test plan!

5.3.3 How to build your bridge

With luck this shouldn't provide you with too much trouble. If you wrote your design specifications with testability in mind, you merely have to apply the check you did when you reviewed the specification for testability in the first place. Take each statement, which should be something like 'When the system clock strikes midnight, the dancer's transportation layer will turn into a pumpkin' and place the words 'Confirm that' at the start of the sentence. Lo and behold, you have your test.

Yes I know, when you get down to the lower levels of specification this may not be so easy. The main ones this technique applies to are the requirements specification, which should form the basis for the acceptance test specification, and the statement of external functionality, on which the system test specification is based. The internals specification, which results in the integration test specification, and the process specifications, which yield the unit test specifications, will not necessarily be so amenable to this technique. But in all cases remember those cross-references that were so painstakingly constructed — now they come into their own. Each test case that you write in the unit test specifications will correspond to one of the statements in the process specification. You can then trace this statement back to the internals specification, and thus you have the essence of the appropriate test for that level of statement already available to you. You can repeat the pattern as you climb back out of the valley of detail, through the SEF layer arriving at the requirements specification. But how should the tests at the most detailed level be constructed? Don't try to run before you can walk. I still need to explain how the testing operation should be organised — before you start doing your tests. If I left the next section till later, it'd be too late and that would undoubtedly be a mark of poor quality.

5.4 Doing the tests

5.4.1 Testing-procedures

These will all depend on your corporate culture, or at least the one you would like to foster. I consider that it is perfectly in order for a project to buck the trend, swim against the stream — provided it's swimming in the right direction. So what should be on the signposts you're following?

We need to consider how best to organise both the people and the software. On the human side of things, I've already advocated the use of programming pairs; let them get on with writing the unit test specifications, but don't forget to review these documents before you allow any testing to take place. Review them against what? Patience, patience — the next few pages will give you a taxonomy of testing techniques, from which you should ensure the programming staff choose enough to cover the software fully.

Organising the software should be straightforward if you spent time up front thinking about the file-directory structure and how you build the system. You may well want to have more than one copy of the system, and will probably have different subsystems at different stages of completeness. This means you will have to start thinking about configuration management. This will initially seem like a very trivial problem, a bit like stock-taking in a shoe shop, no real challenge here. Danger — you'd be quite right to think it's simple, when you first start. But all complex systems are built out of small, easy-to-comprehend building blocks. It's only when you put enough of them together that they start to develop a life of their own and fight back. In truth, there is so much to this issue that I devote a separate chapter to it. All the detail is in there. Try the next paragraph; if it sounds familiar carry on reading here; if it's all a foreign language to you, then take a break from testing and go read Chapter 9 on 'Change Control and Configuration Management' now.

You will need a library tool and a build tool. Ensure that the library tool is configured so that only one person can lock a particular version of a file (at any one time). Also create snapshots of different chronological versions of the whole system; think of these as markers identifying your level of confidence in the different versions of the system. Configure the security of the tool so that only specially authorised people can migrate files into snapshots that represent firmer versions of the system.

Now tie this tool in with the build tool, which should be able to do a complete, unaided build of the whole system whilst the project team goes down the pub for a well-earned jar. The tie-in will mean that the build tool will check to see which files have changed since the last build (these will be ones that have been checked back into the library tool as fully tested and ready for use by the rest of the team); and the build tool will rebuild only the parts of the system that have changed, or depend on files that have changed. This should be a very routine operation, do it every night; as testing tends to be a very high pressure activity, if files are not put in the library for safe keeping and immediately incorporated, there's a good risk that in the headlong rush (which testing may well degenerate into) the files will be overlooked, lost and need to be reworked.

I mentioned this in Chapter 4 'Internals and Coding', but it bears restatement. Ensure that untested software is available only to its tester. Initially use a 'stub', dummy procedure or simulator. Once it's deemed tested, and only then, the process can be 'released' to the rest of the testing team. If other tests reveal problems with this file (that is now in the system), and as a result it needs to be changed, the same rule applies. The file will need retesting; this should be done in the tester's own programming area, and in the meantime the rest of the team should continue to use the old version. Only when the retest is completed can the file be rereleased to the rest of the team. This is where the library tool's snapshot facility comes into its own.

If the last three paragraphs confused you, go and read Chapter 9 on 'Change Control and Configuration Management'. This book has an intended audience of practising professionals. I dived straight in to how to use these tools because some of the gentle readers will no doubt be very familiar with the trials and tribulations of configuration management already; contemporaneously, others will be mystified by the title, never mind the detail. Remember all I am doing, in this book, is basically restating what is 'good practice', so almost everyone will find some section or other very familiar — if so, feel free to skim.

5.4.2 Record keeping

Having talked above about why to keep records, here's how. There are two distinct things to record: test outcomes and bugs. And these are not one and the same, even if the test does find a bug.

I presume that you will generate some sort of typewritten set of test scripts. These may be separate documents corresponding to the test specifications, or part of the same document. No matter, just make sure that the individual test cases in the scripts leave some blank space after each set of instructions for the outcome to be written down.

Before I forget, the instructions should include test environment, timing considerations, input, and expected output. The test environment section describes the other parts of the system and the test harnesses that are needed. Timing — if system response time is critical, how big is the window of opportunity, and how do you know if you've got through it okay? (Beware of using debugging tools that step you through code. I once created a process that kept mysteriously dying. After must frustration the problem turned out to be that it needed to receive its start command within 10 seconds; and I wasn't stepping through the code quickly enough. A case of the debugger adding bugs! — fear not, this sort of glitch is rare, I should've run the code first without the debugger.) Input should be obvious — lots more on that in a moment. Output, almost equally so, but if you're monkeying around deep inside your system, the output from your particular test case may never reach the user interface — so state where the output is actually to be found.

Back to the blank space in the test script. This is for the tester to write down what actually happened. Good old handwriting is better than keeping a file on-line, even if you do have a snazzy multi-tasking windows-based work-station. On-line test records can be more easily tampered with, and the testing record may prove very important should legal proceedings arise at a later date, or just so that the team leader is confident, for instance, that the aileron adjustment subsystem has been fully tested so that it can withstand severe windshear.

More often than not, the person who finds a bug will not be able to fix it at that moment. She may not be able to fix it within the necessary timescale because a lot more tests need to run. The bug may be an incidental bug in a part of the system that the finder is not familiar with, thrown up in the course of a test that was seeking to exercise a completely different area of code. So someone else will have to fix the problem. In addition, the project manager may want to keep a record of the number and location of bugs discovered. All sorts of marvellous things can be inferred from graphs of cumulative bug counts. But none of the above will be possible if the development team fails to keep a record of the bugs found.

The idea location for such a record is, in contrast to the test record, an on-line database. It will need frequent updating, lots of people will want to access it, and reports will be needed from time to time. Not only should it be on-line, in the ideal exquisitely beautiful world of the 'perfect project', it should be a relational database. This provides easy access by whatever key is the most appropriate, and generates reports covering each individual's particular needs at any given moment. So what fields should each row in this marvel contain i.e. what are the column headings? They are:

- *Finder*. The girl who stumbled upon the problem. She'll know the best way to recreate it.

- *Fixer*. The guy who gets all the fun of picking through the hexadecimal core dumps and all the glory of getting the system to damn well do what it was meant to in the first place.
- *Dates*. Well, if these two want to go out on one — fine by me. Meantime, we need to record when the problem was found, when assigned to the fixer, when fixed, and when the fixed version was incorporated back into the test system.
- *Area*. Which part of the labyrinth of 0s and 1s did this little monstrosity rear its ugly head in?
- *Test number*. Which test case actually uncovered the problem. This may be necessary if we want to recreate the bug, or test the fix, given that while out on their date the finder and fixer decide to elope to Guadeloupe and refuse to come back, never mind answer the phone ever again.
- *Nature of problem*. Okay, so what actually is this bug? Provide details of how the system's behaviour departs from the functionality laid down in the specification.
- *Class of problem*. Where it happened (operating system, data, typo) helps with future analysis of where errors are being generated.
- *Source of problem*. Closely allied to the class of problem, this details where the bug arose, in the specification or the coding.
- *Severity/priority*. Helps in determining which bugs to tackle first.
- *Now fixed*. A simple yes/no field so we can identify which ones are outstanding.
- *Files changed*. Which files were amended to fix the problem, and what was changed in them.

This gives us a handle to control the test–bug–fix–test loop. We've decided on the test specifications and test records; it's time to address what the actual tests will do. Yes, what you thought this chapter should have been about right from the start.

5.5 Types of test

Tests can be classified into various groups. These groups may be new to you even though the actual tests look very familiar. Don't, however, be misled, just because I am providing a theoretical underpinning to your testing activities; remember that none of these tests can ensure that your system will be error-free. Each testing technique has its plus points and its minus points; you will need to use an appropriate combination of them to create a thorough and complete set of test cases.

There are two main groupings: static tests and dynamic tests.

- *Static* (or investigative) tests are so-called because the code stays still — it isn't run!
- *Dynamic* tests, on the other hand, involve feeding the software with morsels of data and confirming that the code digests the data as expected.

Static approaches can themselves be split into two groups:

- *Static analysis*, where the source code is scanned by eye for errors or anomalies; and
- *Symbolic execution*, where the code is 'dry-run' using algebraic notation to record the values of variables (rather than genuine data).

Dynamic approaches split into three groups; these reflect the way in which the data that is going to be fed to the beast is chosen:

- *Functionally*, where data is chosen on the basis of the software's external functionality, also called black box because the code is treated as a black box about which the internals are a mystery;
- *Structurally*, where attention is paid to the insides of the code, and how it is structured. Also called white box (should be clear box really!) because we do know something about the insides (and white here is considered the opposite to black!); and
- *Derivatively*, where the design representation is used to construct the test data.

Let's look at all of these in a bit more detail.

5.5.1 Static techniques

- *Static analysis*. At its simplest this is just desk checking the code before it's run. This is best done by someone other than the original coder. No doubt you are familiar with the scenario where you're wrestling with an intractable bug or compilation error but can't see where the problem is. You present the code to a colleague who immediately spots the problem, claiming that the discrepancy was obvious; it stood out from the rest of the code like the glass pyramid stands out from the rest of the Louvre. Once this has been pointed out to you, you see the error too. It would have taken you weeks to find it, since you were now no longer seeing the code as it was, but as you wanted it to be. A second pair of eyes is invaluable.

This staring at the code can be improved by adding some structure to the sessions. A formal review is no bad thing. A culture of ego-less programming needs to prevail, however, if this is to work. A culture of what? The idea is that it is the code that is important and the aim of the review is not to judge the performance of the programmer, but to ensure that the team produces high-quality output. It may be necessary to declare that the review records, which of course should be written, will not be released from the project files to anyone in Personnel, and will not be used when trying to assess the programmer's performance.

All good reviews need checklists of things to look for. In the case of desk-checking code, look for the following:

- Any non-standard or dubious programming practices (remember the coding guidelines that were developed earlier?)
- Logical faults — does the logic flow correctly?

- Uninitialised variables — include global variables and assumptions made about them.
- Unreachable code — is there an IF statement that will never be true?
- Incorrectly calculated array bounds — yes that good old chestnut, especially important with liberal languages like 'C' that don't check array bounds at compile time.
- Variables set but not read — lots of very similarly named variables can cause confusion resulting in the wrong one being in the wrong place.
- Not keeping to interface specifications — is everything called correctly? Are you sending the correct ACKs and NAKs (see Glossary) when so requested?
- Cross-references (this will need what I talk about below). Look for too much naughty close coupling, abuse of global variables, or potential timing and synchronisation problems.

Most of the above can be worried about and worked out with a blunt pencil, but if you are lucky there maybe sharper tools available to you. Most computers and most common languages now come with CASE tools that can do a lot of this static analysis work for you. Pick up the phone and give the nice hardware salesman (who you haven't talked to since January) a bell, and see if there's anything in his (or her) goody cupboard that might save you time here, and do a more thorough job than the team leader's greying matter.

- *Symbolic execution*. Here we are at the half-way house between running a unit and, in the great bright shiny world to come, using formal methods and logic to PROVE a unit is correct. We aren't yet quite that advanced, not on your budget anyway!

It's a little esoteric, so I'll just give you a taste. You need to execute the unit symbolically. You'll hold the values of the variables in algebraic form, and represent the outcome of the program using one or more expressions. Each time you make a decision (in the program) follow both outcomes whilst remembering the condition values that sent you down each of the possible paths. When you're done, you'll have two facts about each path through the program: a list of the decisions made along the path, and algebraic-form values for all the variables at the end of the program. These can be compared with the specification. For more on this see Chapter 8 ('Test Tools and Other Techniques') in Myers [13].

5.5.2 Functional (black box) dynamic techniques

- *Equivalence partitioning*. Here we look at all the inputs for a unit and divide them up into classes of data such that all members of a particular class should be treated equivalently by the program. We have thus partitioned the data into equivalence classes (a good old mathematical term, that will be unfamiliar to you unless you enjoyed the dubious pleasure of taking mathematics at degree level). The basic point is that one representative item of data from each equivalence class will suffice to examine if that class of input is handled correctly, since the program should handle all of that type of data in the same way.

An example may help. If a valid input can be an integer in the range from 0 to 255, then equivalence partitioning will result in input values x, y, z such that $x<0$, $0<y<255$, $255<z$.

- *Boundary value analysis*. This complements equivalence partitioning, because it focuses on the boundaries between equivalence classes. You should aim to devise test cases that exercise the unit with data from the boundary areas of the input variables. In addition you need input data that will exercise the unit at the boundaries of the OUTPUT data.

Back to our previous example. Boundary value analysis would add extra input data in addition to x, y and z. Specifically, it would cause us to choose: -1, 0, 1, 254, 255, 256. If the output data fell into two classes, either greater than 15 or less than 15, you should choose input data that should generate output of 14, 15, 16.

- *Cause–effect graphing*. Equivalence partitioning and boundary value analysis look at each equivalence class in isolation. They do not exercise the unit with different combinations of inputs from different equivalence classes. Combinatorics is a branch of mathematics that can be used here to show that there are an outrageously large number of possible combinations that could be tested. There is a way of getting a handle on this problem, but even the solution is time-consuming. If you have a critical unit or subsystem that you need to test extremely thoroughly, then and only then will this be worthwhile. If so, time for another look at Myers [13], chapter 4 — 'Test Case Design' (glance at figure 4.14 to discover why I am not going into any more detail here on the subject).

- *Random data selection*. Choose some data on a random basis, determine what the output should be (put some numbers into a bit of symbolic execution) and run it. You could use a cheap pocket calculator's random number generator to ensure that you do have genuinely random input. A couple of other more esoteric ways of reaching the same point may be more fun, if a little messy. Round up that infinite group of monkeys who are still busy writing the complete works of Shakespeare and get them to do so on your keyboards. Or put some terminals in a sealed room, get some chickens, yes — chickens, and let them loose in the room for a while; amongst other things they should generate some random input (although the office cleaners may not be very friendly for the next few weeks). Both techniques require that you have a log file facility configured, so that you can record the random input — chickens do not themselves keep high-quality test records. Anyway, removing my tongue from my cheek, we shall continue.

5.5.3 Structural (white box) dynamic techniques

Industry folklore claims that even good black-box testing may only exercise between 50 percent and 70 percent of the code. That leaves 30–50 percent still untested. So to get at those elusive little language statements, we need to do some white-box tests.

These pay attention to the code's internal structure. They are not sufficient on their own because they do not guarantee that we have tested the unit's explicit functionality. Ideally, we would like to exercise every entry-to-exit path in the unit; tough — there are just too many. So we have to be selective. The coverage criteria below can guide us. I start with the least stringent, and get fussier as I go.

- *Statement coverage*. The aim here is to create enough tests so that every statement is executed at least once. It sounds a lot, but actually is pretty minimal; don't settle for less than this. Some of the cases may come from the black-box tests, but you will need extra ones, otherwise you won't be reaching that 30–50 percent of the code that's being so shy and retiring.

- *Decision coverage*. Now you need to generate enough test cases so that each decision has a TRUE outcome and a FALSE outcome at least once.

What? Statement coverage will ensure that every statement and (thus) every decision is exercised at least once. But it doesn't necessarily exercise every decision outcome. For example, the statement

IF X = 0 THEN PERFORM ERROR ROUTINE

is covered with a test case of $x = 0$, but we have no evidence on how the code will perform when $x<0$ or $x>0$.

- *Multiple decision coverage*. This condition addresses the situation where we have code with complex decisions, such as

IF A<B AND (C>D) OR C< >A THEN ...

Here we seek to exercise every possible combination of each of the original conditions in the statement. Oh, by the way, what might be bad about the sample line of test here? If you're not sure, check the coding guidelines in the preceding chapter.

5.5.4 Derivative dynamic techniques

The above techniques have concentrated on what the unit is meant to do (functional techniques) and how it does it (structural techniques). We shouldn't forget how the code was designed. The analysis carried out then can be of great benefit in designing test cases.

- *Decision tables*. These are often used to reason about the way a program is intended to behave. They need to be checked for completeness and consistency before they can be used. Once this is done a little dose of Boolean algebra needs to be applied and a set of test cases will drop out without having to consider all 2 to the power *N* possible combinations. This wraps back into the cause–effect graphing discussed by Myers [13], so I refer the curious reader there.
- *Finite state machines*. These also provide a different way of reasoning about

a program. It is possible to use them as a starting point for deriving possible test cases.

5.5.5 *Applicability*

I have talked about the unit as the item under test. These approaches can of course be applied to the integration, system, and acceptance tests as well. Once one has climbed out of the depths of the valley of detail, and is at the system level (or above), the structural dynamic tests become inappropriate, as you are now trying to test the system's functions without regard to its construction — just like a regular user.

Plan for the unit and integration tests to take longer than the later stages. You will find that the later tests often consist of a subset of the earlier test; and initially you will have to devote time to getting bugs out of the test scripts and simulators, in addition to the bugs in the actual system. If you have done the lower levels of testing thoroughly, the higher levels should be far easier, as you will already have got rid of the majority of the bugs. Indeed, if you find your system tests repeatedly stumbling into problems, then you probably haven't done your unit and integration testing well enough. Acceptance testing should throw up almost no bugs whatsoever.

5.5.6 *A digression*

In rereading Myers for the writing of this chapter, I happened upon a section that I had almost overlooked. I'm fallible too. When did you last question something I've said in this book? But I digress from my digression.

Having expended effort on locating all these problems, they now have to be solved. The name of the game is debugging. Myers summarises the research on the psychology of programming with some very pertinent epithets. They come in two parts: the former concern the identification of the problem, the latter its solution — not necessarily the same thing, and not necessarily carried out by the same person.

First of all use your brain; brute force is a very blunt tool, a sharpened mind is much more likely to solve the problem. Use pen and paper but stay away from the computer; using it only encourages blind stabs in the dark. Don't spend too long on a problem, say 30 minutes for a small program, half a day for a complex system. If you're not succeeding take a break, and let the 95 percent of your brain that you never use have a go. Either your subconscious will come up with a new idea, or at the very least you'll return to the problem refreshed. Try talking to someone else; you may well solve the problem there and then without their saying a word. Use the debugging tools as an aid to thinking, to test a hypothesis, and not as a substitute for thinking. Don't experiment by changing the program; you're cutting the ground out from underneath yourself. And above all remember the concept of ego-less programming, you're human and so bound to make mistakes. Just because the compiler won't forgive you, it doesn't mean that the organisation you work in will behave in the same way.

Having found the bug, bear this in mind. There will probably be more bugs in the vicinity — go look for them. Fix the bug not the symptom; all (not just some) of the original indications that there was a problem should be cleared by your fix. Your fix might not be right, or might introduce new bugs. Test it thoroughly (as thoroughly as the original program was tested, using the same procedures — desk checks, etc.) and retest (regression test) the rest of the program. If you introduce more bugs than you fix, the quality of the code is regressing, hence the term regression test. The bigger the program, the less likely your fix is to be correct, after all there's more to take into account than for a small program. And for goodness sake fix the source code; don't zap the object code, as this would only cause a configuration management nightmare later on. That said, good bug-hunting; and now back to our story.

5.5.7 *Attribute testing*

Oh come on now, there can't be anything else to test for? I'm afraid there is, old chap. So far we've covered the system's functionality, but think back to the design specifications. These included sections on all sorts of non-functional attributes that the system possessed. We need to check that these have been achieved as well.

- *Stress testing*. This involves making sure that the system can indeed handle the load that it is meant to. You know, all those ticketing agents in the Asia–Pacific region, from Osaka, through Macao, to Perth dial-in at the same moment, all wanting tickets for the gallery in the control room for Japan's mission to Mars. As this won't happen for a few years yet, even though this level of loading is in the specification, you need to be able to confirm that the system can handle it. You'll need appropriate test harnesses. And you'll need to do this when you can soak the machine with transactions, i.e. outside regular working hours. You may care to automate this to save spending every hour of your waking life in the office.

- *Resilience*. Basically this is plug-pulling (both physically on the hardware and logically on specific pieces of software). Once pulled, the system should behave as in the specifications, gracefully shutting down and, if appropriate, restarting. The debugger can be used here to introduce nasties in appropriate locations, thus faking certain error conditions. Again, this may need to be done outside office hours.

- *Event logging*. Most systems keep a little (or in some cases horrendously big) diary of all the significant things that happened to them that day. The truthfulness of this needs to be tested. If the resilience and stress tests are run while the machine is home alone, then they will actually be rather good tests of the sufficiency of the event log. Because the log will provide the only clues as to what happened if something untoward occurred.

- *Configuration*. Can you set the system up in the way the specifications said you could? Fairly self-evident really, bot not to be overlooked.

- *Security*. Closely allied to configuration; now it's been created, can any unauthorised so-and-so break into it?

5.6 Final thoughts

5.6.1 *Scholarly aside No. 2*

Can we use measurement to assess the quality of our testing? The research findings I've mentioned earlier [3] have something to say here.

In integration testing, once trivial unit-test errors have been removed (by good desk checking, etc.), a measure of the number of errors per 1000 lines of code (the error rate) can be taken. As each subsystem is added into the test system, the research findings (mentioned in 'Scholarly aside No. 1') show that the cumulative average error rate (the average of the averages) tends to stabilise. So draw a graph, and if there is a sudden departure from an otherwise increasingly well-behaved line, get worried — prod your code more carefully. You could even take the next step and use statistical process control (as per manufacturing industry).

Certain organisations (a big blue one being famous in this regard) now do not allow their software to exit system testing until the cumulative error rate drops below '*n*' errors per 1000 lines. The actual value of '*n*' is less important than the approach that it symbolises.

The research points out that experience indicates that 'conscientious' system testing (i.e. non-safety-critical) uncovers about 80 percent of the bugs in a system. This implies that 20 percent are left to be found during acceptance testing and live running. Therefore, the number of bugs found during acceptance testing should not exceed one-quarter of those found up to acceptance testing. If this isn't the case, then the earlier testing missed bugs and wasn't of a high enough quality.

5.6.2 *QA and QC*

I talked about this at the start of the book. But let's do it again — you might be allergic to reading introductions and have missed this pearl of wisdom.

If the system is large, or will form the basis of a product, then it is well worthwhile to establish a group of people unconnected with the coding to do the system testing. Now you know what they should be called? Correct, not the QA department; that implies that quality is something that is tested for just before the product goes out the door. But quality is designed in right from the start; these people are the QC department. They control it. The only group who would be entitled to call themselves a QA department would be the people who check that everyone in the organisation is paying attention to quality from day one. I know, I'm nit-picking, but if I fail to convince you that there's more to quality than testing for it, then I've failed. But if you read at least one other chapter in this book and act on it, then I am starting to succeed in injecting quality into the whole of your development lifecycle.

5.7 Questions

1. Who will be your testing supremo?
2. How will their performance be judged?
3. Have you planned the production of test harnesses and simulators yet?
4. Have you started writing test specifications yet?
5. How will you organise the testing to ensure that no-one tests their own code?
6. Where will you store the test records?
7. Have you started to create your bug database?
8. When will you know that the system has been fully tested and can be given to the users?

6 Installation

6.1 Introduction

6.1.1 Not now surely?

So should you be reading this chapter yet? Chances are you should have looked at it before now. We've arrived at the stage in this book where the fabric of space–time breaks down. Books are sequential beasts; chapter follows chapter, paragraph trots on after paragraph. We, however, need to bifurcate, in fact split centrifugally in many directions all at once. All the rest of the chapters should be read in parallel. In other words, the issues covered in this chapter (excepting the soliloquy on acceptance) no longer sit comfortably at one point of the development lifecycle. This will also apply to my subsequent musings.

All we can really determine is whether this is the most appropriate moment for you to read this chapter. It's never really too early, but if you are still formulating the user requirements you will be able to translate the concerns I raise into only high-level points in your own development. It's best to have nearly completed the statement of external functionality (SEF); by then you know what you want to build and thus probably what you'll need. Some of the issues raised here might even be quite at home in the SEF or otherwise the development plan or some sort of installation plan.

If you are further down the road, specifying the internals or actually coding and testing, then stop! At least for the few minutes that it will take you to read this, because a lot of the activities involved in installation have long lead-times that may be outside your control. You need to consider these activities now, so that you are not delayed when you need them to happen.

Installation has different characteristics depending on whether the system has been developed in-house or by a separate company. The in-house situation is simpler; a single organisation will face a subset of the issues and problems that arise when there are two companies involved. So this chapter will focus on the latter scenario, and I leave it to the gentle readers, from organisations that do things in-house, to use their native wit and intelligence to extract that which is of relevance to them.

6.1.2 Testing, testing, 1, 2, 3

I know I covered testing in the last chapter. Well, there is an area of overlap between the last stages of testing and the installation of the completed system. The manager of the development and the user have an option as to which comes first — acceptance tests or installation at the system's eventual home.

In the first scenario, the acceptance tests (the ones that must be passed before the users accept the system) will take place at the developers' location. The two groups could be based on different floors of the same building, or the users might have to hop on a trans-Pacific 747 to get to the tests. The users then observe the tests being run on the developers' computers. Once the tests are complete and the users deem themselves happy, then the system is ready to be installed at the users' premises.

In the second scenario the system is taken to the users' location and installed there. However, it doesn't go live straight away, as it still has to be acceptance-tested. Since this occurs at the users' site, it is more likely that it will be done by the users with the developers looking on (in contrast to the above scenario). Once the testing is complete, then the installation process is completed. This can vary in levels of complexity, from leaving the system on the current computer and just allowing the 'real users' to start to use it live; to moving it to a different computer in a separate geographical location.

6.2 Acceptance issues

Where acceptance and installation intermingle, there is a whole raft of extra considerations. I will float these out to you now. If you are really truly sure that your users have already signed on the dotted line or will do so before the system leaves the hands of the developers, and all that is left is to install it and go live, then you may skip the next few paragraphs. However, you might enjoy contemplating all the risks that you are not likely to face, but which could leave others completely stuck in the mud.

6.2.1 'My dog barks, I wanted one that says "Woof"'

If the system is to be tested by the 'real users' then make sure you know who they are. You jolly well ought to by now anyway. The reason is that the users might themselves split into various subdivisions; I outlined them back in the user requirements chapter. Specifically if the system is being developed by a separate organisation (under a contract and all that) you will have to be prepared for the fact that the users who test your system may (if you are unlucky) be completely new to you.

This situation can arise because up until now the members of the client's DP department may have dominated the procurement of the system. They will have visited the developers' offices, they may have sat in on the system tests or dry-runs of the acceptance tests. Crucially they may have been the ones who drafted the acceptance tests. This has been all very helpful for the developers since the DP department speaks approximately the same language (techno-gabble) as the developers. But the client organisation may not have tied the DP department and the 'real users' together tightly enough or often enough. Apart from being rather painful for these two groups, the benefit of having done so is that the acceptance tests would, in such a situation, reflect the prolonged close-quarter contact between the two client groups and thus be a more appropriate test of the system.

The point to remember here is that we aren't talking about clean analytical formal method proofs that the system does what the users ask of it. Instead we have a set of tests, aimed to ferret out bugs from where the users fear they are most likely to lurk, and also aimed at demonstrating that the system actually does what the users want it to do. But the users may not know a great deal about computers, so they will still focus their acceptance decision on criteria they understand. These criteria will be reflected in the requirements specification (RS) rather than the SEF — even though the SEF is nominally (and contractually) the 'specification of last resort'.

But why should all this matter? In the situation where acceptance testing is being done at the developers' offices, the clients' DP departments are the groups most likely to witness tests and to sign to accept systems. After all, they have been the primary point of contact for most of the development. This means that they will, if they can, leave the 'real users' behind at home. The 'real users' will get their hands on the system only after it has already been accepted and then if they have problems they will raise problem reports (more on this in Chapter 7 — 'Support of a Live System'). However, if the testing is being done at client premises it will be almost impossible to exclude the 'real users'. As a result there may be a certain amount of internal friction between those two client departments. But most importantly the 'real users' are very unlikely to accept the system unless it meets what they perceive to be their requirements. What we have here is a question of emphasis. The 'real users' are quite happy with the 200 pages of SEF, they reviewed it, they confirmed to their satisfaction that it mapped correctly back to the RS; now they just happen to place a slightly different interpretation on the meaning of the text!

The developers can't really get around this. I do not advocate locking the 'real users' in a cupboard, and only letting them out after the DP department has signed for the system. The system is intended for the users, who will have to be faced sooner or later, and the sooner the better. Why? Because they will demand change and the later a change takes place the more costly it will be to all concerned.

6.2.2 'My dog barks, I wanted one that says "Meeow"'

Although the above situation sounds inconvenient, it's a mere trifle compared to the nightmare below. It is not unknown for the 'real users' not to have been involved by the DP department and to discover what 'their' system is meant to do only when they come to run their acceptance tests on it. A warning sign of this will have been the fact that the draft acceptance tests (which the developers were expecting to agree to before they were run) remain stubbornly below the horizon. And when they do finally emerge they are vague and written wholly in business-speak.

This lack of co-ordination within the user organisation may have dire consequences since the 'real users' then proclaim that the system fails to meet their requirements. It matches the specifications fine; it just so happens that the specifications are, in the eyes of the 'real users', absolute rubbish. This leaves the developer on a rather sticky wicket. The outcome will depend very much on the fine print in the contract between the developer and the user. It's going to cost someone a lot of money. It is quite likely in this circumstance that the 'real users' are correct, and the system will have to be changed to meet their needs.

The crucial thing to realise in this situation is what has really happened. It cannot be treated like an acceptance test with a lot of bugs found, which the developer fixes and then the client accepts the system, as would be the case when the specification is correct. In our nightmare scenario the specification is wrong, badly wrong! No amount of tinkering at the edges will solve this. There is one sure recipe for compounding this calamity into a disaster — trying to keep to the schedule and treating the problem as a long list of bugs. This will only dig you deeper into the quicksand. The only sensible way out, and it takes courage, is to admit that there has been an almighty failure, and that everyone will have to go back to square one. The problem is that square one is often perceived to be in cloud-cuckoo-land. Why? The cost of going back to the start would be horrendous! However, the cost of chipping away at the calamity that claims to be a system, using patch after bodge after kludge is that in the end the bit-by-bit, bug-by-bug approach will cost more.

6.2.3 Can we talk?

Having worried the stripes off a zebra with my last concern, which I hope and trust you will never actually encounter, let's get back to something which will be of direct relevance whenever a system is acceptance-tested on the users' premises.

The tests may throw up bugs that hold up the testing; these will need to be fixed urgently. The developers, however, will no longer be based on the same computer. They may be down the hallway, a quick junket around the Beltway ringroad from Virginia into Maryland, or separated by an ocean. The developers' computer will, however, still hold the master version of the system. That is where the investigation into the problem and the fix (if the problem turns out to be a bug) will be made. The challenge, however, is getting the fix to the users' system as quickly as possible.

I'll start with the quickest but also most costly approach. Install the same library and building tools on the users' computer and rent a long bit of cable. These days it may well be 'virtual cable' since the link between the developers' computer and the users' computer could easily be via satellite or microwave. The aim is to duplicate the development environment on the users' machine and to create a seamless network between it and the developers'. This is necessary because the developers need to know which version of the software is under test by the users at any moment in time, and which fixes have been installed and which remain outstanding. The issues are very similar to the ones covered in Chapter 5 on 'Testing', and the advantage of the networking approach is that it turns the geographical separation of the systems into a non-issue.

Problems can arise if you take a more cheapskate approach. Failing to link the two sites is a sure-fire guarantee that at some point a crucial bug will arise that needs to be fixed instantly. Presuming that some of the developers' staff are at the users' site, they will go ahead and the make the fix there. In such a situation the source code as well as the object should reside on the users' machine, otherwise there might be a temptation to commit a very naughty sin and zap the object code with a temporary patch. The crucial thing after the fix is made at the users' site is to get the changed code back to the development system, and into the library and building tools; otherwise the two systems may get out of step. They will definitely get out of step if changes are also being made at the development site, because the locking facility of the library tool which prevents two people from changing a file simultaneously will have become totally ineffective. This will have to be addressed by installing a 'manual system' where a copy of the file is locked at the developers' site 'on behalf' of the one being changed at the users' site. Can you feel all the loopholes that are starting to generate themselves spontaneously? The only way they can be countered is by draconian self-discipline by everyone at both sites, and by the scrupulous keeping of records.

Actually getting the changes transferred between the two sites can be fairly straightforward if they are within a few miles of each other. However, if the separation is any greater, then next-day courier services will have to rush tapes up and down the country, and across the oceans of the planet.

On that last note, it's worth reflecting on the fact that 'the empires upon which the sun never sets' have been replaced by a 'global market-place' in which trading never ceases. The same thinking can be applied to your own work should you find yourself in a multinational enterprise spread across the globe. Time-zones are the key, provided the sites are networked. A bug can be raised during the Pacific side of the planet's daytime, fixed on the Atlantic side during the Pacific night, and be ready for retest on the next Pacific morning. However, if there isn't a network in place, time differences could slow turn-around times to the best part of a week.

6.3 Training

I'll have more to say on this in Chapter 8 on 'Documentation', but there is a point or two that relates to letting the 'real users' do the acceptance tests. Whereas in the other scenario the DP department witnesses the developers doing the tests, here the 'real users' get to tinkle the pseudo-ivory of the keyboards. Now the developers have been working with the system for some months, and they know how to use it. Thc 'real users' may not even be computer-literate. So bear in mind that there is a very big dependency here. The acceptance tests cannot start until the 'real users' have been trained to use the system!

If you've not devoted enough time and effort to creating the training courses for them, and not sent good staff along to present the training courses, then that will be self-evident when day one of the acceptance tests is spent, not in running that day's test cases, but in having the development staff (who were too precious to devote to training a month or so ago) explaining the system to the 'real users' as they go along. Moral: plan ahead and don't neglect training. After all, good training builds goodwill on all sides — a commodity that can be absent all too often when a system is being acceptance-tested.

The number of people to be trained, and the time-scale can have quite an impact. You may find it convenient to install two copies of the system, so that while one is being used for inconvenient plug-pulling acceptance tests, its more sedate sibling (clone?) is available for training of the 'real users' not directly involved in the acceptance testing. Training is likely to be spread out over a significant time period simply because the 'real users' still have their 'real jobs' to do. Apart from the situation where you have a green-field scenario (where the processing that your system does was never done before) it will be necessary for some of the 'real users' to keep the old way of doing the job going, and they'll be short-staffed since some of their co-workers will be doing the acceptance testing. So the organisation will be able to spare only a few people at a time to be trained, and training will spread across the whole of acceptance testing and may even overlap with live running.

One consequence of having people who are fresh to the system, even if they've just had a training course, is that they are very good at running inadvertent tests. I've defined these in Chapter 2 on 'Initiation and Requirements' as the sort of silly mistakes an experienced user wouldn't make. So, unless the developers think hard and creatively, they may forget to check that the system can handle the user repeatedly hitting CTRL-C or CTRL-Q. So brace yourself for all manner of marvellous maladies being reported to you down the phone at three in the morning. But do encourage the users to try such tests, because inevitably they will run them eventually; and if they don't try out their theories during acceptance testing, they will on the live system — and the consequences of that could be far worse.

It may be the case that the training system can be integrated into the disaster recovery planning and remain up and running, functioning as a backup system. If this approach is adopted, make sure the two versions remain compatible. Ideally, if the system has been designed well, it will be easy to configure, and it ought to be possible to get the backup system to use the live system's database, merely by changing a few of the file assignments in the configuration file.

6.4 The actual installation

6.4.1 Planning the installation

Having teased out the issues associated with doing acceptance tests within a multi-stage installation, let's now focus on the central issues of achieving a clean high-quality installation.

You won't manage to achieve this without putting pen to paper and writing yourself some sort of installation plan. You will be juggling all sorts of different types of input, all of which will need to be present, functioning correctly and available on the appointed day, if the system is to be considered successfully installed. Some of the issues will already have been decided from earlier stages in the development — inherited from the requirements specification or the SEF. However, you will probably retain considerable scope for using your own discretion.

- *Location*. How and where will the hardware live? The answer to this can range from:

  - comfortable and pampered, the computer room; through
  - neutral, a regular office; to
  - downright hostile, a dusty humid factory floor.

Each environment will place different demands on the hardware.

The computer room option is the most conventional, almost a reflex action. But it's not cheap, and it is worth confirming with the nice friendly hardware salesperson what the environmental requirements are for the particular machine your are going to be using. If you are merely adding an extra system on to an existing machine, then you might be forgiven for thinking that there's nothing to do. Well, go back to the sizing part of your SEF, and check if your current processor can handle an extra 1000 updates to the newly enhanced grommet-distribution database without slowing to a veritable snail's pace. The performance estimates may have been made six or nine months ago; those darling little people in Accounts may in the meantime have expanded their own corporate paperclip-counting database, thus adding a few more straws to the back of your Camel 2000 Supermini. Recheck the estimates.

If it transpires that you will need a processor upgrade, think through the implications. Will it fit in the same box? Will it generate more heat? Will it consume more power and overload your circuit breakers every time the payroll is run? If it doesn't fit in the same box, is there space for it? And remember the legal obligations you are under with respect to safety. You may have a square metre or two to spare, but if you squeeze the buff box in there will you overload the air-conditioning? You've got no more raised-floor space available — will people trip over the power cord? Are there enough fire extinguishers? Will you need extra emergency power shut-off buttons? Go and take a very close look at the safety legislation your organisation is bound by, and make sure you stick to it. You wouldn't want to go live, and then on the following day have to take the whole system down again because the corporate health and safety officer, making her quarterly safety audit, declares the computer room unsafe and gives you only one option — pull the plug!

If your development is a completely new 'green-field' system, you will have to commission a complete computer room. All the issues I highlighted above apply equally in this case. Think about the future; ensure you have enough space under your spanking new raised flooring to accommodate all the cables you'll ever want to wrap yourself in. Prepare in advance to be as fault-tolerant as possible — consider an uninterruptible power supply, which acts as a fallback generator in the event of an electrical power cut or outage.

Think further about fire prevention — inert gas tends to be better than sprinklers or foam for electrical fires. But make sure such a system is configured with appropriate interlocks which make it impossible for the gas to be triggered unless the room is armed. Ensure that it cannot be 'armed' if any door into it is unlocked, and presumably a person is in there. The gas systems can pump out the stuff so quickly there's a good chance anyone trapped inside would be suffocated. It may be necessary, for security reasons, to have key-pad (or some such) locks to prevent unauthorised entry; do not have the same procedure on the inside. It must be possible to turn the handle and escape without any such impediment. If at all possible, ensure that there is more than one exit from the room, in case someone is trapped on the wrong side of a burning computer. Computers spew out disgustingly large amounts of paper; recycling concerns aside, this also constitutes a considerable fire hazard. Ensure that the room is designed so that the paper can be handled, stored, and used without generating a crunchy underfoot carpet of waste.

You may be moving hardware around from time to time. Ensure that you have suitable (low-tech!) equipment to do this; spending a lot of one's working life in a high-tech environment can lead to one forgetting about important low-tech solutions to workaday problems. You don't want the system manager laid up for six months with a slipped disc (in his back, not your machine!) because he tried to carry a heavy box of listing paper.

If the computer you are going to use is robust enough to live in the regular office environment, then only some of the above issues apply. The management of paper is still important, so is power consumption and circuit overload. Keep plenty of easy-to-use fire extinguishers handy, and incorporate training drills covering how to use them into the office safety audits. Last, but far from least, is noise; printer-hoods are a must, loud keyboards can be irritating, so can fans in PCs. If you are looking for a desk top system and have a choice of hardware (the specifications just said PC), then shop around and compare them. If the office hasn't had computers in it before, check the deskprint of the machines; will the staff still have enough space to lay out their work? Can the boxes sit on the floor, and if so will the hard-disks crash more often (since this means they might spin in a vertical rather than horizontal plane)?

What about staff health? Are the keyboards going to be at the correct height and angle? 'repetitive strain injury' is growing as a source of days lost from work — and since there is little in the way of a cure, prevention is paramount. Will the lighting be satisfactory? What about screen glare? And remember the electromagnetic radiation emitted by the screens — the screen should be at least an arm's length away from the person. The issue of radiation-emitting equipment and pregnant women is a political 'hot potato' at the moment. In 1991 the US Supreme Court ruled that it was discrimination to ban pregnant women from such jobs. The option of whether to work in such an environment was a choice that should be left to them. The technology to protect them from danger has, so far, not been developed to any great extent. It is, however, your moral obligation to investigate what steps you can take to protect this category of user, and to ensure that such protection is installed.

Hostile locations can crop up in all sorts of unlikely places. In the middle of a brewery where to maintain cleanliness the whole place is hosed down from top to bottom at 5 a.m. every morning. In an aircraft that can be subject to some very nasty g-forces as it flies through a high-level cloud of volcano dust, all engines stall and it plummets twenty thousand feet, with passengers in free fall, before the engines are restarted and it climbs back to its cruising altitude. I'm afraid (in both senses of the phrase) this is no idle speculation on my part; it did happen once, somewhere above Alaska. Equally, the computer might need to live in an underground metro station, full of strong magnetic fields from the trains' electric third rail and the escalator motors.

So the computer will need to be of a rugged design; delicate disk drives are out! It will need to be protected from bumps, jolts and the intrusion of everything from water to a nasty dose of gamma rays. This scenario would benefit from a little consultancy by a friendly electrical engineer well versed in physics.

- *Connection*. As important as the box are the wires that link it to the outside world. The production of the installation plan is a good opportunity to undertake a cabling audit of your establishment. You'll find a lot of them tucked under carpets, a few sticky-taped to the ceiling, and far too many stuffed into holes in the wall that were never designed to handle the heat that cables can produce. There may well be some mystery cables; they won't be labelled at all, and will mysteriously disappear into the wall never to reappear anywhere else in the building. So what should you be doing? Consider whether your budget can stretch to something a little more high-tech and high-capacity than mile upon mile of co-axial; how about fibre optics? Terminal concentrators have been around for quite a while, but now it should be fairly straightforward for you to plug all the computer's ports into a box with some fibre optics coming out the other end. Run this nice small slim flexible shaft of fibre optics up from the computer room to the users' work space. Plug it into a box and then run regular cables under the floor (and I mean the floor not just the carpet) to floor sockets by all the desks. And ensure that, if there are multiple computers downstairs, everyone can play musical desks and the floor sockets can be reassigned to different computers with the minimum of pain and disruption.

Remember the cabling links to other locations. There's the standby site to be considered. If you've built fault-tolerant redundancy into your hardware, have you done the same for the communications links? Say someone digs up the road outside the office, disrupts the electricity supply to the computer room, the severs the cable linking you to the backup site. Do you have another cable, following a totally different route that can also reach the standby site? If not, why not? Remember it never rains, it pours; you need to prepare for two- and three-point failures as well as the easy-to-think-about one-point ones.

I've touched on disaster planning here. I'll cover it in more detail after covering the rest of the installation plan.

- *Peripherals*. This covers everything that isn't a buff box or a cable. The precise scope will vary depending on what else you have. Most systems will need to consider terminals and printers. But there may be optical character-readers (text scanners), video cameras, light pens, process-control hardware, etc; but whatever there is you will need to ask yourself the same set of questions as you did for the computer itself. Consider power supply: safety, ease of use, and interfacing it to the rest of the system. The more esoteric and unique the peripheral's function, the more complex will be the task of tying it into the rest of the system. Allow yourself plenty of time since you may well be operating in 'ground-breaking mode', i.e. the first person on the planet to attempt this, so who knows what inconvenient surprises may throw a spanner or two into your works delaying you by goodness knows how long? Leave yourself some breathing space.

- *Subcontractors*. The software will probably have been developed by the organisation also leading the installation. This makes the task comparatively simple. A lot of the other stuff, i.e. all the hardware, is more likely to have come from someone else. Result? You'll be dealing with lots of different subcontractors:

  - the computer manufacturers (who will probably supply some but not all of the rest of the hardware);
  - the people responsible for the cabling (probably the users' house services department);
  - the various building contractors that may be involved in upgrading (or building) the computer room;
  - other manufacturers of (or wholesalers for) the more esoteric peripherals that the computer vendor does not sell;
  - the safety authorities, maybe part of the users' organisation, maybe government agencies;
  - the electricity utility company, if you need a lot of power;
  - the telephone company in respect to linking your system to the office down the road;
  - another part of the same telephone company (both parts don't talk to each other) to hook you up to the Satellite link to your Kuala Lumpur down-station;
  - the legal and accounts department to ensure that the agreements with all these people are watertight and financially sound.

Is there a moral here? Not really, other than to assume that before you can plug anything in you will have to precede that action with a goodly number of meetings, and lots of paperwork — don't be taken by surprise.

You should also be planning your office space, how your organise the layout of desks, terminals and printers. It is becoming quite common for organisations to use computer aided design (CAD) tools to elaborate the options available to them when trying to determine what is the optimal and most cost-effective layout for their staff and for the bottom line.

- *Timetable*. This follows on very naturally from my last point. You will need the good old faithful Gantt charts and critical path (PERT) networks. I'll cover these in a little more detail in Chapter 10 'Management of Development'. The single most important aspect in planning your timetable is building in sufficient contingency; however there are no hard and fast rules here — this one's your call. Next comes careful study of your tasks to determine which lie on the critical path. Tasks not on the path can run late but not delay the overall timetable; however any slippage in a critical path task will impact the whole schedule directly. You need to identify these tasks so that enough effort can be concentrated on them to ensure that they are always under control. And if there are any non-trivial slippages (i.e. by more than one week) recheck all the tasks in case this has caused any non-critical tasks to metamorphose into critical ones. Do you start to get the feel that a computer-based project-management tool (rather than just paper, pencil and fingers) would come in handy?

People will be involved in all this — in a fairly heavy way. And to avoid disrupting normal work patterns, most of the major tasks will probably take place overnight or at weekends. Result? Check and recheck your staff availability, and your corporate policies/incentives for working at inconvenient hours.

There are some classic sources of slippage, which if considered in advance can be side-stepped. Installation is the first point at which the documentation is really tested. Are the user guides and, more so, the installation guide(!) correct? If you follow the installation guide's step-by-step instructions and just end up with an inactive heap of 0s and 1s, then get rewriting. If you don't get the documentation correct now, you never will. Also, if you haven't been softcoding your parameters properly this is when your chickens will come home to roost. Specifically, you should have easy-to-alter parameters for the computer's node-name, and the file-directory names; do you? If not, expect trouble.

- *Data entry*. The test systems will be only small pale versions of the full-blown, full-bodied live one. Load-testing will have been done using simulators, so you may have overlooked the scale of the task in setting up the system's database. Try to automate this process as much as possible. If it's to be done within the required timescale, you may need extra temporary staff. Factor this into your planning. You can't go live with half a database.

- *Transition*. The cut-over to live running needs to be carefully staged. When Britain's Independent Television News (ITN) moved into new studios in London's Grays Inn Road in December 1990 they did so with military precision. Michael

Morris, one of ITN's directors, was quoted in *The Financial Times* [14] describing the approach as one 'based on the army notion of "tactical bound operations", where one army division is entrenched before an attempt is made to move a second division'.

Another good example of this was the installation of a new process-control system for one of Britain's major utilities. As it is quite sensitive about possible sabotage or terrorist threats, I cannot identify it any more precisely. No matter, it's the approach, not the organisation, that is of interest here. It had an existing system, which worked satisfactorily but was getting old and needed replacement: however, it trusted this old system. After the replacement system had been acceptance-tested it was installed and started up. However, the old system was left running, and for the first few months it continued to control most of the utility's network, with the new system being phased in gradually. In fact it took eighteen months before the users were confident enough in the new system to transfer all the load on to it, and switch off the old system.

- *Fall-back*. This sounds just like what I've been talking about. But I want to emphasise one other aspect. If there is already a computer system in place, it's quite likely that you'll remember to keep it available so as not to burn your bridges, in case your need to make a strategic retreat. But if the system is brand new and automates a series of tasks that were previously done manually, people may be so enthusiastic about the new system that they overlook the possibility that they may need to fall back to the old way of doing things.

It does happen — I was once in a computer operations room in a major bank in the City of London (the capital's financial district) when the link to one of its main payments systems failed at 2.30 in the afternoon. There were a lot of payments to be made that day, before close of trading, and it was evident that the link to the payments network would not be restored in time. The bank was prepared, and fell back to the old way of doing things. Payment cheques were printed and some of the bank staff sent out, with little black bags handcuffed to their wrists, to dash though the winding mediaeval back-alleys that still crisscross the City and deliver the payments in person. Moral? Be prepared.

- *Facilities management*. It's time for another buzz-word — 'outsourcing'. If the prospect of all the hassle I've been detailing is just too much for you, don't despair. For a suitably lucrative sum all these concerns can be offloaded from both the developers' and the users' plates. The new guys presenting the big plate to the cafeteria's serving hatch are the facilities management experts: predominantly software houses, with the odd accountancy firm thrown in for good measure. They will take the management of your computer hardware and system completely off your hands. This has the delightful consequence of freeing you and yours to concentrate on the less mundane aspects of your organisation and its needs. The downside is that it will cost you money. The pros and cons can only be weighed properly if you go and get a few quotes from these companies, and then do some careful sums. Remember this will involve another set of contract negotiations; be sure to cover who is responsible for any problems which may arise. Think about it, but do so in good time, not at the last minute.

6.5 Disaster recovery

I am addressing disaster recovery now, as a separate topic, because although it should be folded in with your transition and fallback planning, it doesn't stop there. Installation is (hopefully) a one-off task that you will need to do again only if the system is one that runs at multiple sites or else experiences an upgrade.

Disaster recovery, on the other hand, is an issue that you must keep at the forefront of your mind. It is just as important two years after the installation as it was on day one. In fact, given that the organisation will have come to rely on the system after a year or two, its absence — however temporary — will prove all the more traumatic.

The aim of disaster recovery planning is to avoid the scenario I described in the fallback section. A high-quality system should always be available when it is needed.

The current state of the art was very well covered by an article in *The Financial Times* [15] which I will, in part, draw upon while outlining what you should be doing.

The first point is not to underestimate the consequences of a poor-quality approach in this area. The article quotes a David Frost, who is a partner in Price Waterhouse's management consultancy business. In his experience 90 percent of the companies that lose their computer systems and have no disaster recovery plans go out of business. Read that sentence again — out loud.

Causes of trouble come from many sources. Nature is well practised at wreaking havoc; from lightning and storms, to floods and earthquakes. California's Silicon Valley is forever experiencing minor tremors, but the companies there still produce computer chips accurate down to a few microns. They have buildings that can withstand such perturbations and absorb the energy; what about your disk drives? You may not live in an earthquake area, but London experiences regular collapses of its old Victorian sewers; and how about a little bit of mining subsidence?

People are equally good at causing trouble. Fires, power-cuts, or rats gnawing through your cables. Okay, the last one isn't quite human, I know, but can be prevented by human intervention. Then there's the human intervention you don't want. Corporate downsizing and continual reorganisations are now the order of the day. Consequence? Redundant and disgruntled ex-employees, a few well-aimed key strokes, and the organisation could be set back by months (unless you are prepared). It might have been so well prepared that it buried a 'logic-bomb' in the system, just to get its own back should such an eventuality arise. Get out the virus checking software, and maybe even get someone to pore over the code.

And don't forget the spotty teenager hunched over his PC and modem somewhere in Minnesota, poised to deal a bodyblow to systems from Pittsburg to Peterborough.

Chapter 2 on 'Initiation and Requirements' talks about security, and how to try and keep these unwanted guests out. What I will do here is address the situation where your valiant efforts have come to naught, and the aforementioned naughty individuals have gained access to your precious data.

The cure comes in two parts — paperware and hardware. Cure? Yes, we are not talking prevention here; if the prevention had been successful you'd have no problem, no disaster that needed to be recovered from. Cure is the correct word. The paper aspect is a disaster recovery plan, which must cover how each eventuality I've highlighted is to be addressed. It must be kept secure, but not so secure that the only copy is locked in the building which has just been cordoned off following a bomb scare! And it must be kept current; the critical staff who will act on the plan should a disaster occur may well change over time, or even just move house. The organisation's configuration of hardware and software will continue to evolve. The plan must be reviewed every few months, and used as the basis for practice dry-runs. If it's never been tested, the plan will probably fail when you need it most.

The article I mentioned [15] gives a list of possible approaches in respect of the hardware part of disaster recovery provision. They can be enumerated in terms of cost, but cost on two scales. The first cost is in terms of the green foldable stuff — money; the most expensive is at the top of the list. The second is in terms of quickness of response, least 'down-time', and thus most hassle-free continuation of normal operations. Again, the best of these comes at the top of the list. So evidently 'you get what you pay for', the judgement is yours. Consider, though, that the cheapest in folding money may not be the cheapest on the corporate bottom line if it takes two weeks to get back to normal service. Your choice . . .

- *Duplicate*. Here you have a complete duplicate of your live system, in a geographically separate location, hooked into the live system (preferably by more than one route) and running the same software as the live system. If there is trouble, this system can just pick up where the main one left off. One big constraint — the duplicate system must remain just that. The main system cannot be allowed to overflow on to it, otherwise the duplicate may not be able to handle all the processing load when it comes to the crunch.

- *Another buff box*. This is identical to the duplicate system, except that there is nothing running on the standby system. It will take some time to crank it up, and careful thought should be applied to what is loaded first. If the standby has to support multiple applications, the one most crucial to the organisation should be loaded first. With this approach, backups of the live system should be taken with an eye to ensuring that they can facilitate a quick start-up at the standby site.

- *A spare room*. This is the shell in which the standby system would live. A nice cool computer room, with power, air conditioning, and phone lines, but no buff boxes. The computers are installed only if there is a problem. Good point, the corporation doesn't tie up money in hardware it may never use. Bad point, if it does have a disaster, recovery will take longer. Ensure that if the problem arises at 4.30 p.m. on Friday, you don't have to wait until 9.00 a.m. on Monday before the replacement is delivered — review the contracts carefully.

- *Facilities management*. Arrange with a specialist disaster recovery variant of a facilities management (FM) firm to take out an option to use its hardware if you experience a problem. Cheaper than having your own spare room, box or system; but again review the agreement carefully. If a flood hits you and your neighbours, does the FM company have enough staff and machines to support all the victims at the same time?

• *Share and share alike*. This one is kind, risky, but quite cheap. Find a suitably equipped and friendly neighbour, and agree to act as each other's standby sites. Again, do make sure the agreement covers everything, and that your neighbour continues to allow enough space for your applications even when it adds extra functionality to its own systems.

• *Head in sand*. Do nothing, cross your fingers, and cultivate a good job-placement agency just in case. This approach is not recommended.

6.6 Final thoughts

6.6.1 Helping your supporters

I'll say more about support of live systems in due course. But once you've completed your installation and are doing your tidying up, so that the live database will fit, do not delete the acceptance test system. This should be retained as it will be very useful for all sorts of house-keeping tasks.

- You might want to incorporate it into your disaster recovery plans.
- It can be used for training people who, until they're up to speed, could do damage on the live system.
- And it can be used as the regression test platform when bug fixes are delivered.

So as well as the system, keep all the simulators, test scripts, and test-case data. You are going to need them once you've gone live.

6.6.2 Drinkies

Once you've completed the installation and gone live, go and buy everyone a drink, maybe even a meal; they deserve it, you deserve it, and treating people properly never hurts the quality of a system.

6.7 Questions

1. Will the acceptance tests be at your place or theirs?
2. How does this fit with installation schedules?
3. Who are all your players?
4. Do you remember the drill by now — names, addresses, 'phone numbers, and a group caving expedition to the Pyrenees?
5. Will you own up if it's all a total failure?
6. Who will you own up to and what remedy will you suggest?

7. How will you link the developer and user sites?
8. What about training?
9. Where on earth is the installation plan?
10. Who mislaid the disaster recovery plan?
11. What did this author chap claim these plans should contain?

7 Support of a live system

7.1 Introduction

7.1.1 *Alive and kicking?*

Should you read this chapter now? Well there's only one group of people who would be justified in answering negatively and they have nothing but a green field and some ideas.

Everyone else has some sort of system already in existence and its support needs to be thought about now.

This system could be the culmination of months of development effort that have only just been rounded off. On the other hand, it might have been there for many years. Either way you should be thinking about how you can ensure that the system delivers the highest quality service to its users.

In both cases, whether you are merely starting to conjecture about it, or have been ruminating for many days and nights, enhancing the system is almost bound to be on your mind.

Oh yes, and there will be bugs to deal with, on an on-going basis.

This chapter covers all of these areas. They are sometimes neglected as they don't represent the challenging meaty heart of the development process, but attention to them is a 'must' if your system is to maintain its entitlement to the mantle of high-quality.

7.2 Organisational issues

7.2.1 *Going backwards*

This is so crucial that it merits attention ahead of everything else. The moment a system ceases to be a test or training system, and becomes a live production system, it needs to be backed up. This activity forms the first line of defence in the disaster recovery strategy I covered in Chapter 6 on 'Installation'.

It is the most pro-active element as well. Disaster recovery plans spend most of their time sitting dormant on a shelf. The standby site is created, the plan is reviewed every quarter, and practised twice a year; but other than that not a lot of activity is involved. Backups, however, require action every day, maybe even more often.

I use the word 'backup' in as wide a sense as possible. The first question, naturally enough, is what should be backed up? The answer, simplistically, is everything! All the files on the system should be duplicated elsewhere so these copies can be quickly retrieved and put to use should the contents of the 'original' files be lost. Obviously, the files could be considered to fall into various different classes, depending on the nature of their contents. These classes can be enumerated as follows.

- Source code (Cobol, C, FORTRAN, etc.).
- Executables (runnable programs).
- Configuration data.
- Live data.
- Command files.
- On-line documentation.

The precise way each class of files is backed up will vary.

- *Source code*. These files will be needed only if all the excutables are lost, and it becomes necessary to rebuild the system. The backup of these files should not be confused with the holding of source code in a configuration management library tool. The backed-up version of these files is an exact replica of the starting point of the build process that results in the system. They should never be changed, and should be placed in an editor only in 'read-only' mode. Any changes should be made by the organisation that developed the system — the DP department, software house, or any third party maintainers that may have been hired. As a result, it should prove necessary to take new backups of these files only if the maintainers deliver new versions of them as a result of a bug fix or an enhancement.

- *Executables*. These files will be used first if a system is lost. It is essential that a complete set be taken. Occasionally, some files which are not binary object files should be placed in this classification. A good example would be the programs that are used to generate reports about a database constructed using a standard database product. These report files might look like command files, but here I treat command files as the ones needed to build, start, and stop the system. These files may change more often than the source code since it may be necessary to rebuild the system (from the unchanged source files) when a new release of the computer's operating system is installed. Keep the version of the executable from the previous release of the operating system, in case a glitch down the line makes the hardware vendor withdraw the release and forces you to fall back to the previous version of the operating system.

The fact that these files do change without the source changing acts as the starting point for a tempting but dangerous set of actions. I forbade these when I was discussing bug fixing in Chapter 4 on 'Internals and Coding', but let me restate it. Some systems allow the executable object to be zapped, which might fix a bug in a live system. But that fix is extremely difficult to reproduce in other versions of the executable, and the source is now out of step with the executable.

If this is done repeatedly, knowledge of the nature of the differences may become confused. It could be argued that because you have backed up the executable, it is okay to make this kind of fix, since even though the fix isn't in the code, it is in the fallback version of the executable. Although true, this exposes you to a great risk, since if all the backups of the executable are lost in some nasty disaster, then the backups of the source code won't be able to help. There is only one way to ensure this doesn't occur — leave the executable alone.

- *Configuration data*. This is very much part of the live system. It might be accessible via only the system, or it might be in simple edit files. In either case, it as much a part of the backup cycle as anything else. It will need to be backed up more often than the source code and the executables. Depending on how your system is structured you may need to do this every time a new operator is added. As a result, the decision as to whether to back up these files should be an automatic one. The source and executable are done so rarely that their backups can be started by the operators, whereas the configuration files should be included in the command file that runs the backup every night. A check on the files' dates and time stamps showing when each one was last changed should be made. Any that have changed since the last backup was taken should be backed up. In addition, every so often, maybe once a week, all of the files should be done. The first type of backup is a 'partial' one, the other a 'full' one.

- *Live data*. This is what lives in your system's database. It may be necessary to back it up more often than just once a day, depending on the volume of data and how critical it is. Indeed, the backup process should be structured so that if all data is lost the most critical can be reloaded first. This stuff can also be the most sensitive, so appropriate security precautions must be taken. Although there is a high 'churn factor' with the data being backed up very frequently, this is not an excuse for forgetting to take a complete set to the off-site storage facility at regular intervals.

- *Command files*. These are used for building the system, starting it, and gracefully stopping it. They can be easily overlooked since they tend not to be in a specialised esoteric language, but in what people tend to consider to be the rather pedestrian command language of the computer's operating system. The same rule as above applies — back these up whenever they change.

- *On-line documentation*. Very few systems are likely to keep a full set of paper-based documentation at a separate off-site location. Consider the situation where your offices are severely damaged by fire, and you have to fall back on to your backup tapes to rebuild the system. If the fire destroyed your only set of documentation you have a problem; everything must be done from memory, including all analysis for bug fixing and subsequent enhancements. On average, documentation takes up a small percentage of the overall amount of tape (or whatever) used for a backup of the whole system. Adding the documentation in is a trivial task, an extra couple of lines in the backup command file, but it could very well save your bacon.

7.2.2 *Media*

But take a look at the tapes periodically, and copy them on to a fresh tape every six months. Store the tapes as per the manufacturers' instructions — almost undoubtedly in a tape rack in a climate-controlled environment. The environment should be secure, but within easy access to the computer room where the system is located. In addition, a second set of tapes should be stored off-site, in similar conditions. Remember to check and update both sets whenever a change does occur.

I've assumed traditional reel-to-reel tape. That is not necessarily your only option. Systems now come with all sorts of media to store data. You can get removable disk-packs, but if removing these exposes the magnetic surface, be careful not to get dust, sweat, or any other contaminant on them, or the disk may just crash next when you pop it back in the drive. In the PC market there are also removable hard disks which offer high capacity although not letting the oxide see the light of day. While I'm on light, there's optical storage (the close cousin of the CD that's killed off the art of the album cover). These have outrageously high capacity and are easy to transport. The read-only version CD-ROM is still more common than the read-and-write type, so make sure if you buy a WORM (Write Once Read Many) that's what you want.

7.2.3 *Procedures*

Having bent our grey matter to consider what we should be saving in our data Ark, and what the Ark itself should be made out of, how do we herd all the data-packets in? Two-by-two?

There's a big hint in the title to this section. But what characterises a procedure? Boredom primarily — complete routineness; you can do it in your sleep. And here is one occasion when that is exactly what I recommend. All that is required is one good dose of seriously heavy thinking up front and then the procedure should, as near as makes no difference, run itself.

The aim behind the initial cogitation is to ensure that the command file kicks itself off automatically every day, or more frequently if necessary. This can be achieved by running it continuously, in the background, and checking the system clock every so often. It should make very loud and irritating noises if the appropriate storage media are not available to it. And it should not give up on this point. A truly dedicated command file might see fit to call the home of the system manager, to report that the command file cannot get the operator to mount the necessary tapes. Drastic? Overkill? You decide. Aside from handling the magnetic media, the command file should not need any intervention on the part of a human helper; it should decide, on the basis of the time-stamp for each type of file, whether a file should be backed up on that occasion. Also, by consulting the system clock, it should know what day it is, and thus whether it is appropriate to run a full or a partial backup.

Although you are encouraging your command file to stand on its own two feet and fend for itself, a little parental oversight is necessary after the file's done its job. It should, I omitted to mention, be producing a listing (to paper if you like) of all the files it has backed up. Scan this listing carefully; a text-editing program may prove helpful in this regard. You are looking for files that failed to get copied correctly — which can happen if they possess some uniquely irritating file structure which the file-copying command (that your command file invokes) doesn't like. Under such circumstances, all but the most inconsiderate selfish and rude operating systems will at least tell you that the file copy failed, and maybe even why. It is one of life's infuriating little quirks that these will be the most crucial files, and that if you fail to make such a check, the disk they reside on will crash and the files will be lost forever.

Since new file types may appear without your knowing, you need to do the check every day, preferably manually. If you'd rather live fast-and-loose (then goodness knows how you got this far with this chapter) and if you have an operating system that lives 'above its station', then get the backup command file to include a shell-script to search the listing for words like 'error', 'failure', or 'whoops I boo-boo-ed'. The disadvantage of automating this is that you may miss a new error, and then you're back where you started.

Remember the operators are already busy people. To them your pride and joy may be no more than an irritating inconvenient imposition. While designing the backup process go and talk to them, see how they work currently and how the needs of your system can be integrated most efficiently (for them) into their existing schedule. On a day-to-day basis, these may be the first people who notice that something is going wrong with your system (e.g. you might be about to run out of disk-space on your live database) so maintaining good will and fostering a friendly productive working relationship can only be to your benefit.

7.2.4 Practice makes perfect

The moment that the first backup is complete is not too soon to practise disaster recovery. If your system isn't live yet, then do take the opportunity to check that you can rebuild it (from scratch) using only what you've got on your backup tapes. And don't be surprised if you find this takes two or three attempts before the tapes do in fact hold all you need. It's far better to find this out now than when the system is the very backbone of the enterprise.

7.3 Maintenance

7.3.1 How NOT to get in a fix

Now you have a safely backed-up system and are prepared for the problems that the world external to your system will throw at you, we can concentrate on the ones that you have carefully crafted with your own fair hands — live bugs!

The operative word here is 'live'. From the first moment the code was originally hacked out, through the different levels of testing, to the acceptance and training systems, bugs were an inconvenience. A long word but not nearly as worrying as the label that they now acquire. For a live system bugs are lethal. This applies to the organisation that relies on the system, and the developers who built the system. They can grind the whole convoy to a halt, and everyone is faced with little option but to circle the wagons. I'm over-egging the cake here because in one sense bugs at this stage represent a fundamental failure in quality. Ideally, they shouldn't be here. Indeed, I have (implicitly) been exhorting you to dream of achieving one of quality's classic definitions — zero defects.

So what does this mean? You're feeling rotten, guilty, a failure — somewhere down in your soul. There's a lot of emotional baggage here because the system that is our pride and joy is letting us down, and we're to blame for it. No-one likes to admit to their human failings, so we don't. From the point of view of dealing with the situation, we skate over it; it's all problem and no real challenge, and everybody's in a pretty lousy mood. Well? Tough, it's too late now. Although you are perfectly entitled to have a little cry over some spilt milk-shake formulating program, getting all steamed up about it will not solve the problem. The other response of 'no reaction' and carrying on with whatever other tasks you are now engaged with is equally useless. Remember, software development is still a craft; zero defects will come only when we start applying nothing but pure mathematical logic at every stage. In the meantime, in the real world, you the practising profession must get on with your life and the problem must be addressed promptly and thoroughly.

This is one area where procedures are essential. Handling problems is really surprisingly routine; the only unique aspect is the exact technical content of each problem. So if you can establish a procedure to handle the occasions when you are faced with such problems, then your chances of clearing them up more quickly and more successfully will be greatly enhanced. That's what I am about to cover. There will be a great deal of detail, almost overkill, here; but that is deliberate. Your own organisation is unique, so you will have to study closely the steps I outline to see which ones do (or don't) apply to you. I am going to provide you with a framework; you will build your *own* procedures on this, but if you use all of it you'll know enough to earn a degree in advanced scaffolding — which isn't what I intend for you.

7.3.2 Nice homily — what about the details?

Let's just refresh our memories as to who the players will be in today's game. At one end of the field of knowledge we have the *users*; they own the system and aren't worried about the internals, but just want it to do what the specifications or user guides say it should. At the other end there are the *maintainers*; they may have done the development but could be a completely different set of folk. One important member of the maintainers' team is the system's technical authority (TA), who has the responsibility to ensure that fixes are in keeping with the spirit of the system's design.

Refereeing these are a whole host of people; unfortunately none of them are independent, but instead they belong to the management hierarchies that control the two teams. There is only one independent adjudicator, who only gets involved if things reach catastrophic proportions. If the two teams are part of the same organisation then it will be the chief executive officer; if they belong to different companies, then it will be some variety of High Court Judge!

The proceedings will be dominated by pieces of paper, so a good filing system is a 'must'. A database will be helpful for the users, essential for the maintainers. It should contain fields for all the information I suggest is given by the person finding the so-called bug. In addition, there will need to be further fields to track its status and processing; but expect to find that you may need some even more esoteric fields unique to your own particular way of doing business. The movement of these pieces of paper between the players, and the actions that result, can be thought of as phases.

The maintenance team may vary in its degree of dedication. At an early stage in its set-up it should consider if it intends to (or is required to) offer twenty-four-hours-a-day, seven-days-a-week support. Will it dish out bleepers to enable its important staff to be pageable? And will it offer some sort of guaranteed response times?

7.3.3 Discovery phase

A discrepancy is found. Odd word to use, what do I mean? The discrepancy can be considered to be a perceived misfunctioning of the system, *perceived* because it may not be a bug, just a misunderstanding about the way the system is intended to behave, i.e. a feature. Incidentally, the better and clearer the user documentation and specifications are, the fewer misunderstandings are likely to arise. Meantime, it would be rash and unwarranted to call the incident a bug or even a problem — yet.

Now who found this discrepancy? More likely than not it was a user, but if the system is subject to on-going development (more on that later in the chapter), then it could have been one of the development staff. Also, it could have been one of the maintainers who was in the process of dealing with a totally unrelated discrepancy.

Whoever it was, she should already know how to report it. She should be in possession of your distillation of this framework, your own operating procedures. And she should know who to report it to. Ideally, she should have access to your database and be able to enter the details on-line, but this is unlikely to be the case, so she'll probably end up filling in a Discrepancy Report Form (a DRF).

The first thing you need is to know exactly what happened in as much detail as possible, more specifically:

- Who the person was.
- Which team she plays for.
- How that person can be contacted.

- When she found the discrepancy.
- Where the system was located.
- Which version of the system she was using.
- Any reference number she cares to use in classifying the incident.
- The priority she attaches to the resolution of the discrepancy.
- Any deadlines that may be associated with the priority.
- A short title for the discrepancy.
- The functional area within the system where the discrepancy arose.
- The defining document against which the system's functioning was adjudged to be incorrect.
- A full chronological summary of what happened.
- If possible, instructions on how to reproduce the problem.
- The location of any supporting evidence, log files, audit trails, etc.

The manager of the maintenance (MM) team needs to be alerted that this discrepancy has arisen. Receipt of the paper-based version of the form would obviously achieve this, but if the finder is able to enter the details on-line, the MM should be reviewing the database for new discrepancies.

And how does the MM know that the database has new Discrepancy Reports (DRs)? Because the MM was smart enough to configure the database so that finders could get at only certain specific fields. One not available to them would be the status field, and this would default to 'awaiting investigation'. The MM would scan the database to report on new DRs added in the last twenty-four hours.

7.3.4 DRF entry phase

In the other scenario the DRF would dribble out of the fax machine in Maintenance HQ, need deciphering and then entering into the database. Having read the form, so that the MM knows what he or she is talking about, the MM ought to show the finder the common courtesy of acknowledging receipt of the DRF. If feeling brave the MM could pick up the 'phone, but I'd quite understand if the MM preferred to take the weasel-way out and faxed back an acknowledgement.

However the finder is contacted, the MM should ensure that the DRF contents are quickly entered into the database. It helps if the MM has a desk in-tray especially for DRFs!

This seems a very suitable point at which to detail the other fields that ought to be in the database. They cover the specifics of the resolution of the discrepancy, and so should be 'updatable' only by people on the maintenance team. A multi-screen database with all these fields on a screen that is not available to the finder would be one elegant way to achieve this.

So what do we need to note down to facilitate the control of the discrepancy as it chugs its merry way through our procedure?

- The date the maintenance team received the DRF, which may differ from the date on which the discrepancy actually occurred.
- Its internal urgency, never mind whether the finder 'scweams and scweams

until she's thick' (and blue in the face!); you may have other copies of the system with problems that are more urgent. You are entitled to your own determination of how urgent you consider this DR to be.

- The investigator — which one of your sterling chaps are you putting on the job of determining the veracity of the finder's claim?
- The explanation — what the investigator found, in detail.
- The nature of the discrepancy, in one word, bug or feature.
- Its source — requirements-definition error, code-design error, typo, etc. This can be helpful in later analysis of where most errors are being made.
- The effort estimate (if this is a bug) of how many person-days of heart-ache, tears and matted hair it'll take to fix.
- Other organisation that may be responsible for this if the discrepancy is nothing to do with our system.
- The fixer; can you spare your ace investigator, and is someone else actually going to do the rehash of the code?
- The tester; now you know better than to let the fixer test his own work — don't you?
- Which files, and what specifically in them, were changed.
- Which specifications and guides will need altering.
- The current status of the discrepancy, one of:
    - awaiting investigation,
    - being investigated,
    - awaiting review of investigation results,
    - not our problem,
    - awaiting fix,
    - being fixed,
    - awaiting in-house test,
    - being tested in-house,
    - awaiting installation,
    - being installed,
    - awaiting user-test,
    - being tested at user,
    - ready to go live,
    - live at user (maybe = agreed solved),
    - changed code back under configuration control,
    - agreed solved by the user.
- Document status (independent of discrepancy status):
    - no documents need updating,
    - documents do need updating,
    - documents have been updated.
- Date agreed solved by the user.

Obviously, not all fields will be used for each DR, and it is unlikely that every DR will transit through all the states possible in the 'current status' field.

7.3.5 Investigation phase

Once the DR has been entered in the database it can be left to fester. But it shouldn't be left so long that it gets gangrenous; the intention behind leaving it there is not to ignore it until it gets so rotten it smells awful and demands attention, but in fact quite the reverse. Both acting upon it immediately, and leaving it to decay, mean the MM is forced into action. The MM is then behaving reactively. It's far better if the procedure can be so structured that the discrepancy is dealt with pro-actively; no tails wagging dogs around here, thank you very much.

In this case, being pro-active means that the MM should review the database once a day, identify the most urgent discrepancies and parcel them out to one of the team to investigate. The determination of urgency is a subtle and subjective process, whose only real law is that if urgency correlates to the decibel level of the finder's scream, then the MM has failed, stopped thinking, and started panicking. The MM must always take a global perspective and consider all the different sites where the system is running, and out of the whole database of discrepancies — which are the most important? Obviously, if the functioning of a particular system is being severely compromised (it's fallen and can't get up), then it should take precedence, it may even merit instant action, but beware — too many stunts like that and the MM falls into the ruinous reactive rut. An approach similar to medical triage can be adopted. DRs can be considered as emergencies, important, or cosmetic; but unlike a military field hospital, it should be possible to treat even the worst emergency. Beyond that politics will intrude — let's keep everyone happy — and also 'buggin's turn'.

The investigator looks at the discrepancy and fills in the Explanation, Nature, and Status fields in the database. If the nature is *bug* then the explanation need not detail how it should be fixed, only why there is a bug. Otherwise, nature will be *feature*, which means the perceived misfunctioning was actually misperceived functioning! No fix is necessary, just a bit of explanation to illuminate the finder's understanding of the system, and maybe some documentation updates. Status will be *awaiting review of investigation results*.

7.3.6 Review phase

Once a week (or more frequently if so desired) the MM calls a meeting to review all the discrepancy reports (DRs) that are currently on the maintainers' collective plate. Everyone on the maintenance team should be present, but it is absolutely essential that this includes the system's technical authority (TA).

The meeting will proceed to review all the DRs in the database. So it would help if the MM gets the said database to flex its reporting muscles and produce some intelligible summaries of where things stand. What happens to each DR will depend on its status.

DRs *awaiting investigation* will if at all possible be dished out to some lucky soul to pick over the entrails and decipher what the users are whinging about now; the status changes to *being investigated*. What? Me — acting uncharitably towards the users? In the cold hard light of day, unless unusually enthused, this is how the maintenance team will normally approach the DRs that are tossed their way. It will take superhuman goodwill to keep things amicable, but it pretty much goes without saying that if they can be amicable, then the DR resolution rate will be much higher. Anyway, next state . . .

DRs *being investigated* can be skipped over until the investigation is complete and the results are ready for presentation at a subsequent meeting, so their status remains unchanged, but may move to *awaiting review of investigation results* before the next meeting.

DRs *awaiting review of investigation results* should be examined by all the people in the meeting who know something about the area of the system where the DR is alleged to be. In all of the discussions that will follow the TA has the final say — the buck stops with him. A decision should be made as to whether there is a problem here or not; if not, the nature field in the database becomes *feature*, and the status goes to *live at user*. The MM and TA should consider if any documentation needs changing, and amend the database's Document Status field as appropriate.

If there is a problem, then the culprit needs to be tracked down. This is because the discrepancy may be caused by something other than the system the maintainers look after. It could be the hardware, the operating system, the networking software; if this is the case then the status changes to *not our problem* and the MM should send a copy of the DRF to the appropriate organisation.

This leaves the situation where the problem is in the system. The TA (in conjunction with everyone else) should outline the most technically sound approach to solving the problem whilst not compromising the integrity of the system's design (issues such as fanout, close-coupling of modules, segregation of data, etc.). A high-quality system that suffers piecemeal maintenance, at the hands of people who make quick and dirty fixes because time is short and because they are not familiar with the underlying design philosophy, can quickly become a very low-quality system. The status can follow one of two paths; if there is a body to spare it can jump straight to *being fixed*, but if everyone is tied up then it will have to be put on the stack *awaiting fix*. Obviously, this stack is not first-in-first-out; rather it is reviewed and a priority order determined for which problems should be fixed first when the next free body does become available.

DRs that are *not our problem* should none the less be tracked by the MM to ensure that whoever is now responsible for sorting them out does so. This need not occur in the meeting, but if the MM has a responsibility to summarise the status of all of these DRs every week to the rest of the maintenance team, then there's an increased likelihood that the MM will keep chasing the other companies now responsible for resolving the problem. After all, from the user's point of view the maintenance team still has ultimate responsibility for all of the problems, and the poor performance of a subcontractor will reflect back on to the maintainers. Eventually, the status of these DR's should move forward to *awaiting installation* and then progress beyond that in the same way as other DRs.

Once all this has been done the database can be updated to reflect the new information gleaned about this DR.

DRs that are *awaiting fix* can be skipped over — but not so quickly that one question is not asked. If they've been on the *awaiting fix* list for a while, has their degree of cruciality or urgency changed? Is there a deadline by which the user needs this DR resolved? Can this deadline be met if the DR remains unassigned. DR's will leave this state to become *being fixed*.

DRs *being fixed* may need discussion between the fixer and the TA as to the best approach to the fix. This need not occur during the meeting. The fixer should give estimates of how soon the fix, but not the testing of the fix, is expected to be complete. Once the code changes associated with the fix have been done (using the configuration management library tools of course!) the DR's state is then *awaiting in-house test*.

DRs *awaiting in-house test* are subject to the same considerations as those awaiting fix. They should not be left on the stack without periodic review of their urgency.

Why have I included these 'awaiting *x*' states? Am I not overdoing things a bit? No. Next time you arrange to meet some acquaintances for a drink and are waiting for them, be it in a hotel lobby, a railway station, or just a street corner, watch the people going past. Their 'distribution' will not be even; there will be lulls when the area is almost empty, then all of a sudden a whole clutch of people will magically appear and deprive you of your entitlement to a decent minimum of interpersonal space. Next moment they'll all vanish again. DRs are the same, they hunt in packs; indeed for the sake of their convenience users sometimes hoard their DRs until they have enough to justify wrestling with the fax machine. So you will get something like a sine wave of DRs; if you have enough people to handle the peaks, they'll be twiddling their thumbs during the troughs. The only cost-effective approach is to strike a happy medium, accept that there will not always be enough maintainers to keep all the DRs in the air at the same time, but include suitably controlled storage areas for the DRs not being attended to at this moment. This why I include the 'awaiting *x*' states.

Fairly obviously, when someone other than the fixer becomes available (remember the rules for good testing) the state of the DR will become *being tested in-house*.

DRs *being tested in-house* can be skipped; the MM should note the fact that they are still under test, and enquire as to whether any special system configuration is necessary? What regression tests might be appropriate? But otherwise leave well alone. Once the testing is complete (remembering the points made about bug-fixing in Chapter 4 on 'Internals and Coding'), the state of the DR becomes *awaiting installation*.

DRs *awaiting installation* are subject not only to the considerations of the maintainers' schedules and staff availability, but also the convenience of the users. It may well be more sensible all round if the maintainers wait for a number of fixes to stack up and deliver them all at the same time as a minor release. The MM should note which fixes are ready, so that the users can be signalled that there is a delivery ready and waiting for their convenience. Not unreasonably the DR progresses into *being installed*.

DRs *being installed* will require discussion in the meeting to confirm that the necessary facilities are available at the user-site so that the maintainers can do their jobs. It is usual in this sort of scenario for the fixes to be installed on the users' test and training system rather than the live system. This avoids problems with the fix disrupting the users' live operations. Once installed the fix is at the mercy of the users and finds itself *awaiting user-test*. This may last for only a nanosecond, or may stretch out to an aeon or two.

DRs *awaiting user-test* are subject to reverse nagging. Up until this point most of the hassle has flowed from the users to the maintainers; now the situation is reversed. The users will test the fix when they are 'all good and ready'; this depends on how urgent they perceive it to be. Depending on what else is happening this may or may not matter one jot to the maintainers. However, to keep up a sense of professional service it does the MM no harm to be seen to be tracking what the users are doing with the fix they now have, and to give them a gentle prod every so often. Once the users have one of their own bodies to spare, or the 'Deputy Executive Vice-President with responsibility for Thumb Tacks and Information Technology within the Asia-Pacific Basin' has issued a new edict on minimising applications' downtime, they will proceed to test the fix.

DRs *being tested at user* may at first sight appear to need no maintainer action. Wrong. Expect garbled 'phone calls and demands for your three best staff to fly out immediately, as the fix doesn't appear to have solved the problem! The only way to quieten the users and determine the veracity of their claims may well be to acquiesce, but consider installing a link to their system so the maintenance hot-shots can investigate the cause of the users' agitation without the maintenance staff leaving their desks. This is why these DRs will need to be considered at the meeting; neglecting them may cause nasty surprises when staff have to be switched away from other work at the last moment. Eventually, the users will start smiling and the status of the DR can be declared as *ready to go live*.

A DR that is *ready to go live* will need to be tied in to the users' system release management procedures. Some users are happy to add bug fixes every month or two; others draw the line at emergency fixes only, and bottle up all the others for an annual system upgrade. As a result a DR fix may stay in this state for quite a while. It should be reviewed periodically lest it be forgotten and overlooked but, none the less, could prove useful in other work. The DR fix will exit this status when it does go *live at user*.

A DR that is *live at user* may now require the skills of a lawyer. Agreements between users and maintainers vary, but one variety includes a clause that even if the users do not explicitly declare a fix to be accepted, but they run it on their live system, then they are deemed to have accepted it. This issue aside, once a fix is live, the configuration control system will need to be updated to reflect the fact that the users are now running a newer version of part of the system. Once this has been done the DR fix status becomes *changed code back under configuration control*. There are subtleties here that I will address in Chapter 9 on 'Configuration Management and Change Control'.

A DR that has its *changed code back under configuration control* may appear to be all over. However, there may still be some shouting to be done down in the bar (legal or alcoholic? Your choice). It cannot be considered properly closed, even if the contract includes the clause I mentioned above, until the users express their satisfaction. So the MM must review all such fixes and continue to press the users until they confirm that the discrepancy is *agreed solved by the users*.

The *document status* field in the database operates independently of the discrepancy status, and so every DR needs to be reviewed with this in mind. The temptation will always be to say that no documents need updating. If they do need to be, then this is a dangerous path to go down, since at a later date the documentation will no longer reflect the way the system functions and will in fact not be worth the paper it is written on; it may in addition be dangerously misleading.

The document status field is kept separate from the rest deliberately because it may not be feasible to update the documentation for some months. In the interim, individual update sheets are perfectly acceptable, and at a convenient moment ('You what? There's no such thing!') new issues of the specifications and guides can be produced. By definition, there now is such a thing as a convenient moment. Since this approach is pro-active (and allows the documentation to slip beyond the date at which the discrepancy is agreed solved by the user) it, curiously enough, puts the power back in your hands.

The result of this strategy is that the discrepancy can be considered completely wound up only when both the discrepancy status and the document status are satisfied. Until this happens the DR must continue to be reviewed at each meeting.

This marvellous meeting should be minuted by the MM, copiously. The MM should then promptly summarise the said minutes and send a list of the status of every DR to the users. That way, everyone knows where they stand, what is happening, and what the chances are that some people might actually declare themselves happy and contented.

As you can probably infer, the review phase is not a one-off occurrence. Discrepancies will pass through it a number of times during their journey around the maintainers' offices. Although all states tangentially interact with the review phase, I suspect it would be helpful if I just clarified which of the states belong in which of the other phases.

7.3.7 Fix phase

A DR arrives here *awaiting fix*, and remains here while *being fixed*. The fixer should reread the points on bug fixing given in Chapter 4 on 'Internals and Coding'. The database should be updated with the name of the fixer.

7.3.8 Testing phase

A DR arrives here *awaiting in-house test*, and stays here while *being tested in-house*. The crucial aspect of this is to ensure that the tester is not the fixer, and that the testing is thorough enough. Do not neglect non-functional tests, desk checking, and running some regression tests both carefully chosen and randomly selected. Again, update the database, this time with the name of the tester.

7.3.9 Tidy-up phase

A lot happens here, the DR arrives as *awaiting installation*, and then becomes *being installed*. The installation should be accompanied by a release note that details:

- files changed,
- version numbers of new files,
- a new release number for the whole system,
- any external functionality that's changed,
- a summary of the internal code changes, and
- instructions on rebuilds and installation.

The DR fix then is *awaiting user-test*, is *being tested at user* (preferably with samples of live data running on automated test harnesses or simulators), and is then *ready to go live*. Once *live at user*, then *changed code back under configuration control* should happen and eventually the DR is *agreed solved by the user*.

7.3.10 Visual representation

There is a lot to this procedure, it may be clearer if you look at Figure 7.1.

Phase	State	Meta-phase
Discovery	N/A	
Pre-entry	N/A	
Investigation	Awaiting investigation Being investigated Awaiting review of investigation results	Review (Awaiting investigation to Agreed solved)
	Not our problem	
Fix	Awaiting a fix Being fixed	
Testing	Awaiting in-house test Being tested in-house	
Tidy up	Awaiting installation Being installed Awaiting user test User tested Ready to go live Live at user Under configuration control Agreed solved	

Figure 7.1
Support procedure overview

7.4 Enhancements

7.4.1 More faults

You might find it useful to add one other value to the list of acceptable entries for the Nature of Discrepancy field in the database. That valid value is *enhancement*.

No system is static. Even if it is delivered and installed in one fell swoop, rather than the more common phased approach, it will nevertheless start to evolve. In the process of logging down discrepancies in the system, the users are very likely to identify things about the system that they would like changed. Indeed, if a lot of bugs cluster around a particular area this may indicate that a rewrite would be beneficial. Sometimes they may realise that these are enhancements and on other occasions they may think they've found a bug. The affronted maintainers will (as part of the investigation phase) scan the SEF and other associated documents, and much to the chagrin of the users, will declare that the system does in fact function in accordance with the SEF. No bug here, but the description the users give of how they feel the system should behave may strike the maintainers as a surprisingly sensible suggestion. So, under such circumstances, the maintainers will classify the discrepancy as an enhancement request.

Now it should be understood that the maintainers tend to like enhancements. Why? Because bug fixing is usually paid for via a standard percentage of the cost of the original system, winging its way to the maintainers' bank accounts every month. They cannot charge for individual bug fixes. However, an enhancement represents fresh design effort, fresh code, and thus fresh money! This is one of the main motivations.

'All well and good' I hear you say, 'the maintainers just treat the enhancement like a DR and charge for it once it's running live'. True, but there's more to this. Bug-fixing doesn't alter the integrity of the design of the original system, since all it does is bring the actual system into line with the way it was designed to function. Enhancements, in contrast, seek to extend the capabilities of the system, improve its interfaces, and deepen its functionality. Care needs to be taken or else serious problems can result. As with poorly executed bug fixing, the adding-on of enhancements in a piecemeal fashion can rapidly corrupt a high-quality system leaving the users with a low-quality heap of spaghetti!

7.2.2 80:20 again

Enhancements are made to a system because the users discover that it can't do something they need it to. Before they rush headlong into requesting a shelf-full of changes, it could be very beneficial if the users carried out an audit of the way they use the system; they might find that what they wanted was already there.

Most systems are surprisingly complicated, and not many people become skilled in using the system's full functionality. It would not be unreasonable to hypothesise that the classic 80:20 rule applies here, viz 80 percent of the staff that use the system use only 20 percent of its functionality. I doubt that the reverse is even near the truth; the other 20 percent of the staff might use 50 percent of the system but only a minuscule few would exercise 80 percent or more. What am I driving at? Lynne Cheney, Chair of the US National Endowment for the Humanities, once began a speech to a meeting with a tongue-in-cheek reference to her own height, pointing out that in these days of affirmative language she ought no longer to describe herself as short but rather 'vertically challenged' [16]. The same thing can be given different names. If the users think of it as A but the developers called it B then both might think it wasn't in the system. However, a careful study of all the system's capabilities could indicate that the system can in fact already do what the users want; they merely hadn't looked deeply enough into the manuals, or quizzed the developers thoroughly enough. Before you go and try to improve it, maximise the use of what you already have.

7.4.3 *Oh all right, if you must ...*

There are two areas where it may become necessary to enhance the system. There is the 80 percent area that no-one uses much, and it may indeed lack the one little esoteric function that will allow the users to achieve their goal of sending a direct-mail letter to every hamster in Vladivostok.

The other type of enhancement is done to the 20 percent of the system that the users are hammering every day. The aim here is to improve the way the routine operations are done. It is not unusual for the specifications to treat all the activities on a system as being in the same category, whilst it turns out that in real life some are done far more frequently than others. It may not be known until the system has been running for some months which activities will fall into this frequent-use category. But once they have been identified, the quality of the system can be increased by making these activities as user-friendly as possible. This might involve adding a facility to switch between two supposedly unrelated screens simply by hitting a single 'hot-key'. The way colour is used might change, so that mandatory fields in a database have a different background colour to distinguish them from optional fields. As you can doubtless infer, the list could go on; but it can really be written only by the 'real users' after they have some solid experience of the system under their collective belts. This directs the enhancement effort to where it can be of most value.

7.4.4 *Think product*

The key to making enhancements successfully is to treat your system as though it were a product. Some gentle readers may well respond that their systems jolly well are products — good on you squire. These people will have very little problem adhering to the strategy I'm outlining.

A product has to maintain a degree of integrity, internal cohesion, and uniform external appearance. What? Over its lifetime a product will evolve, but it must still retain the same basic look and feel, what the user perceives to be the very essence of the product. If you upgrade your word processor, you are pleased with all the nifty new nuances that have been added, but you want it still to do the basics in the way you are already familiar with. And you want it to be able to handle the old documents that you created three years ago with the previous release of the product.

To achieve a system that does this, the developers are forced to keep to certain disciplines and, to be blunt, behave themselves. They cannot indulge in radical flights of fancy that would change their masterpiece beyond all recognition and they cannot strip out core functionality.

If you apply these disciplines to the way you get your system enhanced, then the changes are likely to be beneficial rather than detrimental. After all, it is quite possible that although you don't have a product it is in some sense a pseudo-product; that is, it is installed at different sites, each of which may be running different releases or configurations of the system. Indeed, you might discover that your system meets a generic need which exists outside (as well as within) your organisation. You could sell the product, although your competitors might balk at buying from a rival. In that case you could sell it to a software house, but arrange to receive some royalties. You might just have a product after all. . . .

So how do we impose these disciplines? You already have the basic tools to hand. Your technical authority (TA) can act as the arbiter of good development taste, vetting any enhancements in the same way as different approaches to fixing a bug are reviewed. Your weekly discrepancy review meeting can be raided and the more senior attendees stolen once a month or so, and turned into a body that supports the TA's enhancement-review role. They themselves can generate enhancement ideas that might be worth bouncing off the users.

You may find yourself adding a lot of functionality; this will provide a real challenge. If you are using the numerical quality measures that I mentioned in Chapter 4 on 'Internals and Coding', you will have already increased your chances of achieving an optimum design that minimises relative complexity. New processes altering the fan-out numbers could increase the relative complexity and so reduce design quality. Keep the rules-of-thumb in mind, continue to limit your fan-out to zero or one or two, and ensure that all modules remain strong (have only a single purpose). So although the aim here is to preserve the existing external functionality whilst adding new functionality, don't be afraid to change the internal design quite radically. Not only will you continue to minimise your relative complexity, but you will prompt yourself to test more thoroughly, and you will avoid the dreaded spaghetti monster.

7.5 Final thoughts

7.5.1 Full circle

You are about to find yourself at the entry point to Chapter 2 on 'Initiation and Requirements'. The number and nature of enhancements may result in one of two challenging approaches. You treat the existing system as the kernel of a whole new system. As I write, the trend seems to be that everyone is giving their tired old mainframe applications snazzy new PC-based user interfaces. This is where having developed good specifications at every level will help enormously. If you are spec-less then it might be as easy to take the option in the next paragraph. However, if that's too drastic, go talk to a few hardware and software vendors, and see if you can find one who has an analysis CASE tool that will look at your current code and working backwards produce a specification (of sorts) for it.

The other option is to ditch the old system, and stare out across the green field alongside which said ditch does run. And look at the green field, see that it is good, wonder and dream about what you'd really like your system to do, and then go and build it — but read Chapter 2 first!

7.6 Questions

1. Do you have a backup procedure yet?
2. Who checks that it is carried out?
3. Have you tried to rebuild the system from your backup tapes yet?
4. Have you created a discrepancy database?
5. Have your formulated your own discrepancy procedures?
6. Does everyone know about them?
7. Are you having regular review meetings?
8. Are you 'thinking product'?
9. Do you dare to do radical redesign when you have major enhancements?
10. At what point is it a good idea to ditch your current system and start your journey around the development loop all over again?

8 Documentation

8.1 Introduction

8.1.1 Yuk! — boring

Juvenile I admit, but it got your attention; and for this chapter that was crucial. While I might have had to restrain eager young readers from chafing at the bit and dashing precipitately into other chapters, which at that moment might not have been wholly suitable for them, quite the reverse is the case here.

Except for a few bizarre exceptions, of which I am one, pretty much the whole software industry has a pathological distaste, dislike and fear of documentation, whether it be the writing of it, the reviewing of it, or merely scanning the text with one's innocent gaze. Frankly, most people would rather jump off the Eiffel Tower without a parachute. Since that is not, however, available as an every-day option, Joe Coder and Josephine Designer resort to the next best alternative — getting on with some real solid work, like writing, testing or (even more fun) modifying programs.

Am I being uncharitable? When did your colleagues last smile at you when you handed them a specification to review? Why is this? What is it about documentation that irritates people and tends to demotivate them?

There is a combination of factors. We have to face the fact that a number of people are just not turned on by documentation. Fundamentally it is static in nature, it just sits there on a desk, cluttering up people's work-space. Software systems, in contrast, are lively active things; prod them and they'll poke you back in return. Even though they may well be meant to, they quite often don't behave the same way twice. They provide challenging problems, problems of a very special nature. Unlike trying to achieve a fair and equitable distribution of wealth amongst all the inhabitants of the planet, which is intractable and whose intrinsic value is open to political debate (about its correctness and efficacy), some people find computing problems much more appealing. They can be cleanly defined, are amenable to careful logical analysis, and can be deemed solved once the necessary steps have been taken.

It is the chance to grapple with this type of challenging problem that attracts most people into the computing industry. And the mind-set that this requires tends not to include a predisposition to the drier activities of writing, reviewing and reading documentation.

It could be said that documentation is not central to the game of computing. Place someone in front of a video-game, and they will drop a coin into the slot and start to play it, lose horrendously badly, then maybe look at the rules etched next to the screen. People prefer window-style interfaces to command lines that require strings of letters to be typed, since the mouse-based system allows the user to get started straightaway without having to wade through reams of muddling manuals. This is good, it's the natural response.

If kids are playing on their own home computer, writing themselves a video-game, they are more likely to enjoy putting it together if they make a first try, play with it for a while, amend it, try again, and continue via a process of creative trial and error until they find something that they're pleased with. A few days later they'll get bored and change the program again. Great! They're having fun. It's most unlikely that they'd enjoy themselves more had they sat down and carefully designed the game, including every last bell and whistle, before they started. This is fine; the only people who get hurt by not having documentation here are the kids, who may end up crying a few tears of frustration when their program keeps crashing. No matter, they'll soon perk up and have another try; it's not as if they've got a deadline by which to produce this game! Step forward a few years, and consider the average student solo-computing project; again computing is still a fun game, and should the student fail to document his or her program correctly, the only thing that really suffers may be the student's grades. Note I said solo-project; if, however, there are other students involved, we arrive at the bridge between the world of self-indulgent computing and (although we may not notice) do in fact cross over into a world of programming in an environment where the developer has social obligations.

The point at issue here is that we are not talking about the game of computing — but the *business* of computing. The provision of systems to meet a perceived user-need is a discipline. It involves contracts, be they internal bargains between two departments within the same corporation, or be they signed, sealed and delivered so that two separate parties become bound by the law of the land. Programmers may have moved from one world (of play) to another (of work), but it is unlikely that they have adjusted their world-view. They didn't choose the job because they enjoy satisfying a series of contractual obligations, they chose it because they enjoy programming. However, unless the organisation in which they find themselves builds upon their student studies and educates them in the implications of the world of business, they will (not unreasonably) continue to practise computing with the same mind-set as they have had ever since they started computing.

8.2 Documentation policies

8.2.1 Corporate cultures

It falls to the organisation to develop an approach to its activities that fosters an appreciation in its staff of the necessity for, and benefits of, documentation. This is a truism. I could have started the chapter with this paragraph, having omitted the preceding preamble. But if I had, the force of it would have been lost.

Let me for one moment clarify what I mean by documentation. It is characterised not by the fact that it is printed out on paper, but rather by the fact that it could be. Subtle distinction I know, but significant. The essence of the approach that values (rather than neglects) documentation, is that it seeks to record information, not ignore and overlook it.

Specifications that are held on-line, readily available to everyone in a development team, but secured so that only the author can update them, count as documentation. If placed under careful change control, and capable of being printed by whoever needs a copy, they even become positively advantageous (more on this in due course).

The issue of 'documentation policy' is thus not one of demanding that every last piece of information be written down, in triplicate, and filed with a double cross-referenced index. Rather, it is part of the wider issue of the organisation's commitment to quality, an appreciation enunciated at the top of the enterprise and handed down the corporate tree. It states that it expects everyone in the organisation to be committed to producing systems of high quality, and that inherent in this goal is an appreciation and acceptance of, and commitment to, the fact that a system is a composite object. It is not just the code, the data, the command files. It is also the thought — codified and laid bare in the specifications; it is also the knowledge that it has been tested thoroughly as exemplified by the thinking that has gone into producing the test scripts; and it is also the guides — clear, concise, complete — that provide the users with a ready reference with which to navigate their way around the system.

Only with such a clear and explicit declaration of intent, backed up by consistent supportive management action, can an organisation inspire its members to believe that they should devote their energies to all aspects of a development project.

You would be perfectly entitled to respond to all this by asking me to come down out of my pulpit, and give some more solid workaday reasons as to why you should focus yourself on documentation. At this juncture, I would point out that (user guides aside) documentation is not an end in itself. It is a means to an end, it is a constituent part of a system, but that system should no more be judged solely on its documentation than it should on its command files. Documentation clarifies, codifies and records thought. That is its function.

Documentation is necessary to achieve clarification of thought because your system is damnably complex. No one person can keep even a small portion of it at the forefront of his or her mind; the only way one can effectively reason about the system is by referring to documentation of some sort.

Inconsistency is the bane of poor-quality systems. Different parts never behave in quite the same way; you are repeatedly caught off guard and confused by a system that presents an inconsistent interface to you and behaves in an inconsistent manner. How do these systems come about? Groups of people, developing the system, exercise just a little too much autonomy for the good of the users' states of mind. This is why, by codifying how a system is to be developed, and what conventions are to be followed, documentation can perform its function and yield a higher-quality system.

When was the most recent collection around your office to get someone a leaving present? Our dynamic societies generate serious levels of 'churn'. Without wishing to milk this phonetic metaphor, people no longer kow-tow to their organisations. A whole career within one firm is a rarity, half-a-dozen job-hops the norm. Result? By the time your development project is complete, half the faces on the team will be different. Word of mouth, and collective team memory, just won't do. All significant decisions and design items need to be recorded for posterity, or failing that for the guy who'll be sitting at your desk next week.

While I'm on documentation's function as the recording of thought, remember that the larger and more complex your system becomes, the less you see of the other team members, but the more you depend on what they are doing. Documentation becomes the primary form of communication. And the larger the system, the longer it will take to develop, and the more turnover in staff there will be. Last but not least, I intimated in the preceding chapter that all systems are subject to maintenance and enhancement, quite often by a completely different bunch of people, so your thoughts need to be recorded for their benefit. Oh yes, and for yours — just in case your forget.

8.2.2 Back to the real world

These exhortations and reasonings are all very well, but don't expect miracles. They have one purpose, and it is less grand than I might be leading you to believe. I have been talking about a 'theoretical average of all programming people', but there is no such thing. Oh, just a moment, I feel another spectrum coming on — one that measures people's disposition towards documentation. At one end I place myself. A prime candidate if ever there was one for the title of docuphile. It's fairly self-evident that I like the stuff — how else could I stand devoting a not inconsiderable number of hours to crafting this very book? Given the choice of writing a memo or a macro, I'd far rather write a memo — they tend not to crash, dribbling octal core dumps all over your desk. That very reason, which for me makes a memorandum into an object of beauty, will revolt the docuphobe! Who, as a result, would place themselves at the other end of my new spectrum. The reasoning behind my discussion of the declarations the leader of the corporation should be making was not to equip him or her with the tools to transform all of the employees into 'out-and-out' docuphiles — not possible. What we seek is just to nudge everyone a little way along the spectrum, a smidgen nearer the docuphile end, so that they can appreciate why documentation is worth doing.

Was all this really necessary? Yes! Well I would say that, wouldn't I? But in all seriousness documentation is easy. It's almost trivial; writing is as old as civilisation itself, and we now have oodles of snazzy desk top publishing tools. We can crank out magnificent-looking masterpieces in the twinkling of an eye. There is nothing inherently difficult in the task of writing documentation which should cause poor-quality material to be produced. At the heart of the battle to produce high-quality documentation is people.

8.2.3 Striking the right balance

By now you must have realised that I subscribe to the philosophy that there are no glib, all-encompassing, one-stop solutions to problems. Rather, my approach could be characterised as 'a little of what you fancy does you good', melded with 'everything in moderation'. The point here being that *high-quality documentation does not necessarily mean exhaustive documentation*. Quality should empower people, not wear them down. High-quality documentation is that which meets the needs of all the people associated with a development, without placing an undue burden upon them.

So, what is appropriate? No easy answers — sorry! But what I do have is the basic tool which you should already be applying to all aspects of the development — forethought. Let's try that again; aforethought, thinking carefully before you act. In this case, actually planning your documentation. And make sure you plan carefully.

8.3 Planning your documentation

8.3.1 This train stops for no-one

Let me take you back through the mists of time to the halcyon days when I was no more than a student. I took the train from York to London quite regularly, and one day overheard a rather apposite conversation.

The ticket collector was making his rounds and asked an elderly gent sitting across the carriage from me for his ticket. The collector looked none too pleased when he saw the ticket — it was for Sheffield, some fifty miles from York. The look on the guard's face unsettled the old man, who said this was the train to Sheffield, was it not? It wasn't. It was the non-stop, high-speed service to London, hurtling through the English countryside at 125 miles an hour. And no, it could not be diverted; however, it could let the (by now confused) old gent off at the next station; the only problem was that the next station was London, 200 miles to the south!

It was obviously a genuine mistake; the gent was getting quite agitated, worried about what his family, patiently waiting over five hours for him on the platform at Sheffield, would think had happened to him. The guard said that British Rail would put him on the first train back out of London to Sheffield; and money worries would be left to later.

But how had this predicament arisen? York Railway Station, marvel of Victorian architecture that it is, is none the less confusing. The platforms are very long. There are tracks that run through the centre of the station but have no platform next to them. These features combine to provide a facility whereby two trains can use both ends of the same platform, and the train in the rear switch on to the middle track and leave first. This results in some strange numbering schemes for the platforms. The mainline down to London isn't even platform 1; it's platform 8. But in addition it's so long that it consists of platforms 8a and 8b. Whether it was confusion, encroaching deafness, or whatever, the pensioner thought he should board the train at 8a, when he probably should have taken the local train to Sheffield standing at 8b. He only discovered his mistake too late to do much about it; he was locked into the rest of the journey. He hadn't been to London in many years and reminisced as the express thundered through the town where he had been billeted prior to leaving for France to fight in the First World War. He had no option but to see his journey through to the end, and then seek a remedy, all because of some confusing numbers.

You could be subject to a similar fate, numerically at least. If you choose a bad filing system for your documentation, and a poor numbering scheme to track it (more about that anon), then you will be trapped into using something inconvenient and counter-productive, which will delay and confuse you for the rest of your development. Big claim? Chances are that as the project proceeds you'll have less and less time to spare, and certainly not enough to reorganise all the documentation.

8.3.2 *I'm not a number, I have a name*

That's as maybe. If, however, you use only names and not numbers to identify your documentation, you will rapidly become a prisoner to your own disorganisation and your development team's multiple mutual misunderstandings. No developers will arrive on your team with a mind resembling a clean slate; everyone will already have their own preferences and prejudices. These will colour what they think should be in particular documents, and what they prefer to call them. You may have quite a cultural battle on your hands trying to get everyone to use your preferred terminology. Luckily numbers are far less emotive.

All your documentation needs to receive an identifying number. And I mean *all*, not just plans and specifications, but minutes of meetings, internal memoranda, delivery notes, change requests, discrepancy reports, terms of reference, and correspondence with the users. This will encourage everyone to think of these items of paperwork as being as important and valid a part of the total effort as the glossiest requirements specification. Plan your documentation with a filing system that allocates a number to each type of document, and plan ahead. Define numbers for all the documents now, leave gaps where you think you may need extra documents, and don't let the fact that (in the end) you may not produce all of these documents stop you from at least planning where you'd file them if you did.

You may end up having multi-part numbers. These can be very useful; taken to their logical conclusion, they ensure that you need never lose another document again. Include numbers identifying:

- The division or group in the organisation that owns the project (its boss is the one whose head rolls should the project go wrong).

- The actual project (that has a separate identity as far as Accounts are concerned).
- The document class, e.g. where it fits in the project's lifecycle.
- The document type, a subnumber locating the document precisely within a particular class of documents (e.g. a specific process specification that belongs to the general class of process specifications).
- A version number for a document that may be issued more than once (sometimes two-part itself e.g. $m.n$, where $n = 0$ indicates a proper issue, and $n <> 0$ a draft version).

You will then be able to mislay the document in any of your organisation's offices, and it should be promptly returned direct to your filing cabinet — magically appearing there without the need for your intervention.

8.4 Document format

8.4.1 I've got you covered

Now all those digits can (and should) appear on every page, in case you drop it on the way back from the photocopier, and not least the front page. While I'm considering clumsy calamities, do make sure that every page is numbered; it does speed collating after you've picked it up from the carpet. Back to the front page — this is where we have to talk a little about control. Try these for size, think of them as a 'pick and mix':

- your organisation;
- your division;
- your project;
- who it's for;
- the document title (with luck some people might even use it);
- a very short synopsis;
- the author(s);
- the reviewers;
- the number of pages;
- how you intend to control it (what? I'll explain in a minute);
- date of issue;
- author's signature(s);
- reviewer's signature(s);
- user's signature(s) (if appropriate);
- validity (when will it self-destruct or quietly sit in the corner and fizzle itself out of date?).

They won't all apply, but if you omit more than two or three you're asking for trouble down the line. Stylistically I leave it to your own good taste to choose how to lay this information out, whether you follow my suggestion and put it on the front cover, or maybe hide it on page 2. But would it be as useful there?

Do I hear sighs of exasperation? I appreciate this sounds like a lot of work every time you write something more substantial than a memo requesting a sharper pencil — have patience. There is another part of this approach to documentation planning and control that will make the whole package significantly more usable. Templates! Having written one document, you can take a copy, delete the information specific to the document, leaving a framework that can be used for all the subsequent documents. Indeed, if you are going to have a lot of people producing documents such as 'process specifications', a template for that particular variant would prove very useful, to ensure that everyone considers all the issues they should. Here the template extends beyond the format, layout, and control information; it also includes the section headings within the document, which can act as aide-mémoires prompting the authors to consider every aspect of the process they are describing.

The aim here is not to turn you into the world's greatest filing clerk; rather it is to sweep out of the way all the boring issues that give documentation a bad name. By sorting all of this out in advance, when you come to write individual documents, the format, layout, and control information will be so familiar that you won't need to expend any thought on them. Instead you can devote all your efforts to the unique aspects of the task you are engaged in.

8.4.2 Hey! good looking?

This is where I indulge in a little cop-out. I've already discussed documentation production in Chapter 2 on 'Initiation and Requirements'. So a quick trip back there should start you thinking about whether you need to order more cheese for all those mice you're about to acquire; otherwise they may not have the necessary energy to help you draw all those snazzy graphics you'd like to impress the users with.

Whatever facilities you plump for, do make sure that they are available to everyone on the project — directly available from their desks. Whenever they feel the urge to pen (or key!) a masterpiece, they should be able to do so. The facilities need not be on the same machine as the one on which the system being developed will run. Do you really want to constrain yourselves with the rather limited word processor bundled with the operating system, when you could all be using PCs hooked into the mainframe?

And it should be possible for these documents to be easily backed up, sent around the office (and world?) by 'e-mail', and placed in a configuration control library tool.

So writing the documentation plan is one of the first things you should do. And, as should be clear, it is more than just an index into the filing system. Consider: how you produce the documentation, what it looks like, how you back it up, how you circulate it, where the templates are, how you number it, and, crucially, how you change it. Change control is covered in detail in the next chapter.

8.5 Document content

8.5.1 *Contents — what about the contents?*

Form and function: so far it's all been form, what about the function? What documents should you be planning to produce? If you have been misusing this book, no, not using it to stop your great-aunt Agatha's piano from wobbling, but rather reading it sequentially irrespective of the stage you have reached in your own particular development, then you will be able to answer this question without any help from me. Go on then.

If, however, you've been an obedient reader, and skimmed, skipped and flipped, then you won't have covered all the chapters that precede this one — good. You deserve to receive an answer. It is, I admit, fairly obvious or, shall we say — intuitive? You nodded? Hey, I'm winning, quality is becoming second nature for you; you're beginning to approach development with quality in mind, without my having to nag you all the time.

Right now then, here's one shopping list and remember to keep control of the (loose) change:

- Documentation plan, check earlier in this chapter if you've already forgotten what it should contain.
- Project or development plan, see the final chapter.
- Requirements specification, you may not have written it, but you sure need to have your own copy — carefully filed.
- Statement of external functionality (SEF), your crucial 'controlling specification'.
- Internals specification, covering how you are you planning to build this marvel.
- Process specifications, if you don't want to give yourself a nasty back injury carrying a heavy one-stop internals specification (that includes all the process-level details) around the office.
- Unit test specifications, if you wrote the process specifications correctly, then just remember the 'Confirm that' construct.
- Integration test specification, same applies as for the internals specification.
- System test specification, ditto here, too, with respect to the SEF.
- Acceptance test specification, again you might not be writing this (the users might . . .), but you definitely need a copy!
- Guides and training material, more on this in a moment.
- Paperwork, comprising
  - contracts,
  - correspondence (external),
  - correspondence (internal),
  - coding standards,
  - change requests.

I have already covered all of these in some detail elsewhere in this discourse; only the guides and training material remain to be examined in depth.

8.6 Training material

8.6.1 *So how do I work this contraption?*

This is the basic user question, and the reason why the user documentation is written. Obvious? Yes, but it needs to be said, because it is no good for the developer to attempt to judge the quality of the user guides. Only the users can tell you if the user guides are high-quality documents. And they are entitled to; you may spend a few months using the SEF, they will spend many years poring over the user guides. They should expect and demand the best, and you should be prepared to involve them from step one. They should help formulate the way the information is broken down into different types of guides, and how the information is presented. This implies they have a say in your documentation tools (word processors!) — true, they do. And the atmosphere will be happier all round, and the quality of the documentation higher, if you acknowledge this and openly invite them in for a brainstorm or two, preferably down the pub!

The single most important point is to realise what function the user documentation is *not* intended to fulfil. It is not, repeat not, a statement of the contractual functionality scheduled for delivery. That requirement is met by the SEF. The user documentation is not about how the system is built, nor how it runs; it is, rather, about how to use the system. We are talking here about documents that are a blend of techno-speak, modulated with a little dash of user-language. The intended audience must always be borne in mind, and that audience is the user community.

This means that it is not a good idea to get the programming staff to write the user documentation; far better to get some documentation specialists in. They will have to climb a learning curve to understand the system which is identical to the one the real users will follow. This makes a separate documentation specialist ideally suited to ensuring that the guides cover everything they need to, in the right order, and in an intelligible manner.

Select documentation specialists who match the current degree of sophistication of the users. No, not whether they prefer brown ale over campari and soda; but how computer-literate the users are. They can be divided into two main groups depending on how they currently do the job. If they already use computers, the documentation specialists are entitled to assume a higher level of computer-literacy than if the users currently shuffle paper all day. This level of literacy should be borne in mind when the guides are written, thus improving their quality by pitching them at an appropriate level.

One other advantage of getting documentation specialists to produce the guides is that they will go straight to the horse's mouth. They will not want to cut and paste chunks of the SEF, they won't even trust the SEF to be true, they would much rather play with a real live (or test) version of the system, and confirm to their own satisfaction that it does what the SEF claims. Hey, good news, you've inadvertently got yourself another random tester.

I talked a moment ago about involving the users; you must make sure that you involve the correct users. It is not uncommon for the user organisation to create a shadow project team, mirroring the roles in the development team. Thus, there is a development project manager, so there is a user project manager; there is a development technical authority, so there is a user technical authority. Marvellous people though these are, in the case of reviewing the user documentation — they're useless. Really? Yes, for the rather odd reason that they know too much. Usually this would rule them in; here it rules them out. They already understand the system, its aims and functions, how these are achieved (e.g. why all level-three screens have a yellow cursor, whilst level-two screens have a blue one).

The people who should be reviewing the user documentation are the actual users. When they come to operate the system, they will not have had much contact with its development. They will have been too busy doing the job the system just replaced. Their requirements will be more demanding than those of the shadow project manager and shadow technical authority. The real users will need to know everything; the authors of the user documentation cannot assume any pre-existing knowledge on the part of the real users. And only the real users can indicate where there is a confusing gap in an explanation; the shadow project manager can use his existing knowledge to fill in the gap, probably subconsciously — not even realising there is a gap. So go make friends with the real users; after all it is their system.

8.6.2 Pass the map

Time to splatter this text with a mathematical concept or two. Don't worry, it's nothing too painful. We have a couple of 'domains'; the first is the mile-high stack of potential user documentation, the other the large crowd of souls that make up the user community. These souls are not all alike, and they need different parts of the documentation stack. What we need to do is establish a mapping (or function) that ties the different types of user to the appropriate documents. What? You though all you needed was a single one-stop user guide. Shame on you, but I bet you'll have excellent muscle structure by the time it's written and you've carried the weight around the office for a few months. Today's buzz word is 'selectivity', in this case teasing out what information is appropriate for what group. But what do we have to give these groups? Try this for size:

- *Administration Guide.*
- *Error Messages Guide.*
- *Installation Guide.*
- *User Guide.*
- *Operations Guide.*
- *System Glossary.*

And what are the groups that we need to map these guides on to?

- *Regular users.* These folk run the procedures (and maybe software, if such exists) that the system will replace. They are the ones who will use the system to do their jobs.

- *Administrators*. Important people. They set up the system after the developers have installed it. They ensure that everything keeps running as it should, reconfigure it when necessary, and generally play the role of surrogate parent.
- *Operators*. The ones without whom none of the enterprise's systems would keep running, but who don't get a great deal of credit; they get the donkey work. However, it is of critical importance that they do their tasks correctly and completely, otherwise the quality of service that the system provides to its users will be significantly compromised.

So who gets what? Or, to look at this question from the other end of the document production lifecycle — which documents are aimed at each group?

The *users* need the *User Guide*, but they also need the *Error Messages Guide*. I will explain more in a moment about why these are separate documents. They should also receive the System Glossary.

The *administrators* need the *Installation Guide*, the *Administration Guide*, the *Error Messages Guide*, and the *System Glossary*.

Meantime the *operators* require the *Operations Guide*, the *Error Messages Guide* and the *System Glossary*.

8.6.3 Are we content now?

Having gone to the trouble of defining so many different varieties of user documentation, I suppose you now want me to explain how they differ. Oh, all right, if you insist.

- *The Administration Guide* is designed to provide the system's superusers with everything they need to know about the system but were too afraid to ask. The operative term here is 'superuser'; these folk are extremely mature (yes, really) and thus entrusted with many important and sensitive tasks, associated primarily with security. This may cover access to data; certainly it will encompass the configuring (and removal) of users from the system. It may involve checking for unauthorised access and tampering.

It is not unusual for these tasks to be done by pairs of people, since the organisation probably won't trust just one of them. To some extent a climate of mutual suspicion is deliberately fostered, and many administrative tasks have two (or even three) stages. The information needed to carry out such tasks should not fall into the hands of people who don't need to know it, so it should be contained in a document separate from all the other ones. Particularly sadistic organisations may require their administrators to read the *Administration Guide*, memorise all of it, and then eat it — if this is the case, it is recommended that non-toxic toner be used in the laser printer, and the output be on rice paper.

- *The Error Messages Guide* is intended as a one-stop reference for all non-sensitive system messages. 'Error messages' is an umbrella title, in that the guide should include all informational messages as well. A message could invite data entry, confirm that the correct data has been entered, confirm that an operation has completed successfully, warn that a minor problem was encountered, highlight that a failure may be about to happen, or whimper that the sky has just fallen in. The point is to have all messages in one place, ordered alphabetically in terms of the text that appears on the screen, print-out or error log file.

The only messages that might not appear here are security-sensitive messages (e.g. 'Unauthorised access to database') which the administrators might not want everyone else to know about; these should be placed in the *Administration Guide* in a specific error messages chapter. Of course, if such an error message mistakenly appears at a regular user's console, then we definitely have a serious failure of quality — with respect to directing of output.

When listed, messages should have a suitably helpful set of explanatory text to accompany them. Doubtless you've already been infuriated, on more than one occasion, by an error message explanation that merely restates the error text without giving any new information. You should try and grade error messages according to some scheme of importance. These levels of importance should be distinguished from each other by what action, if any, it is necessary for the user (or someone else) to take. Consider these possibilities:

- errors which are so serious the user organisation cannot solve the problem, the maintainers must be contacted;
- errors which prevent users from doing what they wanted, and which can only be corrected by user administrative staff;
- errors which prevented users from completing an operation, but which can be corrected by users trying again, right now;
- errors which indicate that a request was carried out, but there may have been some small problem, so users should double check that everything is all right;
- a change of state has occurred in one of the system's components, this may (or may not) be an error;
- an invitation to enter a command or some data is offered;
- a confirmation that a request has been executed without any problems;
- some general piece of information, that may be of passing interest to the users, but needs no user action, is presented.

Choose whichever of these seem appropriate for your system, and give them a numbering or lettering scheme to signify their relative importance.

Now having covered the seriousness of the message, two other pieces of information are crucial. The first is a list of probable causes of this error message appearing; the second is a recommended series of actions. Each possible cause should have some corresponding action to be taken. The first steps of the actions should not necessarily be corrective, rather they should be investigatory — enabling the users to confirm which of the possible causes is the actual cause. Once that has been confirmed, then users can take appropriate corrective action.

- *The Installation Guide* is a half-way house document, which in some respects will be of as much use to the developers as it will for the users. It consists of step-by-step instructions on how to create the system. The starting point is presumed to be at the stage when there are directories full of the necessary files of source-code and build command files. The *Installation Guide* should take the person charged with installing the system from that point to a system, full of real data, that is alive and kicking.

Initially, this document is validated by the development team when it first tries and install the system. It becomes necessary for the users to have a copy because it is quite likely that the developers may send updates to the system, and leave the users to rebuild these new releases.

- *The User Guide* will be the documentation specialists' *tour de force*. It should cover everything Joe and Josephine User are ever likely to need to know — about the system, anyway. Most systems are still terminal- and keyboard-focused. If, however, your particular marvel includes a novel user interface or two (mouse, light-pen, water pistol or whatever), then this should also come within the ambit of the *User Guide*. Indeed, the weirder the device, the more attention it should get.

The aim is to guide, with as little pain as possible, the wary and befuddled user around the maze of screens and options that have just been foisted upon them. Result? Diagrams come to the fore. They are by far the best way of introducing lots of fresh information easily and quickly. Start with an overview of the whole system, including what operations it is meant to perform.

If you have a command-line-based interface, then shame on you. Oops, I got a little opinionated there; it may well be perfectly appropriate for your particular application. None the less, in such a case, do ensure that you do more than merely enumerate the commands. You should show their inter-relationships, and the structure of the data (as it pertains to the user) that you are manipulating with these commands.

Most screen-based systems consist of a hierarchy of inter-related screens, often accessed through menus. Series of hierarchy diagrams are definitely recommended. Before you get down to the detail of individual screens and what you can do with them, it's wise to explain your conventions with respect to how each screen is discussed, and how the information is presented. There may well be some global conventions (no not another G7 meeting) that are worth adumbrating, e.g. the function keys or standard commands that may be used to move you between screens or request help.

When discussing individual screens, bear these guidelines in mind. But remember, if the *User Guide* matches the guidelines but the users aren't happy, then pay attention to the users. After all, they are the ones who will eventually (with luck) pay you. For each screen, after a quick overview of what it does, go ahead and show a copy of the screen image. Column and row numbers around the edges help to anchor fields usefully on to the screen. And remember, what you have here is a static instance of a dynamic screen, so you will have to monkey around with typefaces (and the like) to indicate how various screen elements differ. Specifically, you ought to distinguish between static text and dynamic text (fields); further, the dynamic text can be split down into data supplied by the system, and data supplied by the users. Each field should be discussed in turn, and you should seek to distinguish between those that are initially blank, and those supplied by the system. The ones that are initially blank can be further subdivided into ones that must have data placed in them, and ones that may (at the users' discretion). The fields that are system-supplied can be subdivided into ones that can or cannot be updated by the users. For all of the fields, it helps if some of their other characteristics are highlighted, specifically: whether they are numeric, alphabetic, or alphanumeric (and in this case confirm whether that includes symbols like $, %, etc.). And don't forget cAsE sensitivity.

Once the fields have been listed, their interaction should be detailed. What? Can some be filled in without others? For each field, list which other fields need data for the original one to accept its data. This sort of information can be usefully presented in tabular form.

This is also a suitable point to examine whether any of the standard function keys or commands behave in strange or irascible ways on this particular screen.

And don't forget, after all this spiel, to explain what can be done at this screen and how. It is quite often the case that there may be more than one level of security within the system, so identify what privileges a user needs to be able to tackle a particular class of operation.

And even though you have them elsewhere, include some of the more common error messages that the users might encounter. Unlike the specifications, there is nothing wrong with duplicating information in different parts of the user documentation. This particular bit of duplication may save the exasperated users a trip across the office to consult the only copy of the error messages manual (which is, therefore, superglued to the administrator's desk) every time they encounter an error. And while they are learning about the system, the users will encounter plenty of errors.

- *The Operations Guide* is similar to the *Administration Guide*, but pitched at a lower level, covering the more mundane routine procedures, and excluding the security-sensitive issues that the *Administration Guide* addresses.

Let's enumerate the procedures that this guide should be considering:

- o First and foremost there is daily house-keeping, doing the appropriate preventive maintenance, archiving, and backups.
- o Then there is starting the system, both from scratch (cold-start) and restarts (warm-starts).
- o Complementing this is the art of the graceful shutdown; if done correctly nothing important should be lost or mangled and restarts should be a doddle.
- o Some trouble-shooting procedures to help with the investigation of routine problems would be useful.
- o Next comes what to do in an emergency.
- o And closely related, if the emergency develops into a full-blown disaster, how to recover from it.

Now I've listed all these responsibilities, maybe it will start to sink in just how important your operators are to you and your system.

- *The System Glossary* is an alphabetical list of every single confusing acronym and technical term that is associated with your system, even if only very tangentially. It may not strike you as being really necessary — take a leap of faith, start writing one. The moment it begins to circulate around the developers and the users, you'll be surprised by how quickly it grows, how useful it becomes, and how lost you'd be without it.

8.6.4 So how do I know if these guides are any good?

Fair question. In trying to build a high-quality system we didn't just give out guidelines and tell people to follow them. We did more, we reviewed what they did; in some cases if the urge gripped us we did a little counting, took a few measurements. What about the guides, how do we determine if they are of a high enough quality? There are two sets of actions you can take.

Number one is the good old review. This chapter serves as a starting point for the checklists to be used. Ensure the users are included on the review team, and as well as tracking points raised about the way the information is presented, pay careful attention to points raised on what information is being presented. If a review highlights that a draft version of a guide has a factual inaccuracy (i.e. it doesn't correctly describe the way the system works), then as well as correcting the error investigate how the erroneous information came to be gathered and placed in the guide. It may be necessary to correct the way the documentation specialists go about confirming the veracity of their statements about the system.

The second quality check is a baptism of fire, or (if you prefer) beta test! In this case, the first proper release of the guides will probably be used by the users to educate themselves about the system while they are running the acceptance tests (if they choose to run them). In such a case, the guides will be tested very thoroughly, errors and problems will be found, so a rapid reissue before the system goes live would be in order.

If the real users do not acceptance-test the system, there is one other opportunity for beta testing — user training.

8.6.5 Do you follow my train of thought?

The crux of training is that it should be more than just directed reading of the guides. It should maximise hands-on access to the system and its needs different documentation. Why? Training will fall into different courses for the groups enumerated above, namely administrators, users, and operators. They may share some of the guides, but they each need courses, and course notes, slanted at their particular roles. These notes will be most effective if they take on board one of the lessons from research into the psychology of learning mathematics.

Computing involves grappling with quite a lot of abstract ideas. People can understand a new abstract idea only if it is presented using models or ideas (schemas in research-speak) that they are already familiar with. So design the courses to build on reasonable existing knowledge of the participants — go talk to them beforehand, and ask them what they know! And allow time for new schemas to bed down, sink in, become familiar, before progressing to further new ideas based on the ones only just introduced. If you don't do this, the quality of the course will degrade rapidly. Why? Everyone will be completely lost! It helps if you concentrate on the application as well as the system; you may care about the system, the users care more about the application. And in the end they are the dog, you are the tail; they call the shots, you wag when you're told to. Have fun with your schemas, and (guess what?) the more outrageous the more effective they and you will be. Get to it!

8.7 Questions

1. What's your corporate culture with respect to documentation?
2. What are you planning to do about this situation?
3. Have you planned your documentation yet?
4. Does everyone have a copy of this plan?
5. How do you know they've read it?
6. Where are your templates?
7. Who's writing the user documentation?
8. Why haven't they started yet?
9. How will you know if it's any good?
10. What will you do if it's not?
11. What about the training courses?

9 Change control and configuration management

9.1 Introduction

9.1.1 'Turn and face the strange ch, ch, changes . . .'

So, can you tell the difference between TweedleBowie and TweedleStardust? Confused? Sounds perfectly understandable to me, considering the circumstances. You can step through the 'looking-glass' and on to the chessboard of this chapter if you *cannot* answer the following conundrum. Yes, the entitlement to carry on reading aligns itself with not knowing the answer, more confusion . . . .

That is the heart of this chapter, attempting to resolve this confusion. But first the riddle. I say, I say, I say, pray tell can you elucidate the difference between change control and configuration management? Yes? Very good, I'm most impressed, you may collect 200 small change requests, and go straight to the questions at the end of the chapter. No cheating, you must be able to understand those questions, and in addition generate plausible answers to them (for your own development organisation) and only then can you open the bottle marked 'Drink Me'.

If, however, the riddle or the questions leave you as flustered as the Mad Hatter, then stay seated where you are, put on your best thinking-cap, and prepare to embark on an odyssey of discovery.

9.1.2 Teasing apart the tangle

I guess you'd like me to explain what on earth I'm rabbiting on about. Change control? Configuration management? Aren't they all about the business of making sure that things don't get out of hand, keeping a lid on the pressure cooker of demands for extra functionality, and knowing where we are? Put simply, yes! However, there is (as you've probably guessed by now) a subtlety or two that merits careful consideration.

Change control is the ability to manage changes (to specifications and systems) in an ordered manner. It is essentially a procedure that should be adhered to rigorously, to ensure that changes are not lost, and that the development team isn't bounced into changes that are inappropriate or disruptive to current schedules.

Configuration management is the ability to hold different versions of a system simultaneously, and reproduce any particular version required at a moment's notice. It is the art of careful librarianship, safely storing and cataloguing both the documents and the files that comprise the system.

Both abilities have a fundamental dependency upon which they rest. They cannot be successfully attempted, never mind exploited for their full benefit, unless an appropriate culture is adopted. Culture? Yes, culture: a culture of responsibility. I mentioned in Chapter 8 on 'Documentation' the dangers that the 'school of self-indulgent programming' inflicts on a development. The placing of coding upon a pedestal, and the denigration of documentation to the point where it wasn't even 'real work', would ultimately undermine the underlying strength of the system. A system is a synthesis of many parts, such that when considered as a whole it is much greater than the mere sum of its individual parts. Focusing on one sort of part and neglecting another can be extremely dangerous, and so can failing to realise the importance of what is being done, and the obligation the individual owes to all the other people involved in the system, be they other developers, testers, or users.

This culture of responsibility is, however, unlikely to arise spontaneously. It must be nurtured by the management team, which needs to stress the importance of team-goals as well as solo-goals. Only in such an environment will individual developers gain enough appreciation of the benefits that everyone derives from approaching a development with this culture of responsibility.

Both change control and configuration management are inherently disciplined approaches; in order to work they require co-operation, and a certain degree of selflessness on the part of all participants. CC and CM both involve significant amounts of paperwork (or, if you're lucky, on-line database-work) and the following of rules that slow things down, distract people from the task in hand, and do not obviously give any instant benefit to the person required to obey them.

Educating people about CC and CM is, thus, more than just disseminating a body of knowledge on procedures, techniques, and tools. It involves addressing people and their expectations, what they consider themselves and their performance to be judged against. CC and CM cannot be successfully imposed. If an attempt is made to impose them, they will be an unmitigated disaster, and acquire such bad names that no one will want to see their faces again for a long time to come. CC and CM can work successfully only if people adopt them willingly, buy into them, and feel that as developers they have a stake in the benefits that will flow from the use of CC and CM.

Here endeth the sermon on participative management styles (which ought to be in the next chapter anyway!). Having laid some firm foundations, let's get on with the detail of these two valuable abilities.

9.2 Change control

9.2.1 Money, money, money . . . all you ever think about!

Why have change control? How does it benefit you and your team of tenacious toilers? Put starkly — money, dosh, green foldable stuff. The cost of not having change control can be absolutely prohibitive. However, this may not be apparent on Day One of the project. It is often a lesson that is learned only by bitter experience. If this seems like unnecessary finger-wagging, and you consider my basic argument to be staggeringly obvious, then count yourself lucky. You have just earned the first grade on your way to being a fully fledged 'natural expert in quality'. You have good intuition.

For the less fortunate souls somewhat perplexed by my assertions, I invite you to consider two aspects of development without change control. Let's say you have a spanking new factory that crochets high-fibre, multi-vitamin cardigans, an ingenious new invention that can keep people warm on cold days whilst also providing them with a nourishing breakfast should a heat-wave be forecast. It's your job to automate this wonder of modern engineering. The company that will eventually run the factory engages some building construction experts. Unluckily for you they do not appreciate the limits of your equipment, which although giving a pretty powerful performance, does, however, take very careful programming.

The timescale is tight, but they send you a specification almost straightaway, and you sign the standard industry contract, which leaves a third-party consultant as the final arbiter of acceptability. The statement of external functionality (SEF) is a bit slim but your team leaders agree with their counterparts in the building firm that it seems to have all the information you need to control the one-armed knitting robots. You write the internals specification (IS), and are just about to start coding — but being a good 'quality-aware' project manager you review the IS first. There's only one thing missing, the cross-reference from the SEF, so since time is tight you tell the coders to get on and code from the specification while the cross-reference is constructed. No-one wants to do this particular task — so boring — it's left to you. This is your first lucky break, believe it or not. As you go over the two documents with a fine-toothed comb, you discover that the IS appears to implement different functionality from that in the SEF; also there's a lot more functionality, and it's significantly different. In addition there are some deletions. 'What?!', you exclaim. Some of the SEF's requirements aren't implemented at all. You're shocked; how could your brilliant team be so incompetent? Boiling over into one of your best purple rages this year, you storm out of your ergonomically designed personal work cubicle and give a piece of your mind to each of your team leaders.

They look shocked, and more to the point surprised, by your berating, since they were only doing what they thought was a good thing for the client, and hence the development. Their counterparts at the builders have been ringing them up, on quite a regular basis, and suggesting changes and extra functionality. It seemed like a good idea at the time; after all it improved the system — didn't it? So the team leaders agreed, and amended the internals specification, but left no other written record of the change. However, now it comes out, there might have been some extra requests that the team leaders failed to add, and some other changes were ideas that the team leaders came up with themselves. Result? The development team really aren't sure, any more, what they should be building. Well, it's obvious the SEF is not the correct document, and you have little option but to use the IS as it now stands.

You settle back down into your personally made-to-measure electro-massaging chair, feeling a bit 'frayed at the edges' but sure that the worst is now behind you (so to speak). Wrong! Two months later your installers arrive at the factory; it's all complete, gleaming, ready for the robots to have their software installed. No problems are expected, as the builders have already witnessed the acceptance tests. Now, echoing around the cavernous hangar that will soon hum with the click of knitting needles and the gurgle of mixing bowls, the footsteps of the consultant get louder. He draws closer, shouts across to your installers that the builders are all finished, and if the software can please be loaded then everyone can get on with their knitting (ho ho!). The EPROMs are slotted into place, the big red button given a friendly tap, and lo and behold there is a nasty grinding noise. Quick, the consultant dashes across to the emergency power cut-off. What the hell is this software doing? He demands to see the specifications. Out comes the scrumpled, scribbled-on, copy of the internals specification. He ponders for a moment, lets fly a stream of extremely inventive obscenities, and curses the next seven generations of the builders' offspring. Composure swiftly regained, he explains that the builders got it all wrong; they may know how to build but don't know how to run this sort of installation. There's only one thing for it; as the arbiter of final functionality, he dishes out a new configuration for the control program. And the project has only one choice, erase the EPROMs, catch the bus back to the office, and try and compress changes amounting to six weeks' worth of work into a few days, and with no bugs!

Far fetched? Not on your nelly! Problems of these elephantine proportions can arise all too easily if change control procedures are not in effect. And the later a change has to be made, the more the rework and retest will cost all concerned. So, how can we formulate a suitable procedure on the basis of our experience in the land of warm and chewy Wheeta-Knits? Read on.

9.2.2 Model change control procedures

Rule one is to buy yourselves a photocopier, together with a comprehensive service contract. Then try a fax machine or two. The aim is twofold. Your procedures will need to be written down, and distributed to everyone — on both sides of the developer/user fence. And you need the ability to send each other written communications quickly and with the minimum of hassle. If deciphering faxes is not to your taste, same sort of e-mail system would form a perfectly reasonable alternative.

Infrastructure, in for a penny, in for a pound. You now have the necessary tools; what should you do with them? You need to develop a procedure, based on the fundamental tenet that everything, absolutely everything, should be written down. And you need some information conduits (that term sounds familiar). These conduits are people, yes honestly, and they are limited in number (to two! — one user, one developer) and charged with the task of communicating all information that pertains to changes in anything to do with the development. They are allowed to have deputies, in fact it is essential that they do — do you realise how much it costs to send a fax to a decent hotel in Bermuda these days? The point being that the procedure cannot lapse because one of the partners is missing; it must be adhered to at all times.

All issues under discussion have a two-part lifecycle. They begin as amorphous blobs, vague ideas as yet without form or function. These are 'uncontrolled' issues; they can be batted about between the partners, pretty much at will (though getting the gooey bits out from between the racquet strings may prove troublesome). Once they have solidified into a shape both the users and the developers are happy with, they are formally agreed to, they are signed-off, and become 'controlled' issues. Once an issue is controlled it can never revert to being uncontrolled, and it can only be amended using the change control procedure.

Whenever someone thinks of an amendment to a controlled item, the information conduit partners proceed to send information to each other using a standard form. I'll call it a Tentative Idea Form (or TIF). Very appropriate really as it does indeed offer scope for a minor disagreement. Anyway, since these two people are unlikely to be lovers (although it's not prohibited), their TIF will have a bit more structure than the average lovers' tiff. In particular, it needs a date (this metaphor is running away with itself — solo-eloping?) and a sequential ID number. Both the developers and the users are likely to generate TIFs, so they can have one series of numbers, or two separate parallel enumerations. The TIF should also have a short title, the name of the originator of the idea (who will probably be someone other than one of the conduit partners) and, last but not least, the details of the change the originator would like to take place.

The development conduit partner should review these TIFs on a regular basis. On a big development that might well be the only thing this person does all day; for smaller projects a review once a week should be sufficient. The aim is to consider the technical feasibility of the tentative idea, and the impact that implementing it would have on the development's cost and schedule. Once some numbers have been put to this, the manager of the development should review the TIF. Either he can reject it there and then, in which case it is junked and the paper mutates into a JIF; or the other option is to classify it as something worth pursuing, pursuable in fact, and naturally the Form mutates into a PIF. On a regular basis the development manager, and the users' manager get together and discuss all the outstanding PIFs. Each one is either rejected (RIF!) or agreed to and signed-off, becoming a SIF.

The act of signing-off is crucial to all of this. It represents the culmination of the previous stages of assessment and review, but in addition re-emphasises that the procedure is a formal one. So formal in fact that it should form part of the initial agreement/contract between the users and the developers. Thus changes made without the use of the change control procedure will fall outside the scope of the agreed functionality. Note that both parties are bound by this, the users cannot demand extra functionality unless the developers agree to it and the users agree to the cost and timescale implications of the change; but further, the developers are also bound not to change the functionality of the system unilaterally without the consent of the users.

We have what is known in the jargon of the quality world as a 'complete audit trail'. This particular instance of a change control procedure addresses the control of contractual documents. It can easily be adapted for use on files, within a project team, or for handling feedback about user-guide or similar documentation. It is, however, somewhat labour-intensive, so I recommend that you apply it only to items that must be formally controlled. Determining which ones those may be (other than your contractual specification — usually the SEF) I leave to your skill and judgement.

9.3 Configuration management

9.3.1 You want what?

It's getting dark outside; the precipitation is oscillating between a cold steely rain, and a penetrating whirl of sleet. The day is drawing to a close, you're looking forward to leaving the office, fighting through the onset of winter to reach the warm comforts of home. Just as you are about to go, your boss strides over with a worried look on his face, and explains that International Gooey Foods have just been hit by a burst water-tank at the top of their sky-scraper. They've lost all their computer systems, didn't keep off-site backups, and so you need to build a copy of the system that you installed for them last year. You look up at your boss and exclaim 'You want what?!'

Why this reaction? Because you don't have any configuration management procedures or tools. As a result you have no idea what is in that system; you've made so many changes since it was delivered, and you don't even know if you've got a copy of those files stored away on tape. This is the classic configuration management nightmare; in essence it is very simple — you have no configuration management!

How would things be different if you did have some? There are two points of note. Firstly, you would have all the previous versions of all your files, safely stored and quickly available to you, via an easy-to-use index. Secondly, you would know what combination of these files (and that means probably not all of them) and which versions (which will vary from file to file) constitute the system installed at a particular site. Thus you have the ability simultaneously to hold different versions of a system, and to reproduce any particular version required at a moment's notice.

Notice that I haven't mentioned anything about tools. You could achieve all of this with a large dollop of self-discipline, paper, pencil, card index, and a sizeable tape rack. But then you're not that masochistic — are you?

9.3.2 What, another new toy?

Any software developer who, if not actually in his or her right mind, is at least within striking distance of it, would not attempt the paper-based approach. Such a developer would go and get a CM tool. And excellent fun such playthings can be. What do I mean by a CM tool? What does it do? And how does it do it?

There are various basic facilities you should demand from any likely candidate as a CM tool:

- It must store text (edit) files, with suitable levels of security to avoid their being accidently deleted.
- It must be able to store multiple versions of a file, and reproduce any of these versions.
- It must enable any of these versions to be 'checked-out' to a named developer, and while the file is 'checked-out' no-one else can access that version of the file.
- It must be able to create a 'snapshot' that identifies a particular version of a system in terms of the files that comprise it, and the versions of those files.

There are many extras that could prove useful:

- Some systems can hold build instructions and, when told to do so, rebuild a particular version of a system.
- That type of CM tool is then often able to hold intermediate object and executable (i.e. non-text) types of files.
- Various users of the tool can be configured with different levels of security, both with respect to the tasks they can do, and the files they can access.
- The ability to take commands from a command file, in addition to commands from an on-line user interface, is very helpful.
- A report generator that is able to answer complex queries about different versions of the system stored in the tool can be handy.
- Tying this report generator into the rest of the tool, so that it can be used to generate command files for the tool for complex tasks, can be invaluable.
- A comprehensive comment-prompting feature, which requires you to log a reason in an associated audit trail database for every command you give it, can help in ascertaining why certain decisions were taken.
- The ability to back-out (undo) commands, and remove files, albeit only with extremely rigorous security clearance, is worthwhile.

Okay, so there's your shopping list. But how, you may reasonably ask, does this tool achieve all these tasks?

9.3.3 File storage

The first requirement is that text tiles be stored, and stored safely. They are stored in what can be thought of as a library. This is a directory that is set aside to be used by the tool to hold the files. In fact, it holds copies of the files, which are augmented with special configuration information which I'll explain in a moment. The security facilities inherent in the computer's operating system are capitalised upon. All the files on the system can have various levels of access, often differing in their restrictiveness depending upon what task is to be done (i.e. anyone can read a file, but only its owner, the owning ID, can delete it). The highest level of security is often reserved for the files that hold the computer's operating system; these can be deleted only by the most senior operations staff. The CM tools also make use of this same strict security, and when a new file is added to the tool's library of files, it is given this high level of protection. In other words, once added to the tool's library, it is impossible for even the chief developer or project manager to remove the file, unless they enlist the co-operation of the head of the operations staff. The fact that the operating system is 'used' by the CM tool in this and other ways, means that most CM tools are in fact developed and sold by the vendors of the hardware. If a separate company sells a CM tool for a particular machine, it is likely that the firm will have worked closely with the hardware vendor both to ensure that it makes the most of the operating system, and that the tool won't have the ground cut out from under it (or in the worst case rendered inoperable) by unexpected enhancements in new releases of the operating system.

As should be obvious, if you are on a single-user system (a PC!) there is no sophisticated logon and security procedure for the CM tool to make use of. In such a case, the tool ends up doing the user-authorisation checking for itself.

Before we consider the next requirement I quickly need to adumbrate the rationale behind the numbering schemes that most CM tools use. They could just use sequential numbers 1, 2, 3, 4, . . . , etc. But this allows very little scope for identifying when a major change has occurred in the system and, in effect, a new release has been created. So, instead, most CM tools allow each file to have a two-part version number 1.00, 1.01, 1.02, . . . , 2.00, 2.01, 2.02, . . . , and so on. How many digits are allowed before and after the good old decimal point varies from tool to tool. Often, though, it's two in both cases, i.e. a maximum version number of 99.99. There are systems that allow extra features, providing for flexibility. More on that in a moment. Right now, you know all you need to know to follow the next paragraph.

The next basic requirement is that the tool be able to hold multiple versions of a single file, and be able to reproduce any of them at a moment's notice. This is where things start to get a little smart. Holding a complete copy of each different version of a file would be very wasteful of space, and would not be helpful, since it would not facilitate the production of reports on how these files differ. So the CM tool treats the file rather like a mini-program. When it is first created, i.e. added to the library, the file receives a header and then is stored pretty much 'as is'. See below.

```
Header info
text text text text text text text text
text text text text text text text text
text text text text text text text text
text text text text text text text text
text text text text text text text text
text text text text text text text text
text text text text text text text text
text text text text text text text text
```

```
text text text text text text text text
text text text text text text text text
text text text text text text text text
text text text text text text text text
text text text text text text text text
text text text text text text text text
text text text text text text text text
text text text text text text text text
text text text text text text text text
text text text text text text text text
text text text text text text text text
text text text text text text text text
text text text text text text text text
text text text text text text text text
```

When the next version of the file is added into the library, changes will have been made to it. This version will have a new number. Let's say we started with 1.00, then this new version will be 1.01, and it will include some new text, and (for the sake of our example) some of the original text will have been deleted. The tool does not store a copy of this file; instead it stores the changes, sometimes called deltas. It does this by inserting into the original file control information, which is never seen whenever the file is taken out of the library. This control information is basically a series of IF statements that turns the file into a pseudo-program. See below.

```
Header info
text text text text text text text text
text text text text text text text text
text text text text text text text text
text text text text text text text text
text text text text text text text text
text text text text text text text text
If x > = 1.01
new text  new text  new text  new text
new text  new text  new text  new text
Endif {1.01}
text text text text text text text text
text text text text text text text text
text text text text text text text text
text text text text text text text text
text text text text text text text text
text text text text text text text text
text text text text text text text text
If x < 1.01
text text text text text text text text
```

```
Endif {1.01}
text text text text text text text text
text text text text text text text text
text text text text text text text text
text text text text text text text text
text text text text text text text text
text text text text text text text text
text text text text text text text text
text text text text text text text text
```

The 'x' in the statements represents the version number of the file that the user has asked the CM tool to extract from the tool's library. So, if now version 1.00 was asked for, the original file would be provided; however, if 1.01 was requested, the new text would be included and a line of text of version 1.00 omitted. The file is modified in the same way if 1.01 is then further changed and another version is added to the library, this time 1.02. As you can see below, the IFs become nested, since the new changes can occur in any line of the new file.

```
Header info
text text text text text text text text
text text text text text text text text
If x < 1.02
text text text text text text text text
Endif {1.02}
text text text text text text text text
text text text text text text text text
text text text text text text text text
If x > = 1.01
new text new text new text new text
If x > = 1.02
more new text more new text more new text
Endif {1.02}
new text new text new text new text
Endif {1.01}
text text text text text text text text
text text text text text text text text
text text text text text text text text
text text text text text text text text
text text text text text text text text
text text text text text text text text
text text text text text text text text
If x < 1.01
text text text text text text text text
Endif {1.01}
text text text text text text text text
```

```
text text text text text text text text
text text text text text text text text
text text text text text text text text
text text text text text text text text
text text text text text text text text
text text text text text text text text
text text text text text text text text
```

This means that when a file is fetched out of the CM tool's library it has to undergo a certain amount of processing before it can be written into the directory of the user who requested it. Indeed, if a user asks for the twenty-fifth version of a file, then it may take the CM tool a moment or two to think about (process) it. In terms of efficiency, CM tools work best if only about 20 percent of the file is ever changed; more than that means that the space saving resulting from storing deltas (rather than multiple copies) is minimal, and that the processing time starts to increase. Time may not appear to be a factor for a single file, but a system comprising 250 files might take a couple of hours to retrieve from the library.

It is worth mentioning that incrementing the major number (e.g. 1.05 to 2.00) does not affect the way the IFs occur in the file in the library, and it does not preclude the use of the subsequent 1.*nn* series numbers (i.e. 1.06, 1.07); more, much more, on this later.

9.3.4 There's never a policeman when you need one

As a percentage of the population, the numbers in the police forces of most industrialised countries are minimal. If there appear to be a lot on duty when you see TV coverage of a demonstration confronting a phalanx of them, strategically positioned behind Plexiglas shields, then go wander around the rest of the city in which this crowd control incident is occurring. You won't find many left. In point of fact, they police the populace they serve, by consent. Notice those last words, 'serve', 'consent'. Most of the people, most of the time, exercise self-discipline; the police merely deter and occasionally prevent things from getting out of hand.

It's the same story with the 'check-out' facility that all CM tools offer. They work only in my previously trumpeted 'culture of responsibility'. The tool acts as a gate-keeper, but can be subverted, ignored, and hood-winked. This facility will be of benefit only if it is used in a mature responsible manner. But what is it, this 'check-out' facility?

Its aim is to prevent changes to a file from getting lost. If the tool wasn't present, you could have a situation where two different people, A and B, both take version 1.01 of a file out of the library. They are in contention for the same file. Independently of each other, they change it — in different conflicting ways. Then 'A' puts her version of the file back in as 1.02. The other developer 'B' replaces

Figure 9.1
'Lost change'

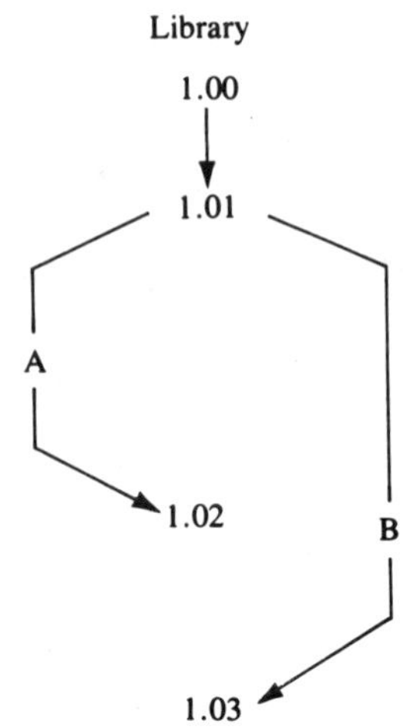

his as 1.03. But 1.03 does not include the changes in 1.02. If this is confusing look at Figure 9.1.

So A's changes would be lost. The only way we can be sure that they will not be lost is to deny developer B access to the file until A has finished. That way B's changes will be made to version 1.02 (rather than 1.01) and so when the next version, 1.03, is added to the library it will include both sets of changes. See Figure 9.2. And yes, you guessed right, this does impose constraints of scheduling. Yes, it can be a pain, an inconvenience, but it is far less troublesome than the problems that may arise later when it transpires that the live system is missing some crucial code because a file was not 'checked-out' while it was being changed, and hence code was lost.

So how does the tool do this? It has a catalogue of all the files in the library. Most tools these days use a relational database for the catalogue; it improves the quality of the reports that the tool can produce. But I digress. In this catalogue, the tool can mark any particular version of a file as 'checked-out' and record the ID of the developer who has checked the file out. The tool then denies all other developers the ability to check-out the same version of the file, until the first developer checks the file back in, in the process making a new version of the file.

It is often still possible to get a 'read-only' copy of that version of the file. This is where the hood-winking can start, but I don't advise it, unless you want to live dangerously. Some tools can be set up to allow multiple check-outs of the same version of a file, but again, unless used carefully, problems can quickly arise.

9.3.5 *Smile for the camera*

The last basic requirement is the trickiest to understand. The facility is needed because it is often the case that different sites can have releases of the system

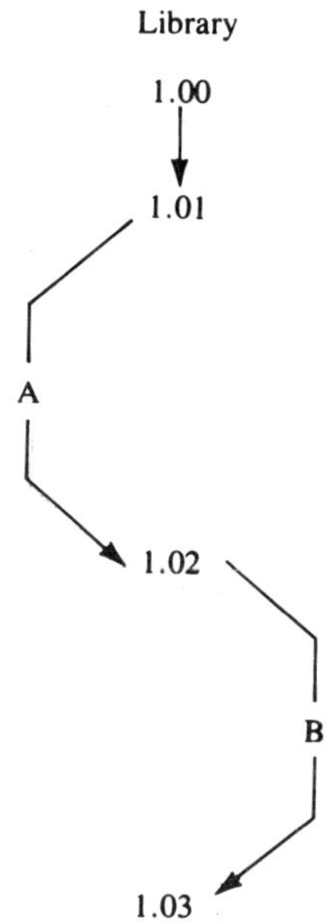

Figure 9.2
'Found change'

that differ not only in the stage of development (i.e. site Z has files from release 2, site Y from release 1) but also in terms of configuration (site Z needs only the chocolate-peanut-tasting subsystem, whilst Y needs that plus the marshmallow-fluffing subsystem). This means that we need to be able to keep track of different 'snapshots' of the system. The facility can also be used to track which versions of the system are under development, unit test or system test. Instead of asking for a list of files (a subset of all the files that comprise the system), entailing having to know and then give each one's version number, you can, by using the snapshot facility, simply ask the CM tool to fetch site X's system out of the library. Figure 9.3 may make things a little clearer.

Figure 9.3 shows a simple system, made up of eight files (A through H). The blobs represent different versions of the files. There are two releases of the system; file A got as far as version 1.06, then release 1 was declared, so all the files were upgraded and their numbering continued from 2.00. It is possible to ask the system for release 1 by requesting it fetch all files; and giving a version number of 1.*, for each file this will get the highest 1.*nn* version.

The only site that is actually on a numbered release is site Y. Of the other sites Z has later versions of some of the files, whereas X has earlier versions of some of the files. Restating, X and Y each have all the files, Z needs only some of the files. Y can be easily retrieved from the system by asking for all files of version number 1.*; this is not possible for X or Z. They need to be identified in some other manner. The wavy lines indicate the 'snapshots' which are named after the sites that X and Z represent. For snapshot Z, the circles around files B and E indicate that B and E are not in Z's snapshot, since they comprise the marshmallow-fluffing subsystem that is not needed at site Z.

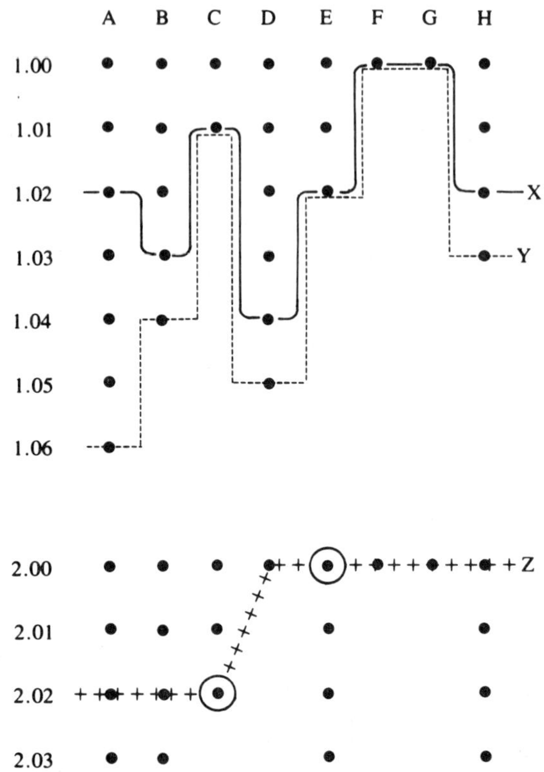

Figure 9.3
Snapshot organisation

9.3.6 Would Sir wish to take the option value package?

Never mind about getting from Aberdeen to Bradford; how about some leather upholstered seats, an eight-speaker CD system, and a voice-synthesising trip-computer that actually tells you your miles per litre. Do you really need all these optional extras? I'll leave that to you and the delightful car dealer, but meantime back at the office you have another set of options to consider. I've already covered the necessities for a CM tool, but what about the optional features? I'll try and provide a little more detail so you can see if they're likely to be of use to you.

- *Build* instructions held in the CM tool are a great time-saver. They force you to think, at an early stage, about how the system should be built properly. They then pay back all this cogitation by enabling you to always have an up-to-date system. In defining the build procedure, you will have created a set of dependency relationships, i.e. which source files copy in text from other library files, which object files result from compiling which source files, and which object files need to be bound together before they constitute an executable. This means that when a new version of a file is checked back into the tool's library, the tool knows which files must be recompiled for the changes to be fully incorporated into the system. This may be only half a dozen, and can be done in ten minutes, much easier than a complete system rebuild. You can run these mini-builds whenever a change occurs, and your system will always be up-to-date.

- *Object and executable* become as important as the source. There is a school of thought which argues that unless one can safely hold executables, identify them with snapshots, and trace them back to the source that produced them, then we are not really managing the whole system, but rather only its inputs.

- *Security* is very useful in a CM tool. Chances are you don't want everybody to be able to delete snapshots, rename files, and even delete files. If access can be restricted to a subset of all the tool's commands, to particular files, and maybe specific versions of these files, then people won't stray into sensitive areas where they're not welcome. And the integrity of your code will be increased.

- *Command files* come into their own when you have a system with hundreds of constituent files. Mistakes will happen if you have to type in every command at a prompt. If, however, you can create command files, preferably using the tool's own report-generator, then you have a more watertight way of carrying out complex sequences of operations and, believe me, tools are very good at requiring you to execute such sequences.

- *A report-generator* is invaluable. You will find yourself wanting to know who has which versions of which files locked? What files constitute which snapshots? What were the changes made between versions 1.05 and 3.02? All sorts of things. And a report-generator that is able to interrogate the tool's database, making use of its relational nature (if applicable), can be a great boon.

- *Comments* can be very useful, because (in case you'd forgotten) you are human. This means you, and the rest of your team, will find it hard to remember the specific reason for every task they carried out with the tool. But unless the tool demands a comment, before it allows a task to proceed, you may well forget to provide one — which you would later discover would be a shame.

- *Backing out* commands doesn't sound very promising, but from time to time the ability to do so will be a godsend. Once again, this is because you are human, and will make mistakes, check-in the wrong files, into the wrong versions, and add them to the wrong snapshots. The ability to unwind your previous command and get it right, without having to resort to hood-winking the tool with bodges, kludges and work-arounds, will keep things a lot clearer.

9.4 Policies on CM tool usage

9.4.1 The solution to all my problems!

Quality is about applying your critical faculties. It is not about slavishly following standards, blindly adhering to procedures, and unthinkingly using tools. If you treat a CM tool as a substitute for your brain, then you are being lazy, devaluing your own grey matter and attributing greater powers to a heap of etched silicon than that heap deserves. Change doesn't control itself; configuration tools don't manage themselves. You must intervene and impose a plan, establish a policy, and (most important) periodically review these plans and policies to determine their effectiveness.

To try and make these abstractions a little more concrete let me detail three different approaches to using a CM tool. I will follow on with some general issues that cut across all three approaches.

I need to lay bare an underlying assumption or two. Specifically, I presume that you have a system that is growing and evolving, that having installed it at one site you are going to install it at another. And that this second site won't be the last, and will differ from the first in two ways. Firstly, the system will have evolved; some bugs not yet fixed at the live site will already be fixed in the newer version, and some enhancements will have been made, so that the second site has increased functionality. Secondly, however, although it may have been enhanced, there may be a different distribution of functionality — back to the question of whether all sites need the marshmallow-fluffing subsystem. And as a consequence of all this, things begin to snowball; you find yourselves planning to install the system at a number of sites, and the development work for each of these sites cannot be done in sequence. Timescales are too tight; you will have to work in parallel. Does this start to sound a little worrying? Good, I've set the stage. There is a basic question you must ask — what is the degree of centrifugalness that my system has? How strong is its tendency to try and grow in different directions at the same time? The stronger the tendency to split, the more you need an approach to manage this — not necessarily to stop it — but to manage it. There are three distinct approaches you can take:

- cohesive;
- oscillatory;
- highly bespoke.

Let's look at them in more detail.

- A *cohesive* approach aims to treat the system very much like a shrink-wrapped, off-the-shelf product. It acknowledges that there may be different features important at different sites, but requires that the system be constructed such that all features are in all versions of it. The different ways of using the system are achieved by configuring it differently when it is installed; all the options are run-time options. So sites take all the functionality in the current release of the system whether they use that functionality or not.

On the plus side this means that maintenance is comparatively easy, since everyone on a particular release has an identical system. The downside is that this approach imposes higher cost and time penalties at the development stage. Fundamentally, all enhancements must be able to work with all other enhancements. Internal contradictions are not allowed. So there has to be very thorough reviewing at every stage in the development process. The technical authority must have a thorough grasp of the whole system, so as to ensure that any new enhancement does not compromise existing functionality, or unduly constrain further developments.

This does, however, make the use of the CM tool fairly painless. Parallel changes (two people subverting the tool and changing the code simultaneously) will not be allowed. All changes must be made to the one 'checked-out' version of the code. There is, though, quite a communication overhead, since the individual charged with changing the code must co-ordinate requirements from different sources (sites, projects). This imposes a requirement of synchronicity upon the different projects; some may have to wait until all the changes have been made for all the sites.

- An *oscillatory* approach is so-named because the system sometimes has only one line of development (like the cohesive approach) but at other times can split into a number of parallel paths. This approach allows different development projects to run at their own pace, freeing them of the synchronicity requirement.

The approach does not, however, allow contradictions to arise. The different paths have their enhancements integrated back into the system, and thus a new release is created. Since all paths are integrated back in, reviews must be undertaken (as per the cohesive approach) to confirm that none of the enhancements will conflict. To be sure that everything does still work after a path has been integrated back in, a full system (in fact regression) test should be undertaken.

This approach can make the use of the CM tool into more of a challenge. It allows multiple check-outs of the same version of a file, to different people. So a tool which permits this, and can track it, is required. I know this sounds like breaking one of the basic tenets of CM tools. However, I am duty-bound to point out that this is a classic example of where the tool should not drive the policy, but vice versa. I have seen this approach work very successfully — in a disciplined environment. It can also make use of one other feature a tool may have, the automatic cut-and-pasting of late changes. What? Consider the situation where version 1.05 of a file is copied forward to become version 2.00, the starting point for release 2. In the meantime a pre-existing project 'checks-out' 1.05 and isn't ready to give it back. When eventually the project is, the version becomes 1.06. But the changes between 1.05 and 1.06 will not be present in any version of the file extracted as version 2.00 or higher. Say the second project eventually creates version 2.01 of the file, and it is now time to integrate the changes from the first project to bring the paths together and create a composite file. Some tools can identify the changes made between 1.05 and 1.06, and in effect 'cut-and-paste' them into a new version (2.02) of the file. See Figure 9.4.

This facility can be dangerous. It can flag a situation where there is a conflict in the text and the 'cut-and-paste' cannot be cleanly inserted. But it cannot guarantee that the new version of the file (2.02) will run correctly. The facility is a glorified editing macro; it eliminates the chance of error that might arise if the changes had to be retyped, but it does not excuse the developer from testing the code. Quite the contrary, the developer is obligated to exercise this composite

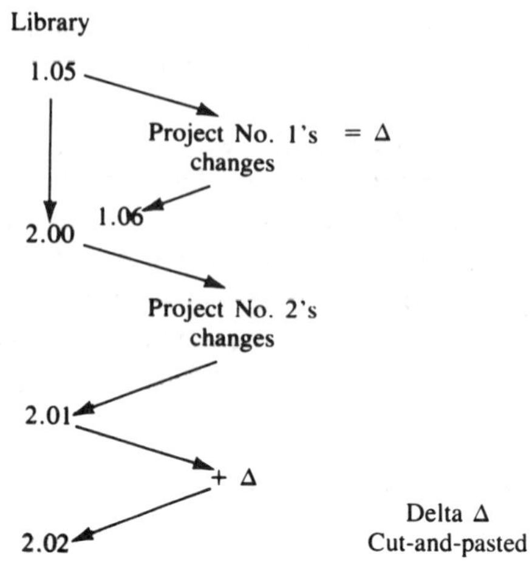

Figure 9.4 Automatic cut and paste

until it's fit to drop, paying particular attention to any possible interactions between the (until now separate) changes made by the two projects.

- A *highly bespoke* approach takes the opposite stance to that of the cohesive approach. It does not require each site to have the same version of the code; rather it allows site-specific releases to be constructed. However, it can become a total muddle unless some discipline is imposed.

This can be done by using in-code configuration symbols. These can differentiate different functional options. It uses a precompiler, which first reads a configuration file to determine which options a particular site is using, then scans the code and creates an appropriate source file for input to the real compiler.

In essence this is conditional compilation. The good aspect is that parallel developments can take place on the same file with no interaction until the configuration symbol controlling that development is made generally available. Up to that stage the code controlled by that symbol is just ignored by the precompiler when it builds systems for other sites. So parallel projects can run without disrupting each other. And this allows for conflicting functionality to exist in the same file, under different control symbols. As a result, complex rules are developed for configuring systems; if a site takes certain options, then it must take others upon which the initial options depended, and further, it cannot take certain specific options as these might conflict with the initial options. As a result the review overhead is less, since changes do not have to be bent and mangled so that they all work within the same version of the code.

The price that is paid for such an approach is that there is no one official version of the system. Since each site has its own unique version of the object code, it will probably have its own unique bugs. Maintenance becomes more costly. It is unlikely that copies of all the different systems at different sites will be instantly available. It may be necessary to reload the appropriate system from a backup tape, or even rebuild it from scratch. One consequence is that the bug fixes can also be added under configuration control symbols.

This approach requires a tool that includes a build facility, since a lot of preprocessing and rebuilds are involved. In addition, the tool should also be able to handle multiple 'check-outs'.

9.4.2 *Which is best?*

'Ça dépend', there is no one approach that suits all systems. I've seen all these work with reasonable levels of success. The technology exists to support all of them; the issue here is policy and planning. You have to decide which development approach and scenario is most applicable to your team, organisation, and style of working. All I can suggest is that having picked one, you stick with it. Chopping and changing will only generate more confusion — and that's the last thing you need.

9.4.3 *Issues*

Cutting across these configuration management approaches you have some other issues to consider. Once again, these do not come with right or wrong answers, but rather require you to apply your thinking skills to determine what is most appropriate for you in your own unique circumstances.

First we have the delivery of bug fixes. Any complex system will generate a number of problems every month; if you're unlucky (or built a poor-quality system!) they'll come along every week. Having fixed them, you have a question on how to deliver them. Apart from the most urgent ones, crucial to the continued running of the system, should you provide a drip, drip, drip of fixes whenever they are completed, or bundle them together into a mini-release? The answer will depend in part on how much regression testing the users will want to do when they receive a fix. But it is also affected by whether there is a CM tool at the user site. Sounds a bit radical. It could be useful, especially if it includes the ability to do mini-builds. It would make the drip, drip, drip style of delivery easier, and could keep a comprehensive record of what executables really are at the users' site.

Next come new enhancements? Should sites which were installed prior to this enhancement being made also receive it? This partly depends on the nature of the agreement between the users, developers, and maintainers. It might be easier to upgrade the site to the newer release, although this could involve a lot of regression testing. The point here is that, if you do choose to reimplement an enhancement on an earlier version of a file, very few CM tools can help you. Although they may be able to copy changes forward, I am not aware of any that can 'cut-and-paste' changes back into earlier versions.

Remember, CM tools do not help you with ensuring that your system maintains forward compatibility. That is, new changes don't destroy existing functionality. A CM tool is only a librarian, you have to ensure through reviews that code doesn't 'burn its bridges', unless you want it to. You may be in a situation where existing sites will never take more recent versions of a system, so you need not worry about forward compatibility. But make such a determination explicitly; don't stumble into a blind alley and find yourself with no way forward.

9.5 Final thoughts

So you should now know what change control and configuration management are all about. You ought to be more enlightened, but you should also feel a little worried. Unless you are naturally given to smug complacency in the face of all challenges, you ought to be wondering whether you are doing enough about addressing issues of CC and CM. If you aren't worried, then you probably haven't read this chapter closely enough; go back to the start, and while you're reading it keep asking yourself how your team deals with each issue. Write down your conclusions, then act on them!

9.6 Questions

1. So what is the difference between TweedleBowie and TweedleStardust?
2. How will you go about fostering a 'culture of responsibility'?
3. What are your change control procedures going to cover?
4. Who are the information conduits?
5. And their deputies?
6. What will happen if you try and live without configuration management?
7. Who's going to investigate what tools you could use?
8. When must they report back?
9. In the meantime, when will all the necessary people meet to formulate a policy on using the tool?
10. How will you seek to enthuse the rest of your team into adopting the ideas of CC and CM?

10 Management of development

10.1 Introduction

10.1.1 'Oh no, not again'

The captain's voice crackles over the PA system. As you'd already surmised, since the plane is now level, you've reached your cruising altitude. You settle back, into your non-ergonomic, body-contorting sedation-device, more commonly known as an airline recliner (!?!), and flip through the in-flight magazine. What catches your eye, while hurtling through the air at 600 miles an hour, 35,000 feet above the small green–blue place we all call home? Surprisingly enough, an article on project management. You had always meant to get around to reading more on this subject, but never seemed to have the time. However, on this occasion, since you're not going anywhere (other than your destination), you realise that this is the perfect opportunity.

You start reading; halfway through the second paragraph the article just disappears — leaving only a pointer instructing you to turn to page 127. You turn the pages, skimming the duty-free ads, glancing at the title of your in-flight movie, but before you arrive at page 127 the PA crackles again, the chief steward announces that lunch will now be served. Too late, you remember airlines only serve food if they are about to hit a nasty patch of turbulence. Right on cue you are buffeted in your seat, the fasten seat-belt sign illuminates, and you start wondering if you should have updated your will. And it doesn't stop; the plane continues to bounce merrily all the way to Bangkok, and the attractiveness of all activities (bar praying) evaporates.

Down on the ground, safely in one piece, you realise that it's happened again. You never did get to read that article. So here's the remedy, this chapter. Should you ever find a copy of it stuffed into an airline seat pocket do contact the publishers! This is the wisdom that you should have been reading last time you were over six miles high.

And who should be reading this chapter? Everyone, not only managers, but the managed. After all, if you're on the receiving end of poor-quality management, you owe it to yourself to discover how you can avoid the same mistakes in the future, and maybe even re-educate your own manager.

So is this the last screed you'll ever need to read on management? No! There is a lot of very good stuff elsewhere, covering both general management and specifically project-development management. Repeating all of that would triple the size of this book, and reduce its usefulness to you. You'll read them in due course; you should.

Meanwhile back at the ranch, you're about to start on a very personal statement, selectively highlighting certain approaches and issues that I feel merit special consideration. The omission of any particular one of your favourite pet topics does not mean that I am advocating that you should ignore it. Remember, although this chapter is about management, the book is about quality. What I am concerned with here are approaches to management that will yield high-quality systems.

10.2 Project performance criteria

10.2.1 Are you a success?

Why? Yes, why? Oh, by the way, did you answer yes or no? And on what particular scale were you judging yourself, your skills, your achievements? And who am I to attempt to judge whether you are a success or not? Actually, I'm a nobody. In this context I am not on the list of your judges. Although I'm about the only person who isn't.

And therein lies the problem. You have many other judges, all of whom do feel perfectly entitled to pronounce upon the success, or otherwise, of the endeavour you are managing. There are the users, lots of them (take another look at Chapter 2 'Initiation and Requirements'). Then there's your own line-manager, your project team, your corporate peers, senior management, the third-party consultants, and — not least — yourself. And what is this problem, other than the sheer multiplicity of overseers? It is the way in which they seek to measure your degree of success.

There are three classic yardsticks against which you will find yourself measured. Time, budget, and specification — the trinity of project management. Most people will use all three (and then some) but, inconveniently, they will assign them varying degrees of importance. Each judge will calculate a 'weighted average' but will assign to each component different amounts of significance.

Each yardstick comes with a point marked on it which acts as your target. There is a date by which the system must be up and running — processing live data. There is a budget which you are allowed to spend, to buy people, materials, consultancy, lunch (?); but this budget has a limit to it. And then there's the specification, the controlling specification (with luck approximating to the SEF described earlier in this book); it is a tricky target to hit, since it comes with many constituent parts. You may not even be sure of whether you have hit this target, unless you have been well behaved and created cross-references between all the levels of specifications and test scripts (only if this is true can you lay claim to having achieved full traceability).

• *Date*. The date is the most tangible of the targets. The people who will worry most about the date are the users; other people may appear to be worrying about the date, but in reality they are concerned about the budget and are equating time elasped with the money spent. This may be the case if the users are in the same company and buy the DP department's time by the week (it all depends on internal accounting systems), or if the users are in a separate company and being charged 'time and materials' rates. However, time will not equal money if the contract is fixed-price, at least not in the sense that an over-run will result in the users paying more. Nevertheless the users might find themselves losing money if the system is delivered late; indeed certain industries have a culture of penalty payments or 'liquidated damages', to cover such scenarios.

So the users will want the project to come in on time. Indeed, they would not object to it arriving early. However, if the estimation was correct (big if) then this might signal that the development was not thorough, it skipped and skimped, and the resultant deliverables would not be of a very high quality.

Your management may behave a little oddly in respect of time. It will understand that meeting the time target, but using more staff than estimated, can bust the budget. So although it will like to present an image of a DP department (or company) that delivers on time, it may be amenable to the argument that not allocating the corporate hot-shot to the project may cause the project to over-run by an (avoidable) period of two weeks but keep it in budget. So do not allow management to judge you solely on this criterion.

The project team wants to be associated with a successful project. It tends to be evaluated in terms of whether it completes its tasks on time, and so it may be eager to keep to the schedule. But the point I have been emphasising throughout this book is that meeting the schedule is useless if the code is of poor quality. Here is where it falls to the project manager (PM) to attempt (and succeed in!) some re-education, and to demonstrate the veracity of the PM's belief in quality by using it as the yardstick with which programmer performance is assessed.

The third-party consultants are paid by the day. They will exhibit a significant tendency towards being just ever-so-slightly two-faced. They will recite the litany of keeping to the schedule, but will lap up all the extra fees that come from every day the project over-runs. Officially they will condemn you; in private they'll love you.

Oh, and you. How about yourself? Do you rate keeping to the schedule as a mark of success? Should you? Would it be better if you bent/twisted this belief into one whereby you were a success if you provided good service to the users, and included keeping to the schedule as one aspect of providing good service?

• *Budget*. The budget reflects the fact that the staff who do your programming cost your organisation money. Your organisation may be a separate company from the users, in which case you constitute a 'profit-centre', and if you don't make a profit you'll be out on your ear. If you're a DP department you are probably required to break even, although now some (e.g. UK clearing banks) are starting to sell their services to other companies. Whatever the circumstances you certainly are not allowed to be a 'cost-centre'.

The budget target may or may not matter to the users. Can you remember what I just said about this in the preceding section? Starkly, if a budget over-run doesn't impact them, they won't care; and more to the point they will still expect the same level of service and quality whether you're over-running or not. Indeed, they may well not be allowed to know, if it's a matter of a separate company's profitability.

Your managers will definitely judge you according to your ability to keep to your budget. The weight they give this will depend on the corporate culture in which you both work; if their senior managers judge them solely on the profitability of their divisions, then they will judge you using only this one yardstick. They may take a slightly longer-term view if your project is creating something which could become a product; you may be allowed to overspend, provided that in the long run all you've done is create a loss-leader, and that the extra expenditure will be recouped by subsequent installations of the same system.

The project team won't even think about money unless you raise the subject. It may be unaware of the underestimation that occurred at the start of the project, and thus be puzzled about why the project is headed for a loss despite the fact the team has been working thirty-six hours a day. You have a special responsibility, to explain the budget disciplines the project is under, but to do so in a manner such that the team doesn't make a complete about-face, ignore quality, ignore service, and come to believe that money is everything.

The third-party consultants are a bit like the users, kept in the dark. Unless you tell them they won't know of your budget, and any problems it has, and won't care.

You, well if you don't make your financial targets, your neck may well be on the line. But if you do bring the boat in on budget, but cost the operation an horrendous stack of groats caused by a never-ending stream of maintenance problems, then your shiny medals will rapidly fade into the dull lustre of more base metal.

- *Specification*. Once you have a signed, sealed specification, you must meet it. But the operative word here is 'meet', which I will clarify in a moment.

The users will use this as their primary yardstick. If the system doesn't meet the specification, expect plenty of blue language and a lot of late nights — you will not have succeeded.

Your managers may or may not view this as important. They will undoubtedly articulate a belief in it, but if conformance with the specification can be achieved only at the cost of a budget over-run, then you'll discover whether they were merely paying lip-service to the concept.

The project team does not think of itself as a financial income generator, project cost driver, deployable Gantt chart resource. Its members think of themselves as programmers. They will judge the project, your project, a success if you implement the specification correctly. To them the project might be even more successful if it exceeded the specification, and delivered some extra (unrequested) functionality. This is where the financial facts of life come into play; you must explain that more functionality does not necessarily equal more success, and can cause a tumble on to the downslope of a catastrphe curve, resulting in financial failure.

The third-party consultants keep the wolves from their doors by ensuring that you meet the specification. They are in some respects the arbiters of the extent to which you succeed in meeting the specification. In fact, they will ensure that you will succeed in this area, as they will bark at your heels, chivvy, and chide you until the specification is met. However, by this point you may have overshot your time and budget.

You? Well that's really your call. Does meeting the specification rank high in your definition of successful project management? Should it? Why?

10.2.2 The fourth dimension

There is one other dimension along which you should assess your degree of success. Guess what — it's quality! My aim in this book is to get you thinking in such a manner that the trinity automatically becomes a quaternary. In fact you should think of quality as being not only one of the four measures of success, but the foremost measure of success.

Now, before you say anything, I am not going to accept bleats that by meeting the specification you have created a high-quality system. As conditions go, meeting the specification is necessary, but not sufficient. A fundamental question is begged by such a claim — is the specification worth meeting? Only if the specification is a high-quality one will the system stand a chance of being of equally high quality.

Measuring quality is not as straightforward as the other goals. So most people don't even attempt to assess their performance on this scale. How should you measure your performance with respect to quality? Remember, there are two aspects: qualitative and quantitative. I have been stressing the qualitative throughout the book; go back and look at some of the checklists, especially near the start; if you'd like to dabble with some numbers, review the advice on design quality and the statistical interpretation of error rates. But, most of all, go and visit the users, and ask them one simple question — are they happy with the system you've built for them?

10.3 Project management techniques

10.3.1 Means to ends

Right then, we've looked at your aims, to build a high-quality system that conforms to its specification, arrives at the users on time, and doesn't cost your boss more than he or she thought it would. How do you manage to achieve this?

• *Administration*. The basic challenge is the volume and variety of things that you need to keep track of. If you're not a natural list-maker, develop the skill (does that make you an un-natural list-maker?). Either you will be on top of the world, or the world will be weighing heavily on your shoulders. In the latter case you will always be running to stay in the same place, interrupt-driven and reactive. The former stance is much more effective; if you are pro-active you call the shots. How do you get pro-active? Always write down everything that happens, where you'll find it again, possibly in a project-diary. Make lists of tasks to be done, and update these as the actions are cleared; such updates only occur if you regularly review these lists, tracking progress on all open tasks. Now you're in the habit of reviewing things, keep going over the checklists (that elsewhere in this book I've prompted you to write), so that you are asking yourself questions about issues and potential problems before they happen, not at a 'project post-mortem' meeting. I appreciate this all sounds too trivial for words, but getting the basics right is fundamental. They provide the foundation upon which all the more sophisticated techniques are built.

Two further points about avoiding chaos and nasty surprises. File all your documentation, including letters and minutes of meetings, promptly and in their proper location (as specified in your documentation plan). And talk to everyone else in the team, keep them informed about what everyone else on the project is doing, and ask them about how they might tackle such-and-such a problem while it's still hypothetical.

• *The work*. Controlling the actual tasks appears trivial, simple, and obvious. But not devoting enough time and effort to doing it properly will result in the whole caboosh boomeranging back on you, when you least expect it.

The idea of partitioning the project into a hierarchy of phases that themselves split down into more and more refinements, until tasks suitable for individuals appear, is now so common as to need little further elaboration. The trick is to use it comprehensively. Ensure that it is drawn up on Day One. It doesn't matter that you'll have only partial information; you can always redraw it later, and if you wait for complete information you'll be chained to your desk until the cows come home. You must focus on the activities, not the people. And you need to consider all activities, not just 'spec'n'codin'n'testin''. There are user-liaison meetings, document-review sessions, planning meetings, progress meetings, report-writing sessions, contract negotiations, and this list is far from complete.

The phases can be borrowed from the classic 'waterfall model', look at the left side of the stepped-valley in Chapter 5, 'Testing', and imagine water cascading down it. The bigger and more complex your project, the more formal you should get, and the more likely you are to need some PC-based tools or work-benches. But don't rush ahead of yourself, and create a fancy schedule that turns out to be useless because you didn't get the work breakdown completely sorted out.

In case the three classic beasts aren't familiar to you, take a quick look at Figure 10.1, which illustrates the difference between, a work breakdown structure (WBS), a PERT network, and a Gantt chart. As you can see, the WBS identifies the tasks

Figure 10.1
Project planning techniques

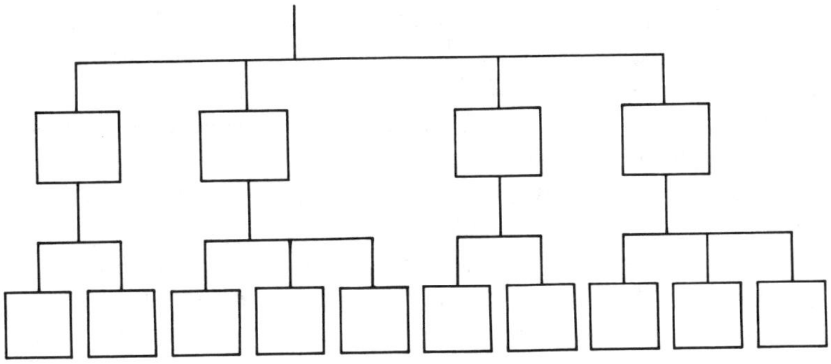

A WBS

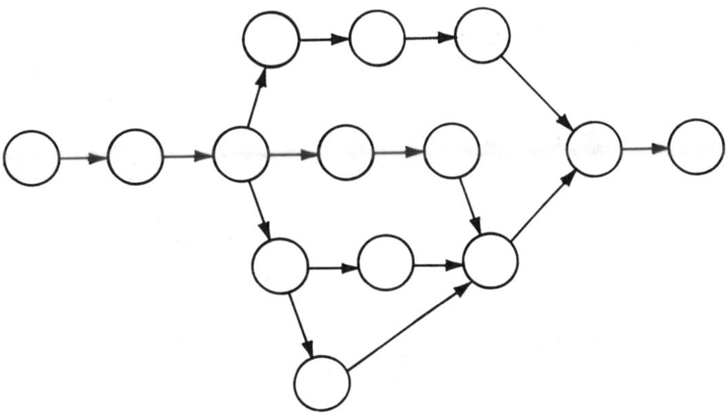

A PERT network

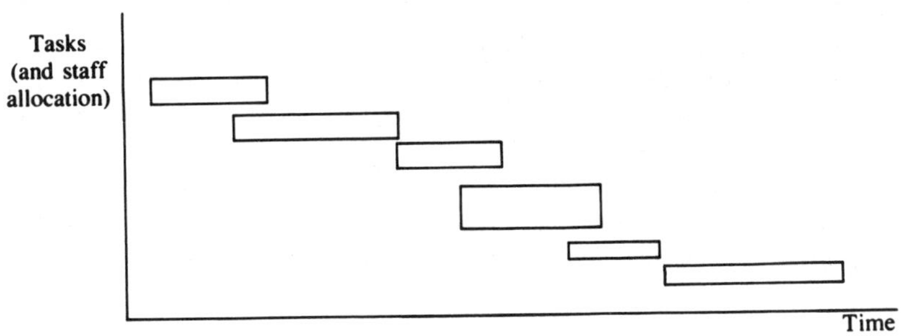

A Gantt chart

(all of them!) and can be refined such that each task can be assigned to a particular individual. There is no mention of time and people, but a WBS can be created without PC-based tools. It tends to help if you give each task a unique code, probably a combination of letter (to represent phase) and number; this can get quite elaborate if you choose to include a code reflecting the subsystem upon which this activity is being carried out.

PERT networks (programme evaluation and review technique) do include time, and they need tools. The nodes (blobs) represent activities, and the arrows represent which activities depend upon the one at the start of the arrow being complete before they can begin (other conventions sometimes reverse this, placing activities on the arrows). Whatever convention is chosen the activities are sequential; you are not allowed to loop back to a previous activity. Lastly, you start to dream up some numbers — this is where the tool helps. You guess how long each activity will take, and with a little mathematical jiggery-pokery your tool will provide you with an estimate of how long the project will probably take, together with earliest and latest start and finish dates for each task. These will give most tasks some latitude; task Z could start anytime between week 10 and week 14 without jeopardising the overall project. It couldn't start before week 10 because even if all the tasks that precede it run fine, they won't be complete until then. If it started later than week 14, it would delay other tasks and hence the whole project. There are various paths through this network; however, one (or more) may be critical. This means that for each task on the path, its earliest start-time and it's latest start-time are the same. So what? Just a mathematical nicety — yes? No, because these tasks have no leeway in when they start; any delay will adversely affect the project. They are critical to the success of the project, and all must run on schedule. If you don't create such a network, you may not realise what your critical tasks are.

PERT networks are good at showing dependencies which the next representation of tasks can't show; however, Gantt charts help to show how the project is actually staffed-up. Most tools can take a database of tasks, and display them not only in PERT network form, but also as a chart of horizontal bars. Each bar represents a task, its length the time it takes to complete the task and, on some tools, its height the number of staff assigned to the task, so that its area equals the person-effort needed. The staff can be identified (on the vertical axis) against each task, and a calendar set up horizontally. This is where the classic waterfall model comes from. However, if the chart includes everyone on the project, it can be difficult for individual staff members to work out what they are doing when. There are two solutions to this: some tools can produce Gantt charts for each person; others will give a list of tasks and dates.

Smart tools not only allow you to insert estimates and create plans, but to add real data as the work progresses. These tools can greatly help tracking, progress-reporting and replanning (should it become necessary).

- *Money*. Whether you are a profit-centre, or only required to break even, you need to track your costs carefully. If you're allowed to be a cost-centre, someone will still want to know if maybe you could cost the enterprise a little less in the future, please, pretty please ...

If you're particularly unlucky you may have to make a guess at the cost of the whole shebang, before you've even started. So what are your costs? There are the buff boxes and other technological gismos (communication links'n'things), people's expenses (lunch — as often as possible), and the expense of people. Warm breathing humanoids will craft this masterpiece, and their time will cost you money. Well, it will in most cases; some DP department heads dish out '*n*' programmers to the development team for this financial year, and they're then yours to do with as you please. But in most cases you'll have to pay for your staff, by the day, if not the hour.

This is where we enter the black art of estimating. You may feel like just guessing on the basis of a combination of gut instinct and previous experience. However, if you'd like to base your estimate on some numerical reasoning, and increase the likelihood that it is an accurate estimate, then read on. There is a classic book in this field by Boehm [17] that most of the ideas I present here come from, and should you wish to delve deeper I advise you to study it carefully (and practise weight-lifting, it covers over 750 pages!).

Let me start with some warnings. Numbers work only if a decision is made at a high level in the organisation to collect the data necessary for their consistent use. The problem is that, although research has found a good correspondence between the number of delivered source instructions (in thousands — KDSI) and the effort and hence cost involved in building a system, it is not at all obvious how given a stark user-requirement one can determine the likely size of the resultant system. What is needed is a quantitative measure of functionality, or maybe complexity, that can be derived from a specification and turned into a KDSI estimate, and thus a cost estimate. Until such a measure hits the scene, you will have to rely on local historic data, i.e. data collected by your own organisation about previous projects, which may allow you to establish a relation between certain attributes of a specification and the eventual size of a system in KDSI. (I have had the term 'function point' drawn to my attention by various people who have seen early drafts of this book. This is not an area I am familiar enough with to write about with any authority, so instead I suggest you read *Estimating with MkII Function Point Analysis* (HMSO, 1991. ISBN 0-946683-53-0).)

Only your own data is really worthwhile because a lot of factors can affect the basic estimating equations. Boehm identifies three distinct software development scenarios:

- 'embedded mode' where timescales are tight but the work is ground-breaking; unusual approaches are necessary, but the system is subject to tight constraints and must adhere fully to the specifications;
- 'organic mode' involves a small in-house team developing a system in an applications area that it is already very familiar with and subject to comparatively lax constraints;
- 'semi-detached mode' is obviously(!) the half-way house between these.

The point here is that borrowing data from a set of organic projects will completely disrupt the estimating for an embedded mode project. Use only your own data.

The data so gathered (or estimated) on the size in KDSI can be fed into a couple of equations to get the effort (in person-months) and schedule (in months). The model that yields all of this is known as CoCoMo (constructive cost model) and can be summarised thus:

$$\text{Effort} = \text{Productivity} * \text{KDSI}$$

Productivity can be affected by personal ability, the complexity of the system, the amount of software that might be reused, and the technology that is applied.

The effort can then be used to derive the time required to complete the development such that:

$$\text{Time} = 2.5 * \text{Fn(Effort)}$$

where Fn(Effort) is a function that raises the effort to different powers, 0.38, 0.35, 0.32, depending on whether the project-mode is organic, semi-detached, or embedded, respectively.

If all this stuff has whetted your whistle, then power yourself full steam ahead into Boehm; you'll have fun. He refines the model for almost every possible variant in a project. However, if this has frightened you, or just plain left you cold, think carefully; might it still be useful? Would it be worth a dabble?

Irrespective of how you derive your estimates, you will have to track the actual cost of your staff against that estimate. A good spreadsheet will help here. More than likely your organisation will demand that you produce monthly reports for your manager covering progress against the plan, notable activities (and non-events!), and a whole heap of numbers. I presume your own enterprise will lay down a standard format for how you should report your costs, so follow it. In the rare situation that you're left to your own devices, take advantage of the number of accountants that there are around these days (one in ten UK graduates!) and get one to give you some friendly advice.

- *People*. Having tied down the admin, got a handle on the work, and figured out the cost of all this, what's left? People! Believe it or not, you are not superhuman; you cannot do the whole project on your own, you need to enlist the aid, help and support of some (indeterminate) number of other people — your project team.

People have been studying the arts of leadership and delegation since time immemorial. Is there really anything new on the horizon that can be added to the existing sum total, which is already overly well documented? Yes, there is some interesting and highly apposite new research [18], conducted by Dr Anna Maria Garden of the London Business School. She investigated what keeps software professionals motivated not only to remain with a particular organisation, but while there to perform at their best. To answer this question she interviewed over 300 professionals spread across eleven companies of varying sizes.

First she confirmed the existence of the standard motivators that resulted in job satisfaction: good pay and perks, chances for education and training, chances for promotion, and clear communication from management. The problem was that satisfaction didn't necessarily equate with motivation. These alleged motivators turned out to be more like hygiene factors; their absence would have demotivated, but their presence did not positively motivate.

Dr Garden then located people who were in a state that she described as 'job excitement'. These people were supermotivated. How did they get that way? Four factors came into play: firstly, having work to do that was not only interesting but challenging; and secondly, having the scope to use their specific skills in the manner they considered most appropriate. The other two factors, although playing a lesser part, were also significant; so thirdly a sense of being able to achieve something useful; and fourthly, an awareness of personally contributing to the success of the employing organisation.

I'm making one of my classic assumptions here. In this case, that you'd like your staff to be supermotivated, which sounds like a good idea to me. Assuming I'm right, the question that all this prompts is how should your staff be managed to facilitate the manifestation of these factors. The study provides an answer to this, but it needs some squaring with the rest of what I've been preaching in this book.

Dr Garden found that the supermotivated staff were managed in a 'strategic' manner, with managers giving them broad direction, objectives, and an idea of the output required. The less motivated individuals were overmanaged and received very detailed instructions about how to carry out every aspect of their tasks. This may sound like a proposal to abandon a detail-orientated check-list-driven approach. Actually, it's not. The embodiment of such existing wisdom in some form of standards or checklists can be very fruitful; the trick is the way the delegation of the tasks is handled.

This aspect of delegation is partly to do with managers' degree of trust in their staff, and their need to feel that they are exercising detailed power and control. It is not necessary to walk a bright individual through a twenty-page standards manual as part of assigning a task. Simply state that you expect the output to conform to the standard, and that the individual's performance will be judged in terms of the quality (as well as timeliness) of his or her work, and that the standard is the arbiter of quality. It is an approach that embodies letting go a little, management that coaches and empowers individuals rather than seeking to nail down their every move.

Let's pour out the cement, get a tad more concrete, and explain how the use of a quality-aware approach, defined in standards or checklists, can be formulated so that it embodies these four motivators. Staff can be given challenging work if you trust them to rise to the occasion; continually assign tasks that stretch them just beyond their current capabilities, and thus show that you expect excellence from them. The very fact that they are tackling something new to them means that they should be devoting all their creative energy to the unique aspects of the problem they are facing. Requiring adherence to a quality-methodology will in fact provide a support framework of successful problem-solving techniques that can be applied to this particular challenge. If implemented sensitively a quality system can empower people and support, not subvert, their own skills and judgement. Communication remains paramount; you should always be talking to your project team, keeping it informed about all aspects of the project, showing it the big picture (this is also good training — some of its members may be project managers one day!). As a result the staff can see their individual effort as part of a bigger meaningful whole, and they get a sense of doing something useful. And by incorporating the use of the organisation's quality system, staff can gain an appreciation of how producing high-quality work enhances the organisation's reputation, and thus how their efforts (if they abide by the quality system) help the overall enterprise.

An extra aid to this is ensuring that whatever personnel development schemes may be in operation are tied into the project as closely as possible. When parcelling out tasks, take note of people's expressed preferences for the type of work they feel would help them to achieve their career goals. And really evaluate people's performance; let them know their performance matters to you, the rest of the project team, and the users. Feed back their performance results into the appropriate appraisal schemes. This is all part of treating them as people, not as units of resource. Respect, consideration, and sensitivity are useful watchwords.

- *Your boss*. Unless you are very unlucky, your boss is not there to give you hassle, but rather support. Just as you should be stretching your staff, he or she will endeavour to stretch you. However, no matter how nasty and devious your corporate politics may become, always keep in mind that ultimately you are both on the same side. If your project plan includes meaningful milestones, ensure that you report on your progress against them, both positive and negative! Always report on a regular cycle (no, not a twelve-speed racer!) weekly, fortnightly, or monthly. Most organisations will require this anyway; but if your's doesn't, that fact alone should act as a warning sign that you should none the less report even more thoroughly, otherwise you may be overlooked by higher management that appears to be stuck in a reactive rut.

Now, you'd expect your staff to alert you, as soon as possible, if they were encountering difficulties that they feared might prevent them from reaching their targets. By their doing so early, you still have the chance to approach the problem pro-actively, rather than in 'fire-fighting' mode. You owe your own manager the same courtesy, and as a result you have the right to ask him or her to take certain actions on your behalf (e.g. talk to his or her counterpart in the user hierarchy if your user-counterpart does not appear to be pulling his/her weight).

Oh yes, keep taking everyone down the pub from time to time. You need to be plugged into the users' grapevine, and be up-to-date on what they 'really' think.

- *Quality*. I've already talked about expecting adherence to quality goals in the section on staff motivation. But quality merits its own section. You have a duty to familiarise yourself with the way your enterprise handles quality issues. What procedures, standards, or checklists does it require you to deploy? How does it require you to assess the quality of the project's work? And for that matter the quality of your own work? How do you know, other than by your boss buying you a second brandy at lunch, that you are a high-quality project manager? And I'm not about to answer that last question. Most of the necessary material is in this book — think of it as a challenge to stretch you a little. Go do it now!

- *Day-dreaming*. Done that last task? Good, then you may carry on. This one can be quite fun, although it should prove unsettling as well, if you are doing it properly. Every week lock yourself away where you can't be disturbed, and let your mind wander — along the highways and byways of catastrophe. Think about what has happened in the past week, what is different now from a week ago. Once you've identified the playing field (level or otherwise) kick a few ideas around on it.

Think about each activity in your work breakdown structure, and imagine that that activity breaks down, goes horribly wrong, operates in 'belly-up mode'! For each of these possible disasters, develop contingency plans, not necessarily in great detail, but just so that you are comfortable with the idea that should X and Y go wrong, you know how you would set about countering the situation. In addition, if you're feeling particularly ambitious, you could even devise some approaches to minimise the chances of such disasters happening in the first place.

- *Reviews*. A few thoughts on reviews would not go amiss. They are essential to ensuring that work is of a high quality. The scene must be set from Day One, stating to your team that irrespective of how it may have worked before, you will not consider any aspect of its work to be complete until the work has been reviewed and its quality demonstrated to meet, if not exceed, the relevant standards.

The idea of ego-less programming is central here. This is where the application of sensitivity comes in. People must consider that it is their work, and not they themselves, being judged. And that the activity, although the meetings are focused on finding errors, is not about picking holes in work so as to 'do down' the programmer, but rather is aimed at improving the quality of the overall system. Finding errors is a pointless activity, if they are not corrected; the ultimate purpose is error correction.

And if necessary, state explicitly that review records will not form part of the input into staff performance appraisals. Indeed, construct a checklist of good performance that includes 'a positive and constructive approach to reviews' as one of its criteria for high-quality staff performance.

- *Lateralism*. I once spent a particularly exasperating evening dashing around and between terminals in Los Angeles International Airport. It didn't help that I'd only just arrived earlier that day and my body clock was still displaced by eight hours. All I wanted to do was sleep, but the person I was visiting had to collect some other guests who were arriving at 8 p.m. (4 a.m. UK time!). With me feeling in need of serious sleep, we arrived at the appropriate terminal, to discover they weren't there. Their plane had been cancelled due to severe thunderstorms in the mid-west, and they'd been switched on to a later flight on a different carrier. Now LAX is big (as in BIG!) so we had to trek half a mile to the other carrier's terminal, to try and meet these folks. Having got there, there was no sign of them. They had been issued boarding cards, but it appeared they hadn't got on to the plane — were they still in Atlanta? We trekked back to the first terminal, maybe they'd caught a later flight on their original carrier, so we paged them, and paged them, and paged them. No luck, where were they? In one last desperate guess we went back to the second carrier's terminal, and there they now were! They hadn't heard our pages, we hadn't heard theirs. Why? Because the pages were limited to individual terminals. But how had they got to LA? It turned out that they'd arrived at their airport so early they were switched on to a flight on the second carrier that arrived in LA before their original one would have arrived.

Now had I been a little less tired I might have thought of these unlikely but perfectly plausible scenarios, and we might have found them a whole lot sooner. I wasn't considering all the alternatives; I'd already dismissed some (including the right one!) too easily, if not subconsciously. You need to consider every option, at every turn, or you may miss something vital. Edward de Bono points out that thinking, lateral or otherwise, is a skill. It can be taught, and should be practised. He explains why it often isn't with the following dilemma: if you're (to be blunt) thick, then teaching you to think is a waste of time; however, if you're bright then you can already think fine and don't need to be taught. De Bono profoundly disagrees with this analysis, arguing that everyone can benefit from being taught to think. I agree, and would advocate you go and read some of his material. It will provide you with a critical edge to handle challenges.

- *Everything*. Meaning what? Meaning that everything must function together if your system is to work properly. To float off into another aeronautical metaphor — although I dislike flying I don't mind 747s so much. They remind me of small intimate cinemas (when they're not bouncing around courtesy of some clear-air turbulence). The wide section of the economy cabin, over the wing, is so large that you forget you're on a plane. When I walk down to the tail, to visit you know where, I get nervous because the cabin narrows, and the floor flexes more. I worry (irrationally!) that while I'm down this end of the plane the tail might break off, and my health would suffer — terminally! Back in my seat, this no longer troubles me, I'm quite happy for the tail to break off, I'm nowhere near it. I take a moment to realise that without the tail the plane would have difficulty flying, and even though I'd be some distance away from the problem, I'd still be affected by it.

What on earth (or in the air) am I driving at? In forgetting that I'd still be affected by the tail dropping off, I'm exhibiting a very useful human skill — selectivity. I'm filtering out things, not paying attention to everything. Now this skill is useful, but not all the time, and definitely not in the middle of managing a project. You'll hit the ground with a nasty bump unless you continually monitor everything, not necessarily in an overbearing manner, but none the less you must do so. The only way to avoid a nasty surprise from creeping out from under the carpet is to check, regularly, under every carpet, to ensure that no-one has brushed anything under there. Okay?

- *The rest of this book*. People other than project managers might need to read only specific chapters of this book. For you there's no such luck; everything in here applies to you. So to supplement the advice I give in this chapter, you should look at and think about the other nine.

10.3.2 Problems, problems, problems

One interesting fact that filtered into my brain by osmosis (i.e. I can't remember where I came across it!) is that everyone faces between ten and fifteen irritants every day of their lives. By irritants I mean small departures from the way we expect or would like the world to run; a train is late, the postal service loses a letter, the car won't start. To avoid becoming completely stressed out, you need to adopt an attitude of acceptance, that the world isn't perfect, and make allowances and work-arounds to deal with these problems.

However, although this is all good stress management, the approach is not appropriate to problems that may arise within your project. Unless you apply for the job as the new chairman of British Rail, you won't be able to do much to improve the way the trains run on time. However, within your project everything is ultimately your responsibility. The danger here is that you try and solve problems with knee-jerk responses. There is a beautifully simple, but very powerful, method outlined in *The New Manager's Handbook* edited by Michael Armstrong [19]. Its aim is to get to the bottom of a problem, and consists of examining the situation in which the problem arose, and asking why this happened. You then have the immediate cause. Looking for a solution at this stage is not a good idea; if you do, you are still treating the symptoms not the disease. You should now consider the immediate cause, and ask the same question, why? You will then get the cause of the cause, good. Ask why again, and keep asking why each time you get to a deeper level of cause; sooner or later you will find you cannot go any further, you will have hit the real (underlying) problem. That is the one you must solve, only then can you be sure you've prevented the recurrence of the original problem.

10.4 Self-management

10.4.1 Fruit flies like a banana

Meantime, back at the ranch, time still flies like an arrow. Managing time is difficult. To maintain my lean and mean body (okay, so I exaggerate — but only a little, honest!), I recently bought one of those cross-country skiing machines, which arrives in a carton, ready for you to assemble. Amongst the stack of metal rods and bright blue extruded plastic I found the instructions, which claimed that the whole thing could be assembled in about one hour. Four hours later, after much struggle, huffing and puffing, I concluded I must have given the wrong 'self-identification information' when I ordered it. The instructions obviously applied only to octopuses with degrees in mechanical engineering.

Time management is trumpeted from almost every roof-top, but we still don't really do much about managing our time consistently. There is a very worthwhile French book [20] (available in English!) that covers time management in both the personal and work spheres of our lives. It advises that we think of time as a spatial resource; we have a cube that fills up each day. The question is what do we fill it with? First, you need to take note of how you fill it currently; if you don't already do so, start to keep a work-diary, and write down in it not only what you do but how much time you spend on it. You might be surprised by how much time is wasted, and how much you spend jumping to someone else's demands.

The book points out that, in general, if we are floating through life on autopilot, we end up in some very bad habits, in regards to assigning priorities to tasks. In general, we do what we enjoy before what we don't enjoy, what goes quickly before what goes slowly, what's easy before what's hard, what's familiar before what's new, and what others impose on us before what we've chosen for ourselves. You need to sit down at the start of each day to assess what you have to do, and at the end of each day to assess what you achieved, how many times you were side-tracked, and how many of those were legitimate diversions of your attention.

To counter these time-slice tendencies of today's world, you need to develop a degree of perseverance. You must build on this diary habit, and engrain daily reviews of the way you spend your time into your routine. Routines are a good way of managing stress, so make this one of your fundamental stress-fighting tools. Identify tasks as having two qualities: important or unimportant and urgent or non-urgent. These will all have to be done at some point in your future, so then plan which are to be done when. Important urgent tasks will come first, these are pretty obvious. Unimportant urgent tasks (getting a cup of coffee, photocopying a memo) tend to distract us. Important non-urgent tasks (writing someone's appraisal report) can slide, all too easily, and if allowed to slide will become important and urgent. Unimportant non-urgent tasks never get done; if you've so classified such a task, do you really need to do it? If so, reclassify it.

Follow this procedure every day, allocating specific parts of your day to each type of task. You will find that, although you can do nothing about the passing of time, you are mastering the management of time because you are using your brain to run ahead of time and work out what best use you can make of your own future.

10.4.2 You, yes YOU!

Having sorted out the way you manage your time, we need to consider some of the other aspects of the way you manage yourself. Remember my question at the start of this chapter. Are you a success? If you answer 'No' to it, then you've got problems. Irrespective of where you are in your life, what you want to achieve, and how much you already have achieved, if you classify yourself as not being a success you are helping yourself to fail. And, more importantly here, the negative attitude you are cultivating will affect your project — for the worse.

Work should reinforce life and the rest of your life should reinforce your work. And you should be aiming to enjoy all of it. This may sound idealistic and naïve, but creeping cynicism can corrode you from the inside out. It hollows out your heart, leaving you cold and detached, unable to appreciate anything, or motivate anybody else. The best way to lead is by example, and in this case that requires passion, infectious enthusiasm, and a sense of enjoyment that covers all aspects of life.

What I am talking about here is cultivating an effective attitude that will enable you to achieve more, because it will provide you with the enthusiasm and energy to go about things. You will be better motivated, and your motivation will rub off on your team. These are basically exhortations to explore aspects of your own personal development. There's plenty on the market about this; one source of information I've found useful is Tony Robbins [21], but choose whatever you find most appropriate for your own needs. But don't just sit there in the corner moping.

Now, it's time for me to get a little personal. How are things between you and your main squeeze, significant other, spouse even? My point of interest here is the negative cycle that can be established by problems, irrespective of their source — home or work — pushing you into a spiral of stress, irritation, and misunderstanding. That last word is crucial; effective communication is important in every aspect of life. However, recent research has shown that men and women constantly misunderstand each other; statements made with the best of intentions are often misinterpreted, causing conflict, stress, and reducing our 'happiness-coefficient'. There is a book [22] by an American psychologist/sociologist that examines this in detail, explains how these misunderstandings arise, and how they can be avoided. Read it. Now is this any of my business? Yes! For two reasons, a poor home life will impact your ability to work at your peak performance levels in the office, thus hurting the project. And the trend towards increased numbers of women in the workplace alters the dynamics of work-related communication. Oh, yes, if you happen to be main-squeeze-less at the moment, the book may help you understand a little more about the way the other half of the population thinks. . . .

Lastly, within self-management we come to something somewhat more solid, maybe even stodgy. Food and fitness. In addition to your mental and social health, a whole-person approach to life would not be complete without examining how achieving the correct level of fitness can improve your energy levels at work. There is a classic in this field [23] from which I will summarise the major findings. Never mind all the stuff about your living longer, not suffering heart attacks, and all that; the reason I'm advocating that you get fit is that it will improve your energy level.

The book points out that the key to everything is being at the appropriate weight. And that is not an absolute weight but rather one where, for men 15 percent, for women 22 percent, of their total weight would be contributed by fat. This means that if you are at your 'ideal' weight and happen to gain muscle, you are allowed to increase your 'ideal' weight, provided the percentage of your body that is fat doesn't overshoot the target. The next point is that adjusting food intake is not the answer; your body can metabolise all food, protein, carbohydrate (and fat) into fat. And your body doesn't know this is the twentieth century; it is still a cave-person's body; cut down on your food intake and it thinks there's a famine on the way, and so proceeds to increase the amount of food it converts into fat, as an energy store.

The only answer is exercise, not to burn off the fat while you run (or whatever), but rather to improve your metabolism, so you burn more fat all day long. To do this you must cause your heart to beat at 85 percent of its maximum safe rate for at least twelve minutes. The actual exercise may take longer since you will need to build up to that rate. Do this three times a week and you will maintain your current level of (un?)fitness, six times a week and you will actually improve. The usual caveat of seeing your doctor if you've been sedentary for the last ten years applies. Anyway the book has lots more; study it or something similar, act on it and you'll have more energy and accomplish more around the office, and probably feel happier as well!

10.5 Quality and academia

10.5.1 Scholarly aside no. 3

It would be most remiss of me if I didn't provide you with a briefing on the theoretical underpinning of quality. There are three notable founding fathers; all three eventually held senior positions in American industry and academia. But before I dive into that, let me just elucidate one of the problems that considering their work causes us. We are creating software; they are all primarily concerned with the manufacturing world. Our problems, although similar, are not the same; specifically they devote a great deal of effort to improving the manufacturing process. This is aimed at minimising the number of errors when an initial version of a product is replicated.

This problem doesn't really arise for software, since replicating a system merely involves duplicating the appropriate files. This whole central area of manufacturing quality becomes tangential to our discussion, and incidentally this is why a lot of articles on quality may seem curiously inaccessible to you. We, on the other hand, are concerned with the issues of correctly constructing a one-off system, providing high-quality service for it (maintenance), and with an issue not really dealt with in manufacturing — maintaining quality when the system is altered. As a consequence of all this, a lot of the measurements taken, and the statistics derived, in the world of manufacturing quality do not have much relevance for us; or at the very least, we need to measure different things and interpret the statistics differently.

W. Edwards Deming is thought of by many people to be the father of the quality-orientated approach to doing business. The key to his approach was 'statistical process control'; this involved measuring how far each copy of an item diverged from its specification. A certain amount of divergence could be tolerated, but beyond that action had to be taken. Although an American, the US was slow to take up his ideas. He was one of the specialists sent to Japan to help its industry rebuild after the Second World War — they paid more attention — enough said.

The closest software developers get to using his techniques are when we take measurements of numbers of errors per 1000 lines of code. We can then set statistical control limits beyond which we do not expect the error rate to stray; if it does, serious investigation of the offending subsystem is called for.

Joseph Juran generated one of the classic definitions of quality, which is often used even by the software fraternity, namely, fitness for use. This had five main components as identified in the *Harvard Business Review*, 'quality of design, quality of conformance, availability, safety, and field use' [24]. Quality of design and quality of conformance convert to whether the specification is up to the requirements of the application, and whether the system meets the specification. Availability translates to reliability and maintainability. Safety is pretty obvious; and field use covers whether the system still meets its original aims once it's in the hands of the real users.

The *Harvard Business Review* [24] points out that:

> Juran recognised that such measures were not likely to attract top management attention; for this reason, he advocated a cost-of-quality (COQ) accounting system. Such a system spoke top management's language — money. Quality costs were costs associated solely with defective product — the costs of making, finding, repairing or avoiding defects.

Since software development is much more of a one-off activity, gathering similar statistics for input into such a measure is trickier. However, the eventual conclusion is pretty much the same — catching an error early in the development (say at design stage) means that correcting it is much cheaper than after it is installed. I would contend that, for software, statistics may not be necessary, since the statement is intuitively obvious. Would you agree?

Philip Crosby articulated that the ultimate goal of quality improvement was zero defects. This is unlikely for software, but his method for reaching this goal is the crucial lesson we need to learn, he 'favoured prevention rather than after-the-fact inspection' [24]. In our language this means review at every stage, rather than test just prior to delivery to the user.

He also identified five states of quality awareness within a company or organisation [24]:

- Uncertainty, the company failed to recognise quality as a management tool.
- Awakening, quality was recognised as important, but management put off taking action.

- Enlightenment, management openly faced and addressed quality problems by establishing a formal quality program.
- Wisdom, prevention was working well, problems were identified early, and corrective action was routinely pursued.
- Certainty, quality management was an essential part of the company, and problems occurred only infrequently.

The question for you is — where is your organisation in this chart?

10.6 General management issues

10.6.1 Changing your corporate culture

If it appears that your organisation is not very far advanced along Crosby's grid, then you might want to try and change your corporate culture. Bear these points in mind. They have filtered down through a number of books, and I repeat them here on the basis of reference [25]. They are in essence pure politics; but then that's what corporate change is all about.

- *Spend time*. Spending time exerts, in itself, a 'claim' on the decision-making system.
- *Persist*. Having more patience than other people often results in adoption of a chosen course of action.
- *Exchange status for substance*. One of the most effective ways to gather support for a program is to reward allies with visible tokens of recognition.
- *Facilitate opposition participation*. Often those outside the formal decision centres overestimate the feasibility of the change; encouraged to participate, they will often become more realistic.
- *Overload the system*. Bureaucracies chew up most projects, but on the other hand, some sneak through; merely launching more projects is likely to result in more successes.
- *Provide garbage cans*. Organisations endlessly argue issues; to induce desired outcomes put 'throwaway' issues at the top of agendas (to absorb debate) saving substantive issues for later.
- *Manage unobtrusively*. Certain actions can influence the organisation pervasively but almost imperceptibly; moreover the resulting change will persist with little further attention.
- *Interpret history*. By articulating a particular version of events, the leader can alter people's perception of what has been happening; whoever writes the minutes influences the outcome.

10.7 Standards

10.7.1 ISO, ISO, ISO

This book wouldn't be complete without some discussion of the international standards that relate to quality. So, who do we call? ISO. Who? The International

Organisation for Standardisation, which for reasons somewhat unclear to me chooses to order its acronym so that it fails to summarise the name in whichever official language (English, French or Russian) it is written. No matter, we all have our quirks; they give life its charm. ISO is based in Switzerland and is a federation of standards bodies (BSI, ANSI, etc.) from most countries on the planet. Technical committees get together and produce standards for all sorts of things, which are often mirrored by standards developed in the individual countries.

For our purposes I'm going to point you in the direction of ISO9001. I choose the ISO version of the standard rather than a country-specific equivalent (e.g. BS5750 in the UK) since I know not where this book may end up; but wherever it does travel, it should be possible for you to lay your hands on the ISO version of this standard. But what is ISO9001? No, not another sequel to the Arthur C. Clarke future history tale of space odysseys, but rather a quality odyssey, produced in 1987.

I've just had a peek at my trusty *Oxford English Dictionary*, and it informs me that an odyssey is 'a long adventurous journey'. As you can tell from the size of my book, there's quite a lot to quality; in fact we've been on quite a long adventurous journey. ISO9001 [26] provides a very useful summary of what I have been talking about.

Let's get to its title *Quality Systems: Model for quality assurance in design/development, production, installation and servicing*. What do you notice about that title? the word 'software' is completely missing; that's because the standard applies to all manufacturing processes from low-calorie salad dressing, through zip-fasteners to software. So I will proceed to give you an interpretation of ISO90001 in the context of software development, and in doing so remind you of the major points you should be considering as you seek to produce high-quality systems.

'0 Introduction'. Usual waffle, but does point out how this standard fits into other associated ISO standards.

'1 Scope and Field of Application'. Covers who should use the standard and when, usually if there exists a contractual relationship between a supplier producing a product (for us an IT system) and a purchaser; the standard being of particular use if the contract explicitly requires the producer to achieve a certain demonstrable level of quality, both in the product and the process by which it is created and maintained.

'2 References'. Other handy ISO standards, covering quality vocabulary and the selection and use of ISO9001 as against other closely related ISO quality standards.

'3 Definitions'. Where the terms used in this standard are defined.

'4 Quality System Requirements'. The meaty bit that defines what should be in a quality system. I'll cover this in more detail.

'4.1 Management Responsibility'. From project managers upwards, the buck stops here. But what should you do when it arrives? You should be concerning yourself with policy, and with ensuring that everyone knows about the quality policy and has the power to take whatever actions may be necessary to enforce that policy. You need to ensure that you have the necessary people to carry out the policy, someone specifically charged with overall responsibility for the policy, and that the policy's effectiveness is periodically reviewed.

'4.2 Quality System'. This states that a policy is no good unless you back it up with a documented quality system, with procedures that cover all the issues listed in the rest of ISO9001.

'4.3 Contract Review'. This goes back to Chapter 2 on 'Initiation and Requirements'; the contract that forms the basis of the delivery needs to be fully reviewed to confirm that all requirements can be met, and a record kept of any changes.

'4.4 Design Control'. This relates to the various levels of specifications, RS, SEF, IS, and PSs. But not so much their content, as ensuring that their production is properly controlled, all the necessary input information is available, that the draft documents cover what they should, that this has been confirmed using (recorded) reviews, and that any changes to the design are made in a controlled and documented manner.

'4.5 Document Control'. This relates to Chapter 8 'Documentation', and emphasises that documents must be adequate before they are issued, not remain available once they become out of date, and that changes made to them must be controlled properly — by involving the original authors if possible, and by clearly identifying changes in reissues.

'4.6 Purchasing'. This is related to the multiple layers of contractors and subcontractors I've talked about. Specifically, it focuses on what should be done should your system include components that you haven't developed yourself. Since this is almost invariably the case in IT, it applies to you.

'4.7 Purchaser Supplied Product'. This short section covers the situation where the client (rather than a subcontractor) provides you with components for the system. You should look after such items properly.

'4.8 Product Identification and Traceability'. This relates to the cross-references I've been harping on about, especially if you have more than one version of the system (with accompanying specifications); this requires you to be able to trace requirements through to implementation. Associated with this is the use of configuration management to identify which version of a system is at which site, down to the level of serial numbers if many sites have the same release.

'4.9 Process Control'. This covers the actual coding of the system, and the provision of suitable coding standards.

'4.10 Inspection and Testing'. This is covered by Chapter 5, 'Testing', and re-emphasises that testing should take place at all stages in the development. It further pushes the point that test records must be maintained.

'4.11 Inspection, Measuring and Test Equipment'. This addresses things like your test harnesses, and requires that they be developed with a similar level of rigour and quality as the system itself.

'4.12 Inspection and Test Status'. This addresses the identification of what stage of testing each component has reached, and for software systems that can be achieved through suitable configuration management tools.

'**4.13 Control of Nonconforming Product**'. This requires that you don't send anything out of the door that is below your levels of acceptable quality, and outlines procedures for handling material that is non-conforming.

'**4.14 Corrective Action**'. This covers the correction of problems, but also goes one step further, requiring you to establish procedures that should prevent recurrences of the same problem.

'**4.15 Handling, Storage, Packing and Delivery**'. Basically, now you've built it, don't break it before it's installed and working. For you that means avoiding getting your data scrambled by an airport X-ray machine, etc.

'**4.17 Internal Quality Audits**'. Not only should you have a documented quality system, you should periodically check that it's working properly.

'**4.18 Training**'. This covers your own staff rather than the users. Indeed, it requires that you develop procedures to ensure that the appropriate people receive high-quality training when they need it; in more concrete terms before rather than after the event.

'**4.19 Servicing**'. This means maintenance, hot-line support, and all that; refer to the relevant chapter.

'**4.20 Statistical Techniques**'. Last, but not least, you are encouraged to use these where appropriate to assess the quality of your deliverables and the quality system itself.

So there you have it. It's coming. More and more organisations are now specifying that they'll deal only with subcontractors who operate quality systems that have been evaluated and declared compliant with ISO9001 (or their national equivalents — BS5750, AS3563 in Australia; identical words, different numbers!). Edicts may soon start emanating from that Diat (or maybe MITI), Strasbourg, and Capitol Hill requiring compliance. So contact your national standards organisation to investigate getting yourselves certified, so to speak.

10.7.2 Measurement and standards

Having just outlined a more formal approach to the material I've covered in this book, I think it is worth making the following point. Don't overdo standards. It is far better to have a limited number of standards, and enforce them properly, than to have a massive all-encompassing set that no one fully understands and which is never properly used.

Remember that if during a review you discover a deviation from a standard, a quality-aware approach implies that in addition to fixing the problem you should also seek to discover why deviation occurred and amend the procedure that implements the standard so that future deviations won't happen.

The same minimalism applies to measurement and statistics. If you try to measure everything you'll get bogged down in a morass of numbers. Determine what would be most useful to you, and thus measure only a few things. Be committed, keep doing this over a number of months, years even; then once you have sufficient historical data you can start to draw useful inferences about the quality of what you are doing and producing.

10.8 Final final thoughts

This book has used a lot of metaphors, similes, and anecdotes that focused on travel and journeys. This is partly deliberate; I want to get you thinking about quality as being like climbing up a down-escalator. If you make no effort you are carried backwards; if you make some effort you stay put; only if you really try will you make progress. Remember, not to decide is still a decision; inaction results in actions in which you don't have any say.

One last travel metaphor — don't miss the train that everyone else is catching, specifically the move towards more formalised development, the 'information systems factory' (ISF). And you don't have to take my word for it, listen to David Talbot [27], in charge of the Software Engineering in Britain's now completed Alvey (Strategic Computing Research Initiative) Programme.

> The concept of the information systems factory is an abstraction. It is the notion of contrasting *ad hoc* software development practices with the notion of a factory with its organisation, investment, tools, and management; and the idea that factories are concerned with things such as getting things out on time, to budget, to specification, to quality, etc. The factory notion undoubtedly was seen as a threat to a number of people who saw programming as fun and did not enjoy the notion of being moved out of their cottages into a bigger and more disciplined environment. The ISF continues to be an articulation of the central concept of software engineering. It remains valid, and it's being pursued.

Indeed, it is being pursued, and with success. The Japanese have adopted this approach, and have sky-scrapers full of programmers following a disciplined approach that generates 70 percent more lines of code than equivalent American programmers, and with fewer errors [28].

So remember, quality is not easy. It requires that you take action, adopt a pro-active approach, a lazy reactive attitude won't yield anything of high quality. Remember the checklist for achieving change. If trying to convert your organisation into adopting a quality-aware ethos feels a bit like nailing jelly to the ceiling, pushing water up-hill with a rake, or kicking a dead whale down a beach; don't get dispirited, don't give up — never give up!

Having just said that, this is where I cease and desist. I've probably talked the hind legs off every donkey on the Costa Brava. . . . Let me leave you with a restatement of the aim of this book.

My intention has been to provoke and unsettle you, thus (I hope) stimulating you into some action. The style may have got up your nose or tickled your funny bone, I don't mind which. Only a response of bland indifference on your part constitutes failure for this book.

10.9 Questions

1. When will you reread this book?
2. Who else do you know who should read it?
3. Have your drawn up your own checklist of what you must do to be a high-quality project manager, yet?
4. What constitutes a successful project, for you?
5. Are you happy with all aspects of your life? And if not, what are you going to do about it?
6. How do you intend to manage
    - the administration,
    - your people,
    - the tasks,
    - your time,
    - your boss,
    - money, and
    - quality?
7. When will you next day-dream laterally?
8. Will you get your own copy of ISO9001?
9. What's the best bit of this book?
10. Why?

Glossary

Summary of computing terms I've failed to define in the text, since I presume most readers will be familiar with them, and since defining them would break up the flow (even more than I already tend to do!). Note — this is not intended to be an exhaustive list of computing terms.

ACKs	Standard abbreviation for positive acknowledgement, used in protocols that enable different computers to talk to each other.
ANSI	American National Standards Institute.
Beta test	Tests of a system in the same configuration as it will subsequently run live, presumes that system tests or acceptance tests are alpha tests; but it is an industry quirk that no-one uses the phrase 'alpha-test' — when they do there's usually an argument about what it means.
BSI	British Standards Institute.
C++	A programming language that is based on the idea of object-orientation, which involves writing programs that are easily reusable in other systems (nothing to do with object files, see below).
CASE	Computer aided software engineering.
CC	Change control.
CM	Configuration management.
Compiler	Part of a computer's operating system that translates the text of source-code programs into files of runnable 0s and 1s.
Cross-compiler	A compiler which runs on one model of computer, but produces executables that can run on a different make or model of computer.
ctrl-c	The pressing of the Control and C keys at the same time.
Deliverables	What you propose to give to the user.
DP	Data-processing.
DR	Discrepancy report.
DRF	Discrepancy report form.

e-mail	Electronic mail, where messages are exchanged on computer without necessarily appearing on paper.
EPROM	Erasable programmable read-only memory, a type of computer chip that can be programmed by storing the program directly in the chip.
Executable	A computer program that has been turned into a set of 0s and 1s and so can run on a computer; often composed of a number of object files.
Fan-out	The number of sub-procedures a procedure calls.
FM	Facilities management, using a third-party company to run an operations computer system.
Functionality	What the system does.
Gantt chart	Standard project planning and control tool that shows tasks and when they are to be done.
Hard-coding	The placing of an actual name or value in a program where a variable could have been.
IPSE	Integrated project/programming support environment, a collection of computer-based tools that all work together to improve the efficiency of creating new computer systems.
IS	Internals specification.
IT	Information technology (not in common use in America).
ITT	Invitation to tender.
Methodology	A proprietary approach to the development of a system, e.g. SSADM (structured systems analysis and design method), Yourdon, etc.
MIPS	Millions of instructions per second — one of the measures of a computer's power.
MM	Maintenance manager.
Modula-3	A programming language.
NAKs	Standard abbreviation for negative acknowledgement, used in protocols that enable different computers to talk to each other.
Object file	A computer program that has been turned into a set of 0s and 1s and but cannot be run until it has been linked together with other object files to form an executable.
On-line	On the computer rather than on paper.
One-stop	A system or document that encompasses all of everything; one only has to make one-stop to gain the information or service needed.

Outsourcing	Delegating a task to someone in a separate company.
PERT	Programme evaluation and review technique.
PS	Process specification.
Pseudo-code	An outline of a process using IF-THEN type statements without conforming to the full syntax of a specific language.
Regression tests	Tests which are reruns of previous tests, repeated because a system has changed, to confirm that the changes haven't damaged existing functionality — causing the quality of the system to regress.
RFI	Request for information.
RFP	Request for proposal.
RS	Requirements specification.
SEF	Statement of external functionality.
Shell script	A file of operating system commands, which is more of a program, added to a computer's operating system by a developer.
Softcoding	The placing of a variable in a program rather than a specific name or value.
SQL	Structured query language, a standard way of extracting information from a type of database known as relational databases; these store information in tables (rows and columns) on the basis that the items of information relate to each other.
TA	Technical authority, for a computer system.
VDM	Vienna development method, a type of formal (mathematics-based) method.
Z	A mathematical language for writing formal provable specifications for systems.

References

[1] *Zen and the Art of Motorcycle Maintenance*, Robert M. Persig, Corgi Books, 1974 (ISBN 0-522-10166-4).

[2] *Removing the Barriers in Manufacturing — Report on the 1990 European Manufacturing Futures Survey*, report by Arnoud de Meyer and Karsa Ferdows, article by Simon Holberton, *The Financial Times*, 21 January 1991.

[3] *Measuring Software Design Quality*, David N. Card with Robert L. Glass, Prentice Hall, 1990 (ISBN 0-13-568593-1).

[4] *Understanding Systems Failure*, Victor Bignell and Joyce Fortune, Manchester University Press, 1984 (ISBN 0-7190-0973-1).

[5] *Systems, Management and Change*, Ruth Carter, John Martin, Bill Mayblin, and Michael Munday, Harper and Row, 1984 (ISBN 0-06-318272-6).

[6] *Age of Unreason*, Charles Handy, Business Books Ltd—Century Hutchinson Ltd, 1989 (ISBN 0-09-174088-6).

[7] Survey by Price Waterhouse, quoted in 'Armed with a secret weapon', John Authers and Gren Manuel, *The Financial Times*, 5 February 1991.

[8] The diagramming technique in Figure 4.1 is a refinement derived from the standard technique of Design Structure Diagrams.

[9] *VAX 11 Structured Assembly Language Programming*, Robert W Sebesta. Benjamin/Cummings, 1984 (ISBN 0-8053-7001-3).

[10] *Mastering Cobol Programming*, Roger Hutty, Macmillan, 1983 (ISBN 0-333-34385-9).

[11] *C Programming — Principles and Practice*, Boris Allen, Paradigm, 1987 (ISBN 0-9488-2515-4).

[12] *Mastering Pascal Programming*, Eric Huggins, Macmillan, 1983 (ISBN 0-3333-2294-0).

[13] *The Art of Software Testing*, Glenford J. Myers, © John Wiley & Sons, 1979 (ISBN 0-471-04328-1). Reprinted by permission of John Wiley & Sons Inc.

[14] 'Plans which contain all the right moves', Lynton McLain, *The Financial Times*, 8 March 1991.

[15] 'Plans for a quick recovery', Della Bradshaw, *The Financial Times*, 29 January 1991.

[16] Lynne Chaney, Chair — US National Endowment for the Humanities, while televised on C-SPAN TV network, 4 April 1991.

[17] *Software Engineering Economics*, Barry W. Boehm, Prentice Hall, 1981 (ISBN 0-13-822122-7).

[18] Anna Maria Garden of the London Business School's high-technology management unit, quoted in *The Financial Times*, 12 April 1991.

[19] *The New Manager's Handbook*, p. 223 edited by Michael Armstrong, Kogan Page, 1990 (ISBN 0-7494-0256-3).

[20] *The Art of Time*, Jean-Louis Servan-Schreiber, Bloomsbury Press, 1988 (ISBN 0-7475-0480-6).

[21] Robbins Research Inc, 9191 Towne Centre Drive, Suite 660, San Diego, Ca, 92122, USA.

[22] *You Just Don't Understand: Women and Men in Conversation*, Deoborah Tannen, Ballantine Books, 1991 (ISBN 0-345-37205-0).

[23] *Fit or Fat*, Covert Bailey, Houghton Mifflin, 1977 (ISBN 0-395-51083-X).

[24] 'A Note on Quality: The views of Deming, Juran, and Crosby'. Copyright © 1986 by the Presidents & Fellows of Harvard College; all rights reserved. Reprinted by permission of Harvard Business Review — Special Collection 'Unconditional Quality'.

[25] *Management of Professionals, Insights for Maximising Co-operation*, Desmond D. Martin and Richard L. Shell, Marcel Dekker Inc. New York, 1988 (ISBN 0-8247-7847-2). Reprinted from p. 255 by courtesy of Marcel Dekker Inc.

[26] The extracts from ISO9001 (BS5750: Part 1, 1987) are reproduced with the permission of the British Standards Institute. Complete copies of the Standard can be obtained by post from BSI Sales, Linford Wood, Milton Keynes, Beds MK14 6LE, or through National Standards Bodies.

[27] Quoted from *Alvey — Britain's Strategic Computing Initiative*, Brian Oakley and Kenneth Owen, MIT Press, 1989 (ISBN 0-262-15038-7).

[28] Reported on 'Marketplace', produced by University of Southern California, broadcast on American Public Radio, on 14 March 1991.

Index